SOUTHERN LITERARY STUDIES
Fred Hobson, Editor

THE
BELLE
GONE BAD

*White Southern Women Writers
and the Dark Seductress*

BETINA ENTZMINGER

LOUISIANA STATE UNIVERSITY PRESS *Baton Rouge*

Copyright © 2002 by Louisiana State University Press
All rights reserved
Manufactured in the United States of America
First printing

Cloth
5 4 3 2 1
11 10 09 08 07 06 05 04 03 02

Paper
5 4 3 2 1
11 10 09 08 07 06 05 04 03 02

Designer: Barbara Neely Bourgoyne
Typeface: Galliard
Typesetter: Crane Composition, Inc.
Printer and binder: Thomson-Shore, Inc.

ISBN 0-8071-2785-X (cloth)
ISBN 0-8071-2836-8 (paper)

CONTENTS

Acknowledgments   vii

Abbreviations   ix

INTRODUCTION: The Southern Lady's Dark Double   1

1   THE BEAUTIFUL SERPENT; *OR*, NOT QUITE EDEN   32
        E.D.E.N. Southworth   34
        Caroline Lee Hentz   54
        Augusta Jane Evans   66

2   WOMEN WITH MOVEABLE WAYS: The Bad Belle
    as Survivor   73
        Ellen Glasgow   82
        Evelyn Scott   95
        Margaret Mitchell   104
        Caroline Gordon   114

3   TO CALL MYSELF AN ARTIST: Destroying the Bad Belle   122
        Eudora Welty   127
        Elizabeth Spencer   141
        Lee Smith   154
        Kaye Gibbons   169

     CONCLUSION: For Whom the Belle Told   178

     Bibliography   187
     Index   199

ACKNOWLEDGMENTS

I am grateful to Fred Hobson, Jack Raper, Linda Wagner-Martin, Margaret O'Connor, Susan Navarette, and Laurie Langbauer of the University of North Carolina at Chapel Hill, to Veronica Makowsky of the University of Connecticut at Storrs, to Michael Hardin of Bloomsburg University, to John Barrett of East Stroudsburg University, and to John Easterly and Jean C. Lee of Louisiana State University Press for their help in revising my manuscript and preparing it for publication. I would also like to thank Virginia Commonwealth University's English Department for giving me a research grant that enabled me to finish my revisions. *North Carolina Literary Review* and *Southern Quarterly* published portions of this manuscript previously and granted me permission to use those portions again here, for both of which I am grateful. Finally, I thank Elizabeth Spencer and Lee Smith for talking with me about their work and for giving me permission to use their comments in this book.

ABBREVIATIONS

WORKS BY AUGUSTA JANE EVANS

B   *Beulah*

WORKS BY KAYE GIBBONS

FF   *Frost and Flower: My Life with Manic Depression So Far*
SU   *Sights Unseen*

WORKS BY ELLEN GLASGOW

ITOL   *In This Our Life*
RC   *The Romantic Comedians*
WW   *The Woman Within*

WORKS BY CAROLINE GORDON

M   *The Malefactors*
SC   *The Strange Children*

WORKS BY CAROLINE LEE HENTZ

MW   *Marcus Warland*
PNB   *The Planter's Northern Bride*

WORKS BY MARGARET MITCHELL

GWW   *Gone with the Wind*

WORKS BY EVELYN SCOTT

N   *Narcissus*

WORKS BY LEE SMITH

LDDB   *The Last Day the Dogbushes Bloomed*
OH   *Oral History*

WORKS BY E.D.E.N. SOUTHWORTH

R   *Retribution*
SR   *Self-Raised*
TB   *The Three Beauties*

WORKS BY ELIZABETH SPENCER

JK   "Judith Kane"
LH   *Landscapes of the Heart*
NT   *The Night Travellers*

WORKS BY EUDORA WELTY

OWB   *One Writer's Beginnings*
OD   *The Optimist's Daughter*
RB   *The Robber Bridegroom*

THE BELLE GONE BAD

INTRODUCTION
The Southern Lady's Dark Double

As Nina Baym has pointed out in *Woman's Fiction,* women writers writing about women dominated the American literary marketplace between 1820 and 1870. Considering the turmoil of this time for the southern states, it may seem surprising that many of the most popular of these women writers were from the South. Readers eagerly anticipated the serial appearances of works of such writers as E.D.E.N. Southworth, Augusta Jane Evans, and Caroline Lee Hentz, now mostly unknown. These novelists expressed a variety of attitudes, sometimes ambivalent, toward the institution that dominated nineteenth-century moral and political debates in the South—slavery. Some, like Southworth, denounced slavery and its moral evils in some novels and portrayed slaves as happy, loyal retainers in others. Some, like Hentz, praised slavery's paternal ideals while portraying actual slaves' discontent. And some, like Evans, avoided referring to slavery in their works whenever possible, as if the institution that was so much a part of actual southern domesticity would somehow sully the domestic scenes they constructed. But regardless of their attitude toward this emblem and tool of southern patriarchy, the writers saw it as their duty to reaffirm the traditional family and gender roles of the white nineteenth-century South. The price for their popularity seems to have been conformity.

The antebellum southern women who wrote for publication reinforced the social structure even though it often necessitated for them a masked stance. Though they may have had conflicting views about the enslavement of another race, they overtly validated the patriarchal family structure of strong, benevolent husband-father and physically weak but morally strong wife-child, a hierarchical configuration that rested on slavery and was wrapped in the Old South's defense of the institution. As Baym explains in "The Myth of the Myth of Southern Womanhood," "The supposed high degree of civilization in the South is specifically attributed to its freedom from drudgery—in a word, to slavery—and consequent freedom for white women to pursue and cultivate the social graces and the arts of life. Southern women, embodiment of these graces, are what the South as a whole has cultivated; they *are* Southern culture." As a result, nineteenth-century southern domestic novelists, as Elizabeth Moss comments, "regularly confronted the inherent irony of their profession: champions of domesticity, they nevertheless led lives that bore little resemblance to the one they recommended to their female audience."[1]

In the works of these nineteenth-century white southern women novelists, however, a character appears who manifests these writers' discontent with the domestic structure they outwardly defended. As a foil to the morally pure heroine of their novels, these writers often employ as villain the southern belle gone bad. A hyperbolic version of the normally coquettish belle, this bad belle is a type of femme fatale—sexually knowing, physically powerful because of her allure, and morally dangerous. She becomes, therefore, the opposite of the ideal southern lady, the mature woman the belle was intended to become. Rather than act as moral exemplar, as a true southern lady should, the bad belle uses her sexuality as a tool to force men to complete her evil, self-serving designs. Rather than act as her admirer's salvation and guiding star, she often leads to his destruction. By applying feminist and psychoanalytic theories and cultural analysis to close readings of southern women writers' texts, we can explore how this figure is linked to ambivalent feelings these writers had regarding slavery and regarding their position as women—often compared to that of slaves—in the patriarchal South and beyond. Though the bad belle has evolved in the works of twentieth-century southern women, its continued appearance marks the ex-

---

1. Nina Baym, "The Myth of the Myth of Southern Womanhood," in *Feminism and American Literary History: Essays* (New Brunswick, N.J.: Rutgers University Press, 1993), 193; Elizabeth Moss, *Domestic Novelists in the Old South: Defenders of Southern Culture* (Baton Rouge: Louisiana State University Press, 1992), 5.

tent to which these social issues of the nineteenth century still shape the imagination of the contemporary southerner. While not an overarching key to these writers' works or to their social and political views, this study offers a reading of an evocative and recurrent character type that suggests authorial commentary on the social roles of southern women.

In creating their belles gone bad, nineteenth-century southern women writers draw on the archetypal figure of the femme fatale that has haunted the creative endeavors of *man*kind from its beginning. In *The Golden Bough,* for instance, Sir James Frazer describes the legend of ancient Assyria's Queen Semiramis, who, because she feared losing power through marriage, "admitted to her bed the handsomest of her soldiers, only, however, to destroy them all afterwards" by burying them alive. Similarly, in one rabbinical literary tradition, Lilith, Adam's first wife, made like Adam from the dust, refused to recognize the male as her superior and was cast out of Eden. Rather than submit to a mortal male's control, she chose to live with the devil and beget demons, periodically sleeping with human men as the succubus. Her visits, the cause of "nocturnal emissions," drained the men of their strength and increased her evil spawn. A similar figure, the Greek Lamia, originally a monster who fed on children's flesh, transformed in later ages into a "shape-shifting snake with a woman's head . . . who seduced young men and sucked their blood." And in some Native American mythology, the origin of the race is linked to the *vagina dentata,* the first woman, whose toothed vagina killed all who tried to sleep with her. After many died, the culture hero used sticks to break the teeth so he could mate with the woman and engender a nation.[2]

Most descriptions of this femme fatale combine an exaggerated ideal of feminine allure with qualities patriarchal culture normally associates with maleness. Like the ideal man, the femme fatale is powerful and intelligent, though she often masks her evil intentions behind a meek (feminine) demeanor. But her womanly beauty is the source of her power. Men are mesmerized by her, usually enchanted by her exotic hair or eyes or her hypnotic voice. John Keats, for instance, who seems to have been obsessed with the dark seductress, returns again and again to the "wild wild eyes" of La Belle Dame sans Merci. In life, as well as in literature, women's hair and eyes

2. Sir James Frazer, *The Golden Bough: A Study in Magic and Religion,* new abridgment from the 2d and 3d eds., Robert Fraser, ed. and introduction. (New York: Oxford University Press, 1994), 649; Maria Leach, ed. *Funk and Wagnalls Standard Dictionary of Folklore, Mythology, and Legend,* vol. 2 (New York: Funk and Wagnalls, 1950), 622–23, 601, 1152.

often are believed to be the source of dangerously seductive power. In Muslim society, for example, a woman must cover her hair and lower her eyes in public so as not to excite the passions of strange men. In the Middle Ages, witches were shaved to rob them of their powers before they were forced to confess. Many myths also corroborate the dangerously hypnotic quality of women's voices. The root of Keats's Lamia's enchanting power, for example, is her beautiful singing. And the siren, the mermaid, and the undine, all beautiful mythic water creatures, lured sailors to their deaths with their songs.[3]

Whatever the focal point of her particular allure, the femme fatale's sexuality is almost palpable, making her irresistible and deadly. Like the vampire or the succubus, she is insatiable, and like these creatures, she coldly (though figuratively) devours her mate after he has served his purpose, increasing her strength from his spent form. In stories devised by men, once her evil intentions become clear, her form sometimes changes, revealing hideously deformed genitals, which mirror her heinous spirit and her violation of gender codes. Spenser's Duessa in *The Faerie Queene,* an evil witch with "neather partes misshapen, monstrous," at first masks her evil qualities to distract the Red Cross Knight from his quest. As portrayed by male writers, the femme fatale embodies the monstrosity society perceives in feminine power. Sigmund Freud blamed this fear of women on the castration complex, the fear that the powerful woman might take the source of male power and the object of her envy, the penis. The witch on the broom, commonly believed to ride the bodies of men at night and drain their strength while increasing her own, is, as H. R. Hays points out, the embodiment of this phallic woman. But another way a woman might drain a man's strength is by simply suggesting his weakness. According to Simone de Beauvoir, woman threatens man because, as the site of his birth and his erotic pleasure, she reminds him of his own physicality, hence his mortality: "In all civilizations and still in our day woman inspires man with horror: it is the horror of his own carnal contingence which he projects upon her."[4]

As Sandra M. Gilbert, Susan Gubar, and Elaine Showalter have pointed

3. John Keats, "La Belle Dame sans Merci" in *The Norton Anthology of Poetry,* 3d ed., Alexander W. Allison et al., eds. (New York: Norton, 1983), 658; Frazer, *Golden Bough,* 769.

4. Edmund Spenser, *The Faerie Queene,* in *The Norton Anthology of English Literature,* 3d ed., M. H. Abrams et al., eds. (New York: Norton, 1975), 361; H. R. Hays, *Dangerous Sex: The Myth of Feminine Evil* (New York: Putnam, 1964), 155–56; Simone de Beauvoir, *The Second Sex,* H. M. Parshley, trans. and ed. (New York: Knopf, 1993), 148.

out, late-nineteenth-century male writers, in response to early feminist and suffragist movements, became even more preoccupied with the femme fatale. These critics cite H. Rider Haggard's *She* (1886), the male quest to annihilate the insatiable female queen, as the prime example of this trend. With the advent of feminism, as the silenced object begins to speak in her own voice, these men see the threatening power of her creativity: representation of the world will no longer rest solely in masculine hands. With angry zeal, male fin-de-siècle writers depict the new woman as an amazon seductress, who, unlike most earlier femmes fatales, is brutally destroyed, definitively silenced.[5]

In American literature, Leslie Fiedler links the fear of the castrating woman with the fear of adult sexuality and responsibility, which can be completely avoided only with Huck and Jim on the raft. Again and again, female characters in American literature are represented as either totally pure and virginal, incapable of passion, or sexually knowledgeable and dangerous. The idea of a female dichotomy of goodness and evil has been around at least as long as the concept of the femme fatale. In fact, Melanie Klein argues that a similar dichotomy is present in the mind of the very young infant and is a necessary precursor to proper ego development. The mother's breast simultaneously supplies all the infant's satisfaction and creates all frustration when taken away. According to Klein, therefore, "in the infant's mind the mother primarily appears as good and bad breast split off from each other." Later, the developing ego realizes "that the loved object is the same as the hated one, and in addition to this that the real objects and the imaginary figures, both external and internal, are bound up with each other." Perhaps the femme fatale who appears in literature by men is a projection of this primal internal conflict created by the infant's first love. Fiedler attributes to James Fenimore Cooper the origin of the convention that the two women be sisters, "thus secretly confessing their kinship." Only when the American ethos itself changes after the disillusionment of World War I does the American Girl become the witch in disguise (Fitzgerald's Daisy Buchanan, for example), the ideal and its antithesis embodied as one, "for wealth is no longer innocent, America no longer innocent, the Girl who is the soul of both turned destructive and corrupt." With the possibility of disguise, there

5. Sandra M. Gilbert and Susan Gubar, *The Madwoman in the Attic: The Woman Writer and the Nineteenth-Century Literary Imagination* (New Haven: Yale University Press, 1979; reprint, 1984), 8–22; Elaine Showalter, *Sexual Anarchy: Gender and Culture at the Fin de Siècle* (New York: Viking, 1990), 9–10.

is the possibility of mistaking the dangerous woman for her pure counterpart, and she becomes even more threatening.[6]

Understandably, this legacy of female representation can also be threatening to the woman writer. As Joanna Russ remarks in her aptly titled essay "Why Women Can't Write," the woman created by male authors is "the Other," and "the Other has no mind at all." Whether angel or demon, she is not even a person, but a projected wish or fear. Without a mind, she obviously has no authority, and so she cannot write. Russ further observes that none of these stereotyped images of women "is of the slightest use as myth to the woman writer who wishes to write about the female protagonist." And in "Aesthetics," Russ comments that "the woman who knows beyond a doubt that she is beautiful exists aplenty in male novelists' imaginations; I have yet to find her in women's books or women's memoirs or in life."[7] In spite of Russ's objections, many women writers do use the femme fatale figure, the dangerously beautiful woman who knows her power, either as protagonist or as the female protagonist's archenemy. And many of the women writers who use the femme fatale figure are southern. Why would a woman writer use this femme fatale figure, who objectifies and vilifies women in general? Particularly, why would those women struggling to write in the late-nineteenth-century and early-twentieth-century South—in a culture that valued a lady's purity and decorum above all else and in which her only proper form of self-expression, silent dignity, made it nearly impossible for her voice to be heard—employ the figure men had so long used as the silent embodiment of female evil and otherness, in opposition to which all important aspects of culture were defined? For southern women writers, at least, I see this figure as a response to the rigid preoccupations of their culture.

This figure of the belle gone bad resembles in many respects the mad or monstrous characters Gilbert and Gubar examine in the works of nineteenth-century British women writers in their well-known study *The Madwoman*

6. Juliet Mitchell, ed., *The Selected Melanie Klein.* (New York: Penguin Books, 1986), 53, 141; Leslie Fiedler, *Love and Death in the American Novel* (New York: Criterion Books, 1960), 282, 301.

7. Joanna Russ, "Why Women Can't Write" in *Images of Women in Fiction: Feminist Perspectives,* Susan Koppelman Cornillon, comp. (Bowling Green, Ohio: Bowling Green State University Popular Press, 1972), 6; Joanna Russ, "Aesthetics" in *Feminisms: An Anthology of Literary Theory and Criticism,* 2d ed., Robyn R. Warhol and Diane Price Herndl, eds. (New Brunswick, N.J.: Rutgers University Press, 1997), 204.

in the Attic. However, there is another explanation for both the bad belles'
and the mad or monstrous women's appearances in works by women writers. At first glance, the similarities may be hard to discern, because whereas
the bad belle is physically alluring, the mad or monstrous character is physically grotesque, and whereas the bad belle is dangerously cunning, the mad
or monstrous character is dangerously irrational. But both figures represent
societal conceptions of women who have stepped beyond the gender roles
defined by their culture. As Charlotte Perkins Gilman's "The Yellow Wallpaper" demonstrates, many nineteenth-century doctors, European and American, believed too much mental activity in women, for which women's
bodies and brains supposedly were unequipped, was the source of the mental illness often labeled hysteria. Gilman creates her madwoman, not as a
way to prove them right or as a way to reflect her feeling of guilt for writing
(the anxiety of authorship Gilbert and Gubar posit to explain the appearance of similar characters in the works they study), but as a way to critique
the absurdity of these beliefs. As Gilman's exaggerated version of her society's image of the woman writer reveals, it is the cure that causes the illness.
She demonstrates that the notions of feminine decorum and limitation are
designed, not to protect women, but to control them and ensure their continued usefulness to men.

The bad southern belles, and perhaps Gilbert's and Gubar's madwomen
as well, function similarly to the madwoman in Gilman's "The Yellow
Wallpaper." Through these figures, the women writers offer a hyperbolic
version, often a parody, of their society's conception of women who have
stepped beyond proscribed roles, and they use these figures as a vehicle for
social criticism. This interpretation draws on Judith Butler's theories of
gender performativity and parody. Though Butler applies her theories to a
critique of compulsory heterosexuality, she also suggests blurring the lines
between queer and feminist theory, and it is in this vein that I adapt her
ideas.[8]

Butler views gender attributes—the characteristic traits society labels as
masculine or feminine—as performative, as behaviors learned through imitation. If gender is viewed in this way, gender identity becomes, not something natural or essential to human beings, but a "regulatory fiction," an
artificial system imposed by culture. Drew Gilpin Faust contends that many
recognized this performative aspect of gender during and after the Civil

8. Judith Butler, *Bodies that Matter: On the Discursive Limits of "Sex"* (New York: Routledge, 1993), 239.

War. As one young woman wrote in her diary, "If only I was a man! I don't know a woman here who does not groan over her misfortune in being clothed in petticoats; why cant we fight as well as the men[?]." "In the theater of war," explains Faust, "gender—with its protections, privileges, opportunities, and responsibilities—had become only a costume." According to Butler, however, most fail to recognize the artifice because the performance is so embedded in culture and necessary to maintain power structures and societal norms. But those who expose the performance, through theatrical exaggeration, gain a political voice at the same time they risk social ostracism. By exposing the performance, the performer exposes and challenges the strategies used to maintain a patriarchal power structure, wresting and reasserting gender identity on different terms. Though Butler refers primarily to the practice of drag, the femme fatale can be seen as engaging in a similar performance, claiming power and blurring gender lines by exaggerating, on the surface at least, typically feminine attributes. Like the drag queen, though, she is really something quite different under her enticing clothes. According to Butler, "The performance is thus a kind of talking back. . . . The queen will out-woman women, and in the process confuse and seduce an audience whose gaze must to some degree be structured through those [patriarchal homophobic] hegemonies, an audience who, through the hyperbolic staging of the scene, will be drawn into the abjection it wants both to resist and to overcome."[9] The femme fatale outwomans women on the surface, and underneath she out-mans men. In doing so, the southern femme fatale, the bad belle, challenges and parodies her society's negative conceptions of powerful women and highlights the hypocrisies and weaknesses of the society that imposes limiting roles on its women.

Why might this parody by southern women writers take the form of the belle gone bad rather than the madwoman, as it did for Gilman and many nineteenth-century British women writers? In the Old South's rigidly structured patriarchal society, sexuality, or lack thereof, was of such great symbolic import in the proper role for women that any violation of that role, mental or physical, brought the suspicion, if not the outright accusation, of

9. Butler, *Gender Trouble: Feminism and the Subversion of Identity* (New York: Routledge, 1990), 141; Drew Gilpin Faust, *Mothers of Invention: Women of the Slaveholding South in the American Civil War* (Chapel Hill: University of North Carolina Press, 1996), 221; Butler, *Bodies that Matter*, 232, 132.

sexual promiscuity. The woman who wrote, therefore, or any powerful woman, ran the risk of being labeled as immoral. Southern women writers parodied this negative image of female power and critiqued the society that imposed it by combining men's worst nightmare, the femme fatale, with southern men's most cherished icons, the southern belle and the southern lady. By exaggerating attributes society deemed inappropriate to the southern belle's gender, race, and class, southern women writers complicated the figure of ideal womanhood the patriarchal system created. Coy and alluring like the traditional belle, the bad belle is also coldly manipulative and far too knowing. Unable to resist her carefully cultivated charms, men who are subject to the dangerous belle's will often meet disastrous ends.

Anne Goodwyn Jones, Kathryn Lee Seidel, and Bertram Wyatt-Brown, adding their recent cultural inquiries about the symbolic stature of the southern lady to the now canonical studies of Lillian Smith, W. J. Cash, and Anne Firor Scott, point out that the white woman's image of purity and goodness was linked to all aspects of the social structure. Jones comments on the social importance of the lady's symbolic quality: "More than just a fragile flower, the image of the southern lady represents her culture's idea of religious, moral, sexual, racial and social perfection." These ideas of racial, moral, religious, and social perfection, because so closely tied to the ideal of the southern lady, were dependent on the society's ideas about sexuality.[10]

The white southern lady was defined in terms of negative sexuality: "Pious—whether aristocratic Episcopalian or middle-class Methodist—the ideal southern lady also acts as a moral exemplar. She embodies virtue, but her goodness depends directly on innocence—in fact, on ignorance of evil. She is chaste because she has never been tempted; in some renditions she lacks sexual interest altogether." The lady is required to suppress all strong passions and to be a guiding example who tames the passions of men. By contrast, her physical frailty emphasizes her white male protector's strength, courage, and class privilege. Wyatt-Brown points out that a woman's chastity was more than just a matter of her personal morality; it also reflected on the honor of the entire household, particularly of its male head. To maintain his status in the community, the patriarch had to retaliate with violence when one of his female dependents was dishonored. Southern so-

---

10. Anne Goodwyn Jones, *Tomorrow Is Another Day: The Woman Writer in the South, 1859–1936* (Baton Rouge: Louisiana State University Press, 1981), 9.

ciety placed the white woman as focal point of its myths about itself, giving her great power as a cultural icon while denying her individual desire or agency.[11]

Smith comments on the debilitating effect of this sexual repression in her autobiography *Killers of the Dream:* "The pain they [southern ladies] denied or tried to displace. The emptiness was the natural way women should feel! Like childbirth pains and menstrual cramps, the sexual blankness of their lives was 'God's way' and hence if you were sensible must be accepted. But some stubbornly called it 'female trouble' and went to the doctors' offices as often as to church, to moan their misery." Interestingly, Smith cites both "childbirth pains" and "sexual blankness," calling attention to the competing ideals of chastity and reproduction imposed on the matron. In her description, southern women endured the pain of sexuality but enjoyed none of its pleasures. Smith identifies sexual emptiness with lack of fulfillment in all realms of the traditional woman's life and says that for many traditional southern women, hysterical physical symptoms became a safe surrogate for sexual expression, as conventional religion became a safe surrogate for mental expression. White women's powerlessness and asexuality went hand in hand.[12]

The limitations of the white woman's place in society created conflict for her, a conflict heightened by the inconsistencies inherent in her role and by the differing social expectations for men and women and the differing roles of white and black women in the South. Tensions associated with the white woman's role began in early childhood. Very young girls were indulged and encouraged to be willful, as were young boys; but as soon as a girl reached puberty, her actions were rigidly controlled, while her brother continued to sow wild oats. Adding to this tension were the somewhat ambiguous expectations placed on marriageable young women through the stereotype of the southern belle. Though the southern lady was regally asexual, the young belle was supposed to be beautiful and flirtatious, but only within carefully prescribed limits. Her flirtations excited male passions, but she was supposed to be, and perhaps often was, innocent of the true nature of those passions. Once married, she was to take her role as asexual moral guide while producing a large southern family, again illustrating the competing ideals of chastity and sexual capacity. Seidel explains in *The Southern Belle in*

---

11. Jones, *Tomorrow Is Another Day,* 9; Bertram Wyatt-Brown, *Southern Honor: Ethics and Behavior in the Old South* (New York: Oxford University Press, 1982), 53.

12. Lillian Smith, *Killers of the Dream* (1949; reprint,: New York: Norton, 1978), 140.

the American Novel that the demands placed upon the young southern girl sometimes created unbearable strain: "A society that prefers its lovely women to be charming and flirtatious coquettes who never yield their purity can create a situation of impossible tension for the belle: she is asked to exhibit herself as sexually desirable to the appropriate males, yet she must not herself respond sexually. She must be as alluring as the Dark Lady, yet as pure as the White Maiden." Though her actions were monitored and controlled, the belle still had the power to wield her carefully cultivated feminine charms to force males to do her bidding. As Thomas R. Dew points out in an 1835 essay published in the *Southern Literary Messenger,* this type of manipulation was the woman's main source of power:

> How is he to be drawn to her side? Not by menace—not by force; for weakness cannot, by such means, be expected to triumph over might. No! It must be by conformity to that character which circumstances demand for the sphere in which she moves; by the exhibition of those qualities which delight and fascinate—which are calculated to win over to her side the proud lord of creation, and to make him an humble suppliant at her shrine. Grace, modesty and loveliness are the charms which constitute her power. By these she creates the magic spell that subdues to her will the more mighty physical powers by which she is surrounded.

Trained from childhood in the arts of allure for the sole purpose of capturing the suitable husbands on which their futures depended, southern belles, as Dew's words attest, share many characteristics with the femme fatale. Historically, both are constructions, engendered by men, (Dew's proud lords of creation) that define women according to the needs they fulfill for men and according to the mystery they represent to men. And both, though at first glance they appear to give power to the woman, end by silencing her.[13]

Typically, southern women were required to abdicate this provisional power once they married. Whereas the belle is the center of male attention and her whims are constantly satisfied, the matron's role is to serve as wife, mother, and moral guide. Her desires are sacrificed for the comfort of others. Southerner Sarah Jane Estes wrote in her diary in 1862, "My own happiness I have never consulted since leaving home for there was little choice.

13. Wyatt-Brown, *Southern Honor,* 231–33; Kathryn Lee Seidel, *The Southern Belle in the American Novel* (Tampa: University of South Florida Press, 1985), xvi; Thomas Roderick Dew, "Dissertation on the Characteristic Differences of the Sexes, and Woman's Position and Influence in Society," *Southern Literary Messenger* 1 (1835): 495–96.

. . . As a mother and a wife I hope I do not consider my own comfort, but live and work for those whom god has given, receiving my reward by making them happy." And in the 1850s, Lizzie Scott predicted that in her upcoming marriage, "my identity, my larger existence will be swallowed up in my husband." Though both roles, belle and matron, were limiting, Minrose Gwin observes that white southern women did not often resist them outwardly: "Since white women were victims of adulation rather than violence, they often internalized stereotypical forms and attempted in great earnestness to become what they were expected to be—faithful standard-bearers of the patriarchy." Though, as Wyatt-Brown points out, white southern women sometimes were victims of domestic abuse, in general their treatment, like their symbolic position, was opposite that of black women, and violence against them was most often the result of resisting their role. Added to the social deprivation this symbolic status imposed was legal deprivation: almost no rights were granted the married woman because it was the duty of her husband to protect and act for her.[14] It is not surprising southern women writers might direct their anger and critique through the figure of the belle, which their society used to tempt them into the restraint of marriage, or that twentieth-century southern women writers create a bad belle who refuses to relinquish her seductive power when married.

Of course, not all southern women writers were once beautiful belles, not all had beautiful daughters, and not all the white female South participated in these social customs. As Wyatt-Brown observes, the yeoman class and the poor whites could not afford to have their women stand idly on pedestals. But, according to Anne Firor Scott, "mythology assured every young woman that she was a belle." The *ideal* of pure white womanhood was still part of the mythos of the entire South, tied closely—especially preceding and following the Civil War—to the ideal of white supremacy, which the planter class employed to keep poor whites satisfied with their lot in life. Nell Irvin Painter points out:

> Sex was the whip that white supremacists used to reinforce white solidarity, probably the only whip that would cut deeply enough to keep poor whites in line. Political slogans that spoke straightforwardly of property or wealth (which not all whites held) had failed to rally whites en masse. However, nearly all white men could claim to hold a certain sort of property, in wives,

14. Faust, *Mothers of Invention*, 35, 140; Minrose Gwin, *Black and White Women of the Old South* (Knoxville: University of Tennessee Press, 1985), 4–5; Wyatt-Brown, *Southern Honor*, 280–83.

sisters, and daughters. When women were reduced to things, they became property that all white men could own. The sexually charged rhetoric of "social equality" invited all white men to protect their property in women and share in the maintenance of all sorts of power . . . in the name of protecting the sexuality of white womanhood.

This dual oppression, which ensured white male dominance, lasted well into the twentieth century and caused the South to resist the women's suffrage movement longer than other regions of the country. As Anastasia Sims states, "If white women became equal participants in the political process, they might choose different protectors or reject protection entirely." Much antisuffrage propaganda in the South equated woman suffrage with black domination. One leaflet enjoined, "Heed not the call of the suffrage siren. . . . Remember that woman suffrage means a reopening of the entire Negro question." Protection of white southern womanhood was not only a means of protecting one's social advantages but also a way of bettering one's social position. The conduct of women reflected on the honor, breeding, and social status of the family as a whole, and any attempt at social climbing through financial gain had to be accompanied by proper deportment. Even the courts presumed that a woman's sexuality was the property of her father or husband, making it very difficult for a woman to press charges for rape without the presence of a male protector. Laura F. Edwards cites the example of Susan J. Daniel, who swore out a complaint in her own name in 1864: "By the end of the case, however, the records referred to her as Mrs. Rufus Daniel. It is unlikely that Daniel herself had much to do with the change. The officials who produced the documentation probably just found it easier to deal with her as the married dependent of a male household head." Because the ideal of womanhood was so rigid, women in general suffered loss of freedom and loss of legal rights.[15]

* * *

15. Anne Firor Scott, *The Southern Lady: From Pedestal to Politics, 1830–1930,* Expanded paperback ed. (Charlottesville: University Press of Virginia, 1995), 23; Nell Irvin Painter, "'Social Equality,' Miscegenation, Labor, and Power," in *The Evolution of Southern Culture,* Numan V. Bartley, ed. (Athens: University of Georgia Press, 1988), 49; Anastasia Sims, *The Power of Femininity in the New South: Women's Organizations and Politics in North Carolina, 1880–1930* (Columbia: University of South Carolina Press, 1997), 156, 178; Laura F. Edwards, *Gendered Strife and Confusion: The Political Culture of Reconstruction* (Urbana: University of Illinois Press, 1997), 211. Also see Cash's *The Mind of the South,* 91–93, 118–19, 148–78, for a discussion of the role the southern ideal of womanhood played in race relations and class interactions in the South.

The act of writing itself violated the sexual taboos that confined the southern woman, which is another reason the writers' critiques of those confines emerged in a sexually dangerous form. As Gilbert and Gubar have pointed out, writing historically has been considered a male act, with the pen representing a metaphorical penis and the male author metaphorically impregnating the female muse to engender art. Writing is explicitly linked to a lack of proper modesty and thereby connected to promiscuity. According to Peggy Whitman Prenshaw, "The double bind that constrained nineteenth-century European and American women generally was especially intense in the American South. For women, honor and good name and 'selfhood' such as might be confirmed by one's society, were attendant upon a woman's acceptance of a private—not public—domain. The act of expressing herself in public in writing, of intruding the female self upon the male-dominated turf, meant risking her standing in her family and acceptance by her neighbors, her church, by the whole wide world as far as she could tell." By writing, a woman places her thoughts and feelings on display for public consumption, just as the prostitute places her body on display for public consumption. Nineteenth-century southern poet Catherine Edmonston explained her reasons for not publishing her work in terms of feminine propriety: "Then indeed you would forget a woman's first ornament, modesty. Women have no business to rush into print; so wide an arena does not become them." Writing meant public exposure and a risk of one's reputation as a lady.[16]

Nineteenth-century southern educational trends illustrate this concept. Steven M. Stowe, in his study of elite women's education and family feeling in the Old South, notes that when it came to reading and writing, women and men were trained differently: "Women were told that they were particularly susceptible to language, almost to the point of having a preternatural affinity for words." Even in the modern South, Eudora Welty confirmed the erotic power and potential threat of words when she wrote of her mother: "She read Dickens in the spirit in which she would have eloped with him" (*OWB* 17). Women, therefore, had to be more careful of what they read and to whom and of what they wrote. Scott states, "In at least one [nineteenth-century] school girls wrote their English compositions on

---

16. Gilbert and Gubar, *Madwoman,* 3–4; Peggy Whitman Prenshaw, "The True Happenings of My Life: Reading Southern Women Autobiographers" in *Haunted Bodies: Gender in Southern Texts,* Susan V. Donaldson and Anne Goodwyn Jones (Charlottesville: University Press of Virginia, 1997), 444; Faust, *Mothers of Invention,* 166.

such subjects as modesty, benevolences, and the evils of reading novels."
This linguistic double standard mirrored the sexual double standard imposed on women.[17]

The act of writing for southern girls was a carefully monitored activity, linked to courtship rituals. One of the primary functions of schooling for girls of the planter class was learning to write appealing and decorous letters. Popular letter-writing guides, "premised on the power of lovers' correspondence and the sorrows that followed misused words," gave "taut and guarded letters as models." A regular correspondence between a young woman and a young man was an indication of a serious courtship and was often the "most tangible token of regard" in their premarital relations. For the young southern woman, writing was exposure that made her vulnerable, and it indicated an intimacy that the proper girl's family had to monitor and control.[18]

In *The Newly Born Woman,* Hélène Cixous explores the parallels between linguistic and sexual silencing that are boldly illustrated in the Old South. Cixous sees the hierarchical binary oppositions (such as Sun/Moon, Day/Night, Culture/Nature, Active/Passive) on which Western "theory of culture, theory of society, symbolic systems in general—art, religion, family, language" are based as symbolically linked to "the couple, man/ woman." Under this system, the masculine element is always privileged, while the feminine element is debased or negated: "the logocentric plan had always, inadmissibly, been to create a foundation for . . . phallocentrism, to guarantee the masculine order a rationale equal to history itself." For the woman artist, the struggle to free herself in language is intertwined with the struggle to free herself sexually. To rebel against one form of constraint, she must also rebel against the other.[19] The southern woman who chooses to create art, then, adds to the inherent tension of her position as sexless icon the tension of discovering her own thoughts and summoning a voice with which to speak them, a voice that can be heard within her patriarchal society.

17. Stephen M. Stowe, "The Not-So-Cloistered Academy: Elite Women's Education and Family Feeling in the Old South" in *The Web of Southern Social Relations: Women, Family, and Education,* Walter J. Fraser Jr., Frank Saunders Jr., and Jon Wakely, eds. (Athens: University of Georgia Press, 1985), 94; Scott, *Southern Lady,* 7.

18. Stowe, "Not-So-Cloistered," 99, 100.

19. Susan Sellers, ed., *The Hélène Cixous Reader,* preface by Hélène Cixous, foreword by Jacques Derrida (New York: Routledge, 1994), 38, 40.

The southern reception of some women writers' works further links writing to the crossing of sexual boundaries. Diane Roberts notes that some nineteenth-century southern women writers metaphorically "saw writing as cross-dressing: Caroline Gilman recalled her unauthorized first publication with shame, saying 'I wept bitterly, and was as alarmed as if I had been detected in men's apparel.'" Though Gilman was not a willing participant, her comment echoes Butler's description of the drag queen's performance as a form of talking back, highlighting through violation the artificiality of gender conventions. By writing, Gilman usurped male power, almost as if she had stolen a man's pants. Similarly, after the publication of *Uncle Tom's Cabin*, proslavery southerners attacked Harriet Beecher Stowe as a shameless woman, connecting her "not just with philosophical offenders but sexual offenders." Roberts further comments on a respected male southern writer's attack on Stowe:

> [William Gilmore] Simms characterizes Stowe's authorship: "the petticoat lifts of itself, and we see the hoof of the beast under the table." . . . Here the cross-dressed author becomes a devil disguised in women's clothing. The image of the petticoat lifting "of itself" is supernatural and demonic . . . . However, something else reveals itself when the petticoat of the female author rises; the "hoof of the beast," the "mark" of the devil also signifies the "mark" of the female, that is: the genitals. The woman who speaks or writes "in public," who makes herself a "display" like a prostitute, in effect flaunts her genitals. She shows what no lady even admits to having; she unveils what her culture covers in layers of skirts and mystifies in language. As well as violating the conventions of her gender, according to her critics, Stowe violates the definition of the body assigned her class and race.[20]

Simms's reference to Stowe's imagined monstrous genitals links her to earlier representations of the femme fatale such as Spenser's Duessa. If a woman chose to reject her role as pure, voiceless lady, she ran the risk of being labeled as that person's opposite, the whore.

Perhaps the most important reason the southern woman writer's dark double—the vehicle through which she parodies society's negative conception of powerful women, such as herself, and critiques that society in general—takes the form of the sexually threatening bad belle is race. As mentioned

20. Diane Roberts, *The Myth of the Aunt Jemima: Representations of Race and Region* (New York: Routledge, 1994), 60–62.

previously, the white woman's role, dependent to a great extent on her lack of sexuality, was linked to all important aspects of southern culture, and no aspect of southern culture was more volatile in the nineteenth century than race. As social and literary critics have observed, in this culture, which placed such great symbolic importance on the white lady's purity and goodness, there was a ready-made dark double, the black jezebel. According to Sara M. Evans, "Southern colonists brought with them the fundamental Western myths about female nature which embodied a polarization between the virgin, pure and untouchable, and the prostitute, dangerously sexual. This dichotomy, associated with images of light and dark, good and evil, gradually took on concrete reality with the emergence of a white planter class based upon a racial slave labor system." Nineteenth-century proslavery apologist William Harper explains the necessity of this dichotomy: "The tendency of our institution [slavery] is to elevate the female character, as well as that of the other sex, and for similar reasons. In other states of society there is no well-defined limit to separate virtue and vice. . . . Here, there is that certain and marked line, above which there is no toleration or allowance for any approach to license of manners or conduct, and she who falls below it will fall far below even the slave." The line to which Harper refers is, of course, the color line. In a society where whiteness represented purity and innocence, sexuality itself was blackness. Smith describes her childhood understanding of the body to show that even on a white body, the genitals were black: "[P]arts of your body are segregated areas which you must stay away from and keep others away from . . . . You cannot associate freely with them any more than you can associate freely with colored children." Based on the assumption that blackness equaled sexuality, white society believed black women were sexually promiscuous. As Edwards observes, during Reconstruction the *Oxford Torchlight* often reinforced this belief in its pages: "The *Torchlight* scattered its references to African-American women liberally through its pages, where they appeared as the inversion of the elite ideal: promiscuous seductresses, heavy drinkers, hard fighters, ignorant housekeepers, and inattentive mothers." White men bolstered their belief in the black woman's inherent promiscuity with racist misunderstanding of African cultures and with projection of their physical desires, which their white wives' culturally imposed inaccessibility left unfulfilled. Though in the southern mythology the promiscuity supposedly gave black women power over men, the texts of many southern women, black and white, indicate that at least some realized the men really retained all the power for themselves. White men, not constrained by the same rigorous standards as their wives, often seduced or raped black women.[21]

Some white women did resent the black woman's supposed immoral behavior. In her autobiography, former slave Harriet Jacobs relates her mistress's jealous response to Dr. Flint's pursuit of the young Harriet. Though his lust is unrequited, Mrs. Flint is incapable of attacking the head of her household, so she conveniently blames Harriet and takes her frustrations out on the helpless slave. Mary Chesnut, a planter's wife from South Carolina, wrote in her diary that the white women were "as pure as angels, tho' surrounded by another race who are the social evil!" Elsewhere, she referred to black women in the household as prostitutes. And Elizabeth Fox-Genovese, citing an anonymous Georgia slave narrative, recounts a white woman's decapitation of her female slave's child, because the white woman believed it to be her husband's child as well. Most wives of slaveholders, however, were also conscious that their actions were, in some ways, more rigidly controlled than their slaves'. As Gwin notes:

> Real southern women of both races, bound by their dichotomous images in the popular mind and, in the case of black women, by actual enslavement, often viewed one another as missing pieces of a female identity denied them by the patriarchal culture. Female narrators of slave narratives reveal their yearning for the chaste respectability of their white sisters, while the diaries and memoirs of the white women show their intense jealously of the stereo-

---

21. Sara M. Evans, "Women" in *The Encyclopedia of Southern History*, David C. Roller and Robert W. Twyman, eds. (Baton Rouge: Louisiana State University Press, 1979), 1353; Donaldson and Jones, "Haunted Bodies: Rethinking the South through Gender" in *Haunted Bodies*, 2; Smith, *Killers of the Dream*, 87; Edwards, *Gendered Strife*, 135. Elizabeth Fox-Genovese, Gwin, Jones, Roberts, and Seidel also discuss the symbolic binary opposition of black and white women in southern society. For a discussion of the southerner's continued ties to Europe, see Daniel R. Hundley's *Social Relations in Our Southern States*, edited and with an introduction by William J. Cooper Jr. (Baton Rouge, 1979); William R. Taylor's *Cavalier and Yankee: The Old South and American National Character*, (1957; reprint, Cambridge, Mass.: Harvard University Press, 1961); Clement Eaton's *A History of the Old South* (New York: MacMillan, 1949); Winthrop D. Jordan's *White over Black: American Attitudes toward the Negro, 1550–1812* (Chapel Hill: University of North Carolina Press, 1968); George M. Fredrickson's *The Black Image in the White Mind: The Debate on Afro-American Character and Destiny, 1817–1914* (New York: Harper and Row, 1971), Wyatt-Brown's *Southern Honor*; and Estill Curtis Pennington's "Anglo-American Antebellum Culture," in *The Encyclopedia of Southern Culture*, Charles Reagan Wilson and William Ferris, eds. (Chapel Hill: University of North Carolina Press, 1989).

typical sexuality of the slave woman. Each is only one half of a self. What is so terribly ironic is that the missing piece of self so fervently desired by one race of women seems to have caused so much suffering for the other.

Jacobs, for example, laments her inability to remain chaste, illustrating the African American woman's envy of her white counterpart's lot in southern life. Chesnut records in her diary her resentment, which seems to stem, not from her jealousy over white male and black female promiscuity, but from her inability to be similarly promiscuous. And Gertrude Thomas, another wealthy planter's wife, writes, "While no man was without sin he was still empowered to cast the first stone at his wife or sister, for a woman of the planter class who had fallen was cast aside beyond recall."[22] We can further compare the restrictions on women's writing to sexual ties between the white man and the black woman, which isolated the white woman. The whiteness of the male was allowed to mix with the blackness of sexuality (as Smith points out, sex itself was black), just as the male phallic pen mixed with the blackness of ink, but the white woman had to be sheltered from the taints of both. But the presence of the dark double in the white southern woman writer's works indicates her rejection of this double standard. It is through the character of the belle gone bad that white southern women writers comment on the abuses and hypocrisies enacted against white and black women by the southern patriarchy.

Because miscegenation was a topic no proper lady should discuss, however, let alone write about in her novels, the evil seductress in southern women's novels usually is not portrayed as a black woman, but as a dark foreigner, often Italian, with fiery blood and magically seductive powers, qualities also attributed to the African slave. As in the works of male romantics, such as Keats, the hair and eyes are hypnotic talismans of this femme fatale, but these aspects of the southern figure have a dark, exotic quality similar to conventional descriptions of the mulatta. By placing in their novels a disguised version of the black female, whom their society believed to be immoral and destructive, the authors not only create female

---

22. Harriet Jacobs, *Incidents in the Life of a Slave Girl*, Maria L. Child, ed., introduction and notes by Walter Teller (New York: Harcourt Brace Jovanovich, 1973); C. Vann Woodward, ed., *Mary Chesnut's Civil War* (New Haven, Conn.: Yale University Press, 1981), 31, 29; Fox-Genovese, *Within the Plantation Household: Black and White Women of the Old South* (Chapel Hill: University of North Carolina Press, 1988), 325; Gwin, *Black and White Women*, 11; LeeAnn Whites, *The Civil War as a Crisis in Gender: Augusta, Georgia, 1860–1890* (Athens: University of Georgia Press, 1995), 26.

characters who can step beyond the proper confines of ladyhood, but at the same time the authors critique those who impose the confinements.

In one sense, the dark figures are surrogate selves, allowing the seemingly conventional (except in the fact that they wrote) writers to vicariously experience some of the dark lady's sexual freedom and control over men in the exploratory realm of fiction. Toni Morrison has observed a similar phenomenon in American literature by white males. Examining such American classics as William Faulkner's *Absalom, Absalom!* and Edgar Allan Poe's *The Narrative of Arthur Gordon Pym of Nantucket,* Morrison asserts that the black population was used as a symbol to articulate the repressed fears of the white culture. White Americans, says Morrison, defined themselves in contrast to the "otherness" of the black slave and imaginatively explored through African Americans that which they feared or which their culture denied to them. African Americans became a shadow population, who not only had a distinctive color but a color that "meant" something. According to Mae Henderson, black women, by virtue of both their race and sex, "exist as the ultimate Other whose absence or (non)being only serves to define the being or presence of the white or male subject. The black woman, symbolizing a kind of double negativity, becomes a *tabula rasa* upon which the racial-sexual identity of the other(s) can be positively inscribed."[23]

Also, by establishing a link between representations of themselves in their writing and their supposed opposite, white ladies shook the social structure that imprisoned black and white women in obverse but equally limiting roles. Nineteenth-century woman's rights advocates from outside the South overtly acknowledged an ironic connection between white women and slaves. Margaret Fuller, for example, pointed out the illogic of arguing that women were too frail to participate in government when pregnant female slaves were forced to work in the fields all day. As Karen Sanchez-Eppler explains, Fuller's words "achieve a double efficacy, simultaneously declaring the physical strength of the woman and implying the need to protect the exploited slave." This connection was more problematic in the South, where slavery was part of the socioeconomic system, and southern writers

---

23. Toni Morrison, *Playing in the Dark: Whiteness and the Literary Imagination* (Cambridge, Mass.: Harvard University Press, 1992), 37–38; Mae Henderson, "Toni Morrison's *Beloved*: Re-Membering the Body as Historical Text," in *Comparative American Identities: Race, Sex , and Nationality in the Modern Text,* Hortense J. Spillers, ed. (New York: Routledge, 1991), 69. Ralph Ellison made an argument similar to Morrison's almost forty years earlier in "Twentieth-Century Fiction and the Black Mask of Humanity," in *Shadow and Act* (New York: Random House, 1953).

could not risk making such bold claims. Southern men also acknowledged the similarly subservient status of slaves and white women, but in most of their writing the status was presented as one that should be protected, not changed. As the editor of the *Augusta Chronicle and Sentinel* wrote in 1861, all of Augusta's citizens must join to resist the "domination of a fanatic, puritan horde of agrarians, abolitionists and free lovers." The North not only threatened to free white men's slaves (through abolition) but also white men's wives (through free love).[24] In the works of southern women writers, a disguised dark double paradoxically embodies both the freedoms the white woman is denied and the general subjection of womanhood through the abuses of white male power.

The bad belle challenges the one-sided, abusive distribution of power. The character serves as a vehicle for disguised social criticism in the works of southern women writers, a way for them to confront the injustices perpetrated against black and white women by the patriarchal South. Via the bad belle, these writers call attention to weaknesses of the men in charge, chief among their sins the sexual abuse of African American women. The belle gone bad uses her sexuality to control the male, attacking him at the source of his patriarchal power, the phallus. Though the nineteenth-century southern woman writer eventually destroys her dark double, she leaves in the bad belle's wake a weakened power structure. The seducer's manipulations prove the southern gentleman to be weak and vulnerable instead of the tower of strength and courage he is supposed to be.

African American southern women writers, however, did not employ the bad belle. As emotionally charged as the dark seductress figure was for the white lady, it was more so for the African American. The character served as an excellent shadow figure for the white lady because through her the lady realized an escape from her pedestal and undermined the patriarchy that had placed her there. But this figure could not be a shadow figure for the southern African American woman because the dominant culture saw it as her true identity, using it to justify sexual abuse, deny her basic human rights, and even to deny her humanity.

According to Deborah E. McDowell, the "network of social and literary

24. Margaret Fuller, "Women in the Nineteenth Century" in *The Heath Anthology of American Literature,* 3d ed., Paul Lauter et al., ed. (Boston: Houghton Mifflin, 1998), 1: 1720; Karen Sanchez-Eppler, "Bodily Bonds: The Intersecting Rhetorics of Feminism and Abolition," in *The Culture of Sentiment: Race, Gender, and Sentimentality in Nineteenth-Century America,* Shirley Samuels, ed. (New York: Oxford University Press, 1992), 96; Whites, *The Civil War as a Crisis in Gender,* 18.

myths . . . about black women's libidinousness" prompted "a pattern of ret-icence about black female sexuality [that] dominated novels by black women in the nineteenth and early twentieth centuries." The project of an-tebellum southern African American women writers such as Harriet Jacobs and Phillis Wheatley, for example, was to prove the moral worthiness of African American women, so the stereotype of the jezebel is one they would disclaim. As contemporary southern African American writer Alice Walker states in her novel *Meridian,* "black women were always imitating Harriet Tubman—escaping to become something unheard of," proving their strength of character while maintaining moral purity. Alternately, African American women writers of the late nineteenth and early twentieth cen-turies often employed the tragic mulatta character, portraying the beautiful young heroine as the helpless victim of white and black men, as in Nella Larsen's *Quicksand* (1928) and in Ann Petry's *The Street* (1946). Both im-ages, the strong Harriet Tubman imitator and the tragic mulatta figure, un-dermine the stereotype of the libidinous and seductive black woman.[25]

The sexuality of southern women was first a preoccupation of male south-erners, and the works of male southern writers, some of which employ-ed the bad belle character, reinforced conventional moral expectations. Nineteenth-century women writers revised this character from its appear-ance in the works of earlier male writers, and these feminist revisions seem to have influenced in turn later male creations of the character. In general, the bad belle who appears in the works of early male southern writers is one-dimensional, someone who might fascinate or horrify the author and reader but not someone with whom they could sympathize or identify. The reader does not see, and presumably the author does not imagine, the vul-nerabilities that lie beneath her beautifully frightening exterior. In addition, because politics was the realm of men and because they used this character to reinforce cultural norms, male writers saw little need to disguise the moral-political messages to which the bad belle characters contributed.

Augustus Baldwin Longstreet, for example, makes use of the belle gone bad in a story from *Georgia Scenes* (1835), "The Charming Creature as a Wife." As the title suggests, the tale uses a shallow, vain coquette to warn

25. Deborah E. McDowell, Introduction, *Quicksand and Passing,* Nella Larsen (New Brunswick, N.J.: Rutgers University Press, 1986), xii–xiii; Alice Walker, *Meridian* (New York: Harcourt Brace Jovanovich, 1976), 105.

the reader that it takes more than charm and looks to make a good wife. Though the story's social commentary is explicit, it avoids the darker side of southern social relations, ignoring slavery altogether. The unlucky husband serves as the point-of-view character, with whom the author intends the reader to sympathize even while lamenting his poor judgment in choosing a wife. We never see into the motivations of the title character, Evelina, and we are encouraged to imagine she has none, other than selfish vanity.

Enchantresses also figure in the poems of southerner Poe. But the reader has no hope of seeing into the thoughts of such dark ladies as Lenore ("The Raven"), Ulalume, or Annabel Lee because they are already dead, and in death they serve as the ultimate one-dimensional projections of their creator's fears and desires. Like the classic femmes fatales discussed at the beginning, these dead beautiful women threaten to seduce their narrators with the dual allure of sex and death. We also see the archetypal distinctions between the fascinatingly dangerous dark lady and the drably pure fair lady in Poe's short story "Ligeia." Here the dark seductress, the narrator's first wife, poisons the fair second wife from beyond the grave to return in her successor's body and reclaim her beloved. The story reveals not only Poe's obsession with the dark lady but also his suspicion that the two types are one and the same. Critics most often interpret these works psychoanalytically rather than politically, supposing the dark women to reflect the darker side of Poe's unconscious mind or an obsession with women resulting from his mother's early death.

In the works of the nineteenth-century southern women writers discussed in the next chapter—Southworth, Hentz, and Evans—the belle gone bad reflects a more complex mixture of psychological and political motivations. These women authors could see themselves more plainly in both the good and bad female characters. And as the women's journals reveal, they often recognized problems in the social structure (even as they outwardly defended that structure) before the men in power were willing to acknowledge them. Chesnut proclaimed in her diary that she hated slavery and that it would not last, and as early as 1862, she suspected that most southern planters were more talk than action and lacked the stamina to win a war. In 1858, Gertrude Clanton Thomas wrote, "Southern women are I believe at heart abolitionists." Many southern women, however, silenced their opinions, because they knew that possessing any political opinion was improper. For example, Faust quotes a letter from Lucy Wood, written in 1861: "Her objections to disunion, she explained to Waddy Butler, arose from her fears that an independent southern nation would reopen the African slave trade, a policy she found 'extremely revolting.' Yet as she elaborated her position, detailing her disagreements with the man she intended to wed, Wood abruptly and revealingly interrupted the flow of her argument. 'But I have no political opinion and had a peculiar dislike to all females who discuss such matters.'" The conflict between the white southern woman's private thoughts and society's expectations surfaces in the characters she creates. The southern woman writer's feelings for her dark double—as manifested by her treatment of this character—seem ambivalent. Unlike that of her male contemporaries, the woman writer's treatment of the belle gone bad reveals a disguised and unconventional political message. Though she often destroys the bad belle in the end, the southern woman writer first carefully explains the unusual past and internal motivations that forced the seductress into her wayward existence. Therefore, the bad belle in the southern woman writer's works is not, as she often is in the works of men, a one-dimensional figure. Laura Mulvey argues that the fetishization of parts of women, such as hair, eyes, lips, or legs, creates a one-dimensional quality in cinema: "One part of a fragmented body destroys the Renaissance space, the illusion of depth demanded by the narrative; it gives flatness, the quality of a cut-out or icon, rather than verisimilitude, to the screen."[26] This fetishization also contributes to the one-dimensional quality of the femme fatale narratives written by men. The women authors create tension in their narratives by adding depth and personality to their female villains while still calling attention to the conventional physical sources of her power. The reader's focus constantly shifts from the hypnotic surface to the complex interior, forcing us to see the artificiality and shallowness of that surface by which men are enthralled. The writer also ensures that the reader feels sympathy for her character, often making her a victim of the patriarchy seeking revenge. Because the writer so carefully creates sympathy for the character, a haunting cry of social protest resonates with the bad belle's death.

One of the reasons nineteenth-century southern women writers associate southern conceptions of race with the belle gone bad, though it had not been an issue in the writings of earlier male southerners, is that women had

26. Woodward, *Mary Chesnut's Civil War,* 29, 88, 246, 365–66; Whites, *The Civil War as Crisis in Gender,* 25; Faust, *Mothers of Invention,* 10; Laura Mulvey, "Visual Pleasure and Narrative Cinema" in *Visual and Other Pleasures: Language, Discourse, Society* (Basingstoke, England: MacMillan, 1989), 20.

the luxury of writing during the time of greatest social upheaval in the South, while most of the men did not. As Elisabeth Muhlenfeld observes, "The nearly twenty years that were consumed in preparation for secession and in civil war, defeat, and reconstruction produced little first-rate traditional literature."[27] After the war, however, some male writers revisited the social issues of the past, recognizing the problems caused by southern racial and sexual conventions women writers had hinted at earlier.

In the novel *The Sins of the Father* (1912), for example, Thomas Dixon, uses a femme fatale character to point out the dangers of miscegenation. Cleo, a beautiful octoroon, seduces an upstanding southern gentleman, causing upheaval in his family, which leads to his death and that of his frail, innocent wife. Dixon's treatment of this character, though similar to that of nineteenth-century women writers, differs in important ways. First, whereas women writers only hint at mixed blood in their femmes fatales, Dixon overtly states at the beginning that Cleo is the product of an "unnatural" union. Though her features are very light, as light, it seems, as those of the bad belles employed by the women writers, Dixon states that her African ancestry is plain in both her appearance and her actions. Second, though Cleo desires Major Norton because of love and gratitude for his having saved her from a Klan raid, Dixon refuses to present her in a sympathetic light. He repeatedly refers to her as a savage beast, even as she cares for Norton's legitimate son, and he describes her desire as "the sinister purpose of a mad love that had leaped full grown from the deeps of her powerful animal nature."[28] Making Cleo's racial heritage an overt plot element not only makes Dixon's political message more obvious than that of his female predecessors, it also makes his message more conventional, particularly when it is combined with a lack of sympathy.

The traditional southern dichotomy, which assigned domestic concerns to women and political concerns to men, accounts for the necessity of subtlety in the women's works. But in addition to treading on male territory, these women undermined that territory in their treatment of the belle gone bad. By blurring the distinctions between femme fatale and lady, the women writers hint at miscegenation while calling attention to the confining spheres

27. Elisabeth Muhlenfeld, "The Civil War and Authorship," in *The History of Southern Literature,* Louis D. Rubin Jr. et al., eds. (Baton Rouge: Louisiana State University Press, 1985), 178.

28. Thomas Dixon, *The Sins of the Father: A Romance of the South* (New York: Grosset and Dunlap, 1912), 42.

allotted to all women, white and black, revealing that white ladies were not much freer than their slaves. Also, by offering sympathy to the bad belle, the women writers indict the system. Whereas Dixon's novel portrays Norton and his family as helpless victims of Cleo's dangerously unnatural combination of white intelligence and beauty with African scruples and animality, the women writers make it clear that their male heroes' (and their society's) treatment of women in the past has led to the heroes' (and perhaps the society's) eventual downfall. As the antebellum women writers had revised the figure of the bad belle from earlier literature by men, Dixon perhaps revised the figure he saw controversially portrayed in the works of earlier southern women writers, making its political import more orthodox.

This type of conservative message was mirrored in much of the literature written between the Civil War and World War I, which often either attacked the South's changed political and social structure, as did Dixon's work, or romanticized the culture of the past, as did the works of Joel Chandler Harris and Thomas Nelson Page. But the period between the two world wars, the Southern Renascence, is generally recognized as a time of rebirth in southern literature, accompanied by a new critically introspective eye, as evidenced by the works of Ellen Glasgow, Thomas Wolfe, Faulkner, and others. Some of the male writers of this period employ the bad southern belle character in ways that differ from their male predecessors and their female contemporaries.

Faulkner, for example, repeatedly returns to the figure of the willful and dangerous coquette. For instance, *Soldier's Pay*'s (1926) Cecily and *Sartoris*'s (1929) aptly named Belle use their beauty and feminine charm to manipulate and conquer the men who surround them. Faulkner uses the power these women have over men to reflect the male effeteness he viewed as a characteristic of the postwar society. These characters comment more on twentieth-century disillusionment and ennui—and the personal fears and weaknesses that debilitate modern men—than on specifically southern social structures. As were the bad belles in the works by earlier male writers, though, these women are one-dimensional entities, forces, like war itself, that destroy uncomprehending men, not fully drawn, complex characters. The reader comprehends the bad belles' feelings no more than do her male victims, and the author appears to be unconcerned with internal motivations. Unlike his male predecessors, however, Faulkner does not punish his bad belles at novel's end. This lack of retribution, like the bad belle's domination, reflects the powerlessness of modern man, victim of the shallowness and dissolution of the twentieth century.

In his later work, however, Faulkner employs the bad belle differently. Temple Drake of *Sanctuary* (1931) is a beautiful and willful coquette who takes great pleasure in cruelly manipulating her fraternity boyfriends. In this novel, the bad belle is punished for her actions through her rape and imprisonment in a brothel by the bootlegger Popeye. Faulkner described this novel as a potboiler, designed to titillate readers and make money, and most of the characters, including Temple, lack psychological depth. But in the sequel, *Requiem for a Nun,* published twenty years later but set eight years after Temple's rape, Faulkner revisits the character to explore her thoughts and to offer through her a critique of the South's treatment of women. As Temple—who describes her younger self as "the foolish virgin"—explains, her traditional southern upbringing caused both her youthful cruelty to men and her eventual downfall: "No, Temple was the optimist: not that she had foreseen, planned ahead either: She just had unbounded faith that her father and brothers would know evil when they saw it, so all she had to do was, do the one thing which she knew they would forbid her to do if they had the chance." Sheltered, as were most well-brought-up southern girls, from the knowledge of the world and its dangers, having all important decisions made for her by her father and brothers, and spoiled in all her whims, Temple is not "prepared to resist [evil], say no to it," and she cannot foresee the consequences of her actions.[29]

Tennessee Williams similarly portrays the southern belle's modern fate through Blanche DuBois in *A Streetcar Named Desire* (1947). Taught to value only luxury, charm, and her power over men, Blanche is left with nothing when her youth and beauty fade, as did her family's wealth. Though she attempts to continue her self-serving manipulations, her eventual destruction speaks to the crimes of the social structure that created her as much as to her own. Like Faulkner, Williams emphasizes the traditional belle's lack of preparation for the corrupt modern world through Blanche's rape by Stanley, the modern man, and her subsequent commitment to an insane asylum.

Williams's and Faulkner's sympathy for the belle gone bad and their use of the character as a vehicle for social criticism are similar to nineteenth-

29. William Faulkner, *Requiem for a Nun* (New York: Random House, 1950; reprint, New York: Vintage, 1975), 113, 118, 117.

century women writers' use of the figure. Perhaps, as Carol S. Manning claims, the nineteenth-century women writers' early-formed critically introspective glance indicates that an unrecognized Southern Renascence had already begun among women writers of the antebellum South.[30] It is interesting to note that Williams and Faulkner banish their femmes fatales, Williams sending Blanche to an insane asylum and Faulkner sending Temple to a brothel. For Temple and Blanche, the authors link inappropriate sexuality to madness, a connection also explored by nineteenth- and twentieth-century women writers.

Women writers of the Southern Renascence return to the belle gone bad, but their use of this character displays a different attitude toward society than that held by their female predecessors and male contemporaries. In the 1920s, as the Southern Renascence began, war and foreign travel had broadened the minds of many young southerners and helped bring social change, but there was still much to protest in the society. Women had acquired the right to vote, but the southern lady was still a cherished ideal, and lynching and rape of blacks still occurred in her name, the former to protect her from black men, the latter to protect her from white. Jim Crow and sharecropping kept blacks a class of serfs in the feudal agrarian structure, with white men still holding all the power. Cash wrote in 1941 that the modern South "is a tree with many age rings, with its limbs and trunk bent and twisted by all the winds of the years, but with its tap root in the Old South" and that its "characteristic vices in the past. . . . remain its characteristic vices today."[31] During this period of literary flowering and somewhat greater social freedom, southern women launched protests against patriarchal standards through such means as antilynching organizations. At the same time, the southern women writers' use of the belle gone bad evolves to show the authors' changing attitudes.

In the works of the writers discussed in chapter 3—Ellen Glasgow, Evelyn Scott, Margaret Mitchell, and Caroline Gordon—the bad belle is not destroyed, and sometimes she even triumphs. These Southern Renascence women writers attack the South with strong, angry divas rather than with pathetic, beaten former debutantes, such as Temple Drake and Blanche

---

30. Carol S. Manning, "The Real Beginning of the Southern Renaissance," in *The Female Tradition in Southern Literature,* Manning, ed. (Urbana: University of Illinois Press, 1993), 37–56.

31. W. J. Cash, *The Mind of the South* (New York: Knopf, 1941), x, 440.

DuBois. The bad belles' wanton, unpunished destruction of others reflects the authors' rage against the culture that created restricting roles for women and demonized those who stepped beyond conventional bounds. Though the writers may not always approve of the their characters' actions, they usually explore her motivations fully and seem to view her manipulations as necessary strategies in a corrupt and threatening world, where the patriarchy's promises of honor and protection prove false. Through this stronger bad belle figure, Southern Renascence women writers attack the patriarchal standards more openly than their foremothers, but they still perpetuate the negative image of strong women being a mysterious threat to men.

Some recent southern male writers have been directly influenced by Southern Renascence women writers' portrayals of the belle gone bad. Mitchell's Scarlett O'Hara, particularly, has become America's stereotype of the southern belle and has influenced subsequent portrayals of southern women. Truman Capote's Holly Golightly of *Breakfast at Tiffany's* (1958) shares Scarlett's survival instincts, her ability to recreate herself from nothing, and her ability to manipulate men without being strongly affected by them. And Carol Templeton Hollywell, the main character of Willie Morris's *The Last of the Southern Girls* (1973), is a self-described admirer and imitator of Scarlett O'Hara. Displaced from her Arkansas homeland, she thrives on the manipulation of power in Washington, D.C. After many affairs and a failed marriage, Carol finally meets the seemingly perfect man and returns with him to the South to help with his senatorial election campaign. But Carol rejects Jack Winter when his campaign fails, not wanting to be associated with a loser. Like Scarlett, she plans, at the novel's end, to return to her home ground—now Washington—to reclaim her power, leaving a broken man in her wake.

Contemporary southern women writers, however, do not rest so easily with the image of Scarlett O'Hara. But the continued presence of the bad belle in the works of these recent southern women writers indicates that they still struggle to free themselves of rigid social constraints and to speak their own voices. One contemporary writer, Elizabeth Spencer, spoke of this struggle in a recent interview. In her upbringing, she said, "it was considered that men did all the interesting things out in the world and women were pretty much reduced to a domestic pattern or minor careers. The whole idea of a woman in the arts must have horrified my family at first.

They admired English women who had artistic careers, but no southern women were supposed to be encouraged in that way."[32] The contemporary southern women writers discussed in chapter 4—Eudora Welty, Elizabeth Spencer, Lee Smith, and Kaye Gibbons—attempt to finally distance themselves from the attitudes and inequities Spencer describes.

In these writers' works, the dark double is a sexually manipulative mother figure whom the heroine, a young artist, must destroy in order to accept her feminine power as a positive force. Though these contemporary writers destroy their bad belles, the character's death does not reinforce patriarchal standards, because the heroine moves off on her own, independent of both the bad mother and the controlling male characters. To achieve the subjectivity from which to create independently, the southern woman writers must first destroy this vehicle of their predecessors' repressed rage, the vehicle that is also the image through which society silences or vilifies powerful women. By killing off the stifling stereotype, the contemporary women writers purge the negative images unintentionally perpetuated by literary foremothers. They finally free the mind and voice of the woman artist. With the exception of Welty, the earliest, these contemporary writers also attempt to free the woman's body from the sexual limitations that, for the Old South, were emblems of her powerlessness in all social realms.

In *The Dragon's Blood: Feminist Intertextuality in Eudora Welty's "The Golden Apples"*, Rebecca Mark describes feminist intertextuality as the "confrontation of, and transformation of, patriarchal myths and masculinist texts." By using the belle gone bad in their works, southern women writers confront and revise not only men's earlier literary representations of women but also the patriarchal myths that inform southern culture itself. In earlier literature by men, the dark lady is a "mysterious seductress who embodies the double threat of sex and death, the archetype of the Eve or Lilith who brings evil into the world."[33] Southern women writers change the relationship between this character and her world. By pointing to the similarities between the belle gone bad and her proper counterpart, and by showing the circumstances that lead to the bad belle's actions, southern women writers indicate that the dark lady does not bring evil into the world, but

32. Betina Entzminger, "Interview with Elizabeth Spencer" *Mississippi Quarterly* 47 (1994): 602.

33. Rebecca Mark, *The Dragon's Blood: Feminist Intertextuality in Eudora Welty's "The Golden Apples"* (Jackson: University Press of Mississippi, 1994), 4; André Tridon, *Psychoanalysis: Its History, Theory, and Practice* (New York: B. W. Huebsch, 1919), 95.

that the world—in this case, the South—forces evil upon the dark lady, and that all women are similarly victimized by the patriarchy's abuses. As women writers revise earlier representations of women, they also revise the culture's understanding of itself and of its women, subtly upturning its conventions, just as the bad belles upturn complacent lives in the women writers' works. It is ironic that a culture that has denied authority to its women has been so influenced—as twentieth-century male writers' portrayals of women reveal—by these women's revisions of their roles in that society. Finally, it seems, contemporary southern women writers are revising the belle, bad or otherwise, out of existence.

1 THE BEAUTIFUL SERPENT;
OR, NOT QUITE EDEN

In the 1850s Northeast, many women took up the abolitionist cause, speaking and writing for the public in a way women rarely had done before. Critics of the abolitionists, sometimes even people sympathetic to the cause, often condemned the improper public involvement of female members, believing that those of the more delicate sex should only provide support behind the scenes while men should carry on the real political rallying. As Blanche Glassman Hersh points out in *The Slavery of Sex: Feminist-Abolitionists in America,* the feminist movement in America developed alongside the abolitionist movement, partly in response to this unfair criticism and partly because of abolitionists' attempts to gain more women supporters by showing similarities between the plight of women and that of slaves. Women loyal to the South had to distance themselves from newly emerging feminists who linked their cause with the ending of slavery. In *Sociology for the South* (1854), George Fitzhugh expressed the southern fears that linked the two issues: "The people in our Northern States, who hold that domestic slavery is unjust and iniquitous, are consistent in their attempts to modify or abolish the marriage relation." Instead of embracing the ideals of individualism and autonomy upon which northern feminists based calls for social reform, then, southern women, as manifested in the popular novels written by and for southern women, embraced in the decades before the Civil War a hierarchical domestic structure. Catherine Clinton suggests that southern patriarchs consciously steered women's energies toward domesticity to protect the power structure: "If women's attention wandered from the welfare of their families and their husbands' slaves and other property, it might stray to a critical attack on society."[1] Some domestic novels, however, through the character of the bad belle, managed to focus on the home and critique society at the same time.

Regardless of her true feelings about slavery, the woman who wrote and hoped to continue living in the South had to guard against offending southern readers. Roberts asserts, "If a woman writer was seen in some quarters as a prostitute, displaying herself for her male patrons, then a woman writer who involves herself with the issue of race becomes doubly tainted. She commits literary miscegenation." The coupling of white womanhood with blackness was the greatest taboo of the Old South, violation of which was believed to threaten the entire social order. But nineteenth-century southern women writers had to shy away from more than issues of race. Because southern concepts of family and social hierarchy were so intimately tied to concepts of race and because rebellion against the woman's traditional place in the hierarchy was so closely identified with northern abolitionism, the writers also had to avoid fictional assertions of feminine independence. Though women writers did win wide audiences in the nineteenth century, they were also attacked by male authority figures on moral and artistic grounds. Baym points out that contemporary clergymen impugned the moral messages of these writers' works because the clergy felt threatened by what they saw as the writers' attempts to do the clergy's job, a task for which these women were deemed unqualified. Male writers of the time showed their distress at the "apparently sudden emergence of great numbers of women writers . . . in expressions of manly contempt for the genre, its authors, and its readers."[2]

Accused of moral and literary transgressions, these women writers had to protect their social reputation and ensure continued book sales by endorsing, ostensibly at least, the values and social structure of their readers. But how did they manage the physical and philosophical conflicts between real-

---

1. Blanche Glassman Hersh, *The Slavery of Sex: Feminist-Abolitionists in America* (Urbana: University of Illinois Press, 1978); Faust, *Mothers of Invention*, 6; Catherine Clinton, *The Plantation Mistress: Woman's World in the Old South* (New York: Pantheon Books, 1982), 11.

2. Roberts, *Myth of Aunt Jemima*, 20; Nina Baym, *Woman's Fiction: A Guide to Novels by and about Women in America, 1820–1870*, 2d ed. (Urbana: University of Illinois Press, 1993), 23.

ity, as manifested by their own talent and that of many other black and white women, and the value system society forced them to uphold? One subtle way they managed these conflicts was through their characterizations of the bad belle. These sexually dangerous characters in many of the nineteenth-century writers' novels are associated with art, explicitly connecting artistic expression with other social dangers of the dark seductress. This character thereby parodies the conservative society's image of the artist herself: a dangerous woman taking on male power. She serves as a commentary on the perceived menace of feminine power.

E.D.E.N. SOUTHWORTH

One of the most popular American novelists of the 1850s and 1860s, Emma Dorothy Eliza Nevitte Southworth (1819–99) illustrates the tensions between ideology and profit. Born in the Washington, D.C., area, Southworth spent most of her life in Maryland and Virginia, and most of her novels are set on wealthy Upper South plantations. The name with which she signed her works, E.D.E.N. Southworth, seems to indicate a deep personal identification with the Edenic settings she described, but was probably more a reflection of nominative luck and marketing strategy. Though Southworth was a staunch Union sympathizer during the Civil War, her biographer points out that "in her picture of slavery she had endeavored in the 50s to propitiate her readers on both sides . . . , [and] she maintained a similar policy in the 60s, that of writing for her reading public and avoiding any such bitter issue as might gainsay her popularity." During the war, many women admired and envied writers, such as Southworth, who were able to earn a living. As one prospective newspaper contributor, Susan Cornwall, asked, "But if I can realize anything from it should I not try to succeed in order to aid my dear husband in his labors?" Despite conventions of modesty, money had to be earned in whatever way possible during hard times. But apparently, keeping references to the race issue out of her novels was not enough to protect Southworth from censure in her home region, and one contemporary's comments underscore the risks to reputation suffered by the woman writer: "They [Confederate sympathizers] never forgave her loyalty and probably never will, and while Mrs. Southworth has lived a life of perfect chastity, yet her fate is that of every other woman who rises above the common place or above her first station in life—more or less slander, and envy at her heels."[3] Southworth's detractors challenged not only her loyalty to the South but, apparently because of her life in the public eye, also suspected her virtue. It is not surprising that this woman writer, and others like her, chose the femme fatale figure to parody society's attitude toward female power.

Southworth's attempt to assert her values despite her fear of censure from the community appears most clearly in her first novel, *Retribution* (1849). Though her later novels suppress her antislavery sentiments, this is clearly an antislavery work. In the novel, the belle gone bad is painted in very bold (and very dark) colors, and her presence allows Southworth to suggest even stronger criticism, which, if stated plainly, would have offended readers north and south. But the fact that Juliette, the sexually manipulative bad belle, possesses Southworth's talent for writing, along with other artistic accomplishments, indicates the writer's identification with the character and suggests a commentary on her region's attitude toward all powerful women, most visible of whom is the woman artist.

The main plot of *Retribution* describes the life of wealthy orphan Hester Grey, an unattractive but sensitive and good girl, and her beautiful and evil friend Juliette, both of whom eventually marry Hester's guardian, Colonel Ernest Dent. Southworth's criticism of the slave system, however, is introduced through a familiar and sentimental subplot involving a beautiful, seventeen-year-old slave, Minny Dozier. Daughter of her master, Mr. Dozier, and a quadroon slave, Minny receives all the material and emotional benefits of her father's guilty conscience. Though Minny describes her master-father as a kind and loving man, Southworth hints at his large defects of character. Thinking to absolve Mr. Dozier of cruel and oppressive deeds, Minny explains that it was not his tyranny that killed her mother, but his obsessive and excessive love that broke her rebellious heart: "She was not his wife, not his willing mistress, but his slave" (*R* 36). Though Minny finds no great fault, the reader recalls Mr. Dozier's uncontrollable passion for the mother as Minny relates how as a child she slept in her father's bed every night until he gave her a room of her own, a separation that caused her to weep for a week. The modern reader is reminded here of Isaac McCaslin's

3. Regis Louise Boyle, *Mrs. E.D.E.N. Southworth, Novelist* (Washington, D.C.: Catholic University of America Press, 1939), 42; Whites, *The Civil War as Crisis in Gender*, 29; Boyle, *Mrs. E.D.E.N. Southworth*, 16.

discovery in Faulkner's "The Bear" that his grandfather had fathered a child with a slave woman and subsequently seduced his own mulatta daughter. As William Bedford Clark points out in "The Serpent of Lust in the Southern Garden," miscegenation was a popular rallying point for abolitionists, and these sexual sins became "a convenient fictional symbol for expressing the South's broader guilt over the whole question of bondage and the racial wrongs arising from it."[4] Mr. Dozier's libidinous character is further emphasized when his heavy drinking and late hours contribute to his early demise—before he has gotten around to freeing his daughter.

Prior to Dozier's death, Minny, aged fifteen, had married a French opera singer and become pregnant with his child. Not long after, her husband leaves the country to attend to business, Minny goes into labor, and her father dies—all in a single day. Mother and newborn child are separated to be sold by greedy relatives, the beautiful and nearly white Minny as a concubine. Colonel Ernest Dent at this point finds and purchases Minny to save her from "a fate worse than slavery" (*R* 29). In this conventional tale, Southworth indicts the major sins of the slave system abolitionists traditionally focused on: the separation of slave families, the arbitrary distinction of slave status, and the sexual exploitation of slave women. However, it is in a seemingly safe haven that Minny's interactions with Hester, Ernest, and especially the seductress Juliette allow Southworth to challenge the icons of southern culture, the self-sacrificing matron, benevolent patriarch, and beautiful belle.

Through the matron's relationship with Juliette Summers and through her similar relationship with Minny Dozier, who becomes an ironic counterpart for the dark seductress Juliette, Southworth criticizes Hester Grey, the first Mrs. Dent. Ironically, Minny the slave never (as far as we are told) sinks to the stereotypical sexual behavior imputed to those in her position, while Juliette, the supposed best friend and would-be successor to Hester, exceeds the stereotype of misconduct through her evil manipulations. Though they are not explicitly compared in the text, Juliette and Minny are paired characters in many ways. Upon first introducing Juliette, Southworth describes her exotic beauty in detail:

> Her abundant and shining black hair was trained to droop in large smooth, glossy ringlets on each side of a face whose richness of complexion could only have come from Italy. But the glory of that matchless face were the large black

4. William Bedford Clark, "The Serpent of Lust in the Southern Garden" *Southern Review* 10 (1974): 806.

eyes, with their long black fringes, so dusky and brooding one instant, so melting and suffused the next, and suddenly so resplendent with light and soul, and upon occasion, so fierce and flaming in anger. There was a mesmeric spell in those eyes. Indeed, the sinister and inviting coquette had once in an unguarded hour asserted that she had "only to look into the eyes of a man to make him love" her. (*R* 13)

Juliette has the hypnotic eyes and hair traditionally attributed to the femme fatale, and the darkness of her features makes her that much more dangerous and exciting. Though Minny is described in far less detail and in far less regal terms, the descriptions of the slave and the belle are quite similar: "[U]pon an elegant black pony, sat a young girl, the most lovely little creature I ever saw . . . the beautiful little girl, with her jetty curls, and dusky eyes [that] drooped till the long black lashes rested on the dead white cheeks" (*R* 29). Here, Hester describes Minny in diminutive terms, but she is in fact seventeen and already a wife and mother. A stereotype contradictory to the one that viewed slaves as libidinous and seductive is one that portrayed all slaves as childlike, too simple and inferior to be threatening. This convention seems to have influenced Hester's view of Minny. Both Juliette and Minny have dark curls and "dusky" eyes, but the slave is described with "dead white cheeks," while the exotic blood is plainly evident in the "rich complexion" of the Italian.

As many southern literary and cultural critics have pointed out, southerners inherited European conceptions of the symbolic moral values of lightness and darkness. Winthrop D. Jordan notes, "Long before they found that some men were black, Englishmen found in the idea of blackness a way of expressing some of their most ingrained values. . . . As described by the *Oxford English Dictionary,* the meaning of *black* before the sixteenth century included, 'Deeply stained with dirt; soiled, dirty, foul . . . Having dark or deadly purposes, malignant . . . Indicating disgrace, censure, liability to punishment, etc.'" Though not as dark-skinned as Africans, Italians suffered some of the same bigoted associations. Northern Europeans saw Italians as fiery, emotional, and libidinous. Especially after the early nineteenth century, when many poor Italians emigrated to England, Britons accused Italians as a whole of drinking, carousing, and fostering vices in the community.[5] These

---

5. Jordan, *White over Black*, 7; Lucio Sponza, "Italians in London" in *The Peopling of London: Fifteen Thousand Years of Settlement Overseas,* Nick Merriman, ed. (London: The Museum of London, 1993), 130.

prejudicial stereotypes are similar to those southerners imposed on African Americans during the nineteenth century. By creating Italian seductresses, Southworth, and later Hentz, could draw on the similar racist conventions and approach blackness without risking the scandal that might be provoked by a more explicit treatment of miscegenation. While the presence of Minny does confirm past miscegenation, the act occurs entirely off stage and is condemned by all characters in the present action of the novel. Through Juliette's duskiness, however, Southworth undermines the stature of those normally beyond all censure, the benevolent patriarch and the self-sacrificing matron.

The patriarch Ernest fits the image of the southern gentleman described by Daniel Hundley, an observer of southern culture, in 1860: "The gentleman, . . . in addition to being finely formed and highly educated, was firm, commanding, and a perfect patriarch. . . . The weakness and dependence of women was thrown into bold relief by his virility and mastery of his environment." Hester reveres Ernest like a father, and he rewards her obedience and conformity to his wishes with a marriage proposal. Southworth soon reveals, however, that this gentleman may not be all that he appears. Though Hester never loses her reverence for Colonel Dent, Southworth introduces doubt for the reader soon after the engagement. Marcus Derby, a young man who has befriended Hester since her arrival at the plantation, warns her against the marriage: "*He is not*—this demigod of yours—what you take him to be. He is a cold, hard, black, marble Colossus, whose altitude will intercept the dear sunlight of heaven itself from your life, and in whose damping shadow you will wilt and wither and die" (*R* 27). As his name suggests, the patriarch has a major defect of character. Hester, however, gladly follows through with the marriage and continues to behave as a proper wife, forming her thoughts after those of her husband. Hester plays to perfection the role of the good southern wife described by a university president in 1835: "She must resolve at the outset never to oppose her husband, never to show displeasure, no matter what he might do. A man had a right to expect his wife to place perfect confidence in his judgment and to believe that he always knew best."[6]

When less than six months after the marriage Colonel Dent purchases Minny Dozier and sends her to Hester's estate, Marcus sneeringly alludes to what he believes to be the sinful purpose of the acquisition: "'Well!' said

6. Scott, *Southern Lady*, 14, 6.

he, 'what do you think of your handmaiden; fair to look upon, is she not? *Colonel Dent* thinks so, I know. Hagar, or Zilpah, or Bilhah, is her name?'" (*R* 30). Hester, however, believes only what Ernest told her, that he purchased Minny "with the purpose of saving her from a southern slave dealer" (*R* 29). Though Southworth never confirms that Dent has illicit desires for Minny, Marcus places doubt in the reader's mind. And Hester's refusal to entertain the suggestion is similar to the willful ignorance for which Chesnut criticized her contemporaries: "[E]very lady tells you who is the father of all the mulatto children in everybody's household, but those in her own she seems to think drop from the clouds, or pretends so to think . . . there are certain subjects pure-minded ladies never touch upon, even in their thoughts."[7] On the surface, Southworth condemns Marcus's implications and praises Hester as a good, trusting, loving soul, who takes Minny in almost as a sister, but the reader begins to wonder whether Hester is perhaps too trusting for her own good.

The reader's doubts increase when, immediately after Minny's introduction, Hester's hereditary malady, blindness, mysteriously begins. Southworth never overtly draws the connection between the two events, and a period of at least one year is supposed to have elapsed in Hester's life, but the chapter that ends with Marcus's accusations is followed immediately by the news of Hester's blindness and the unforetold birth of her daughter. The blindness is temporary, lasting only several months. Hester blames its onset on excessive excitement, but the reader wonders if the hidden implication is that Hester closed her eyes to what was going on around her only to open them to find a new baby in the household, for it is the morning after the birth of the child that Hester's eyesight returns she wakes to see the infant sleeping between herself and her nurse, Minny Dozier.

Suspicions of Dent's unspoken liaison with Minny increase in hindsight when the reader sees Hester's figurative blindness to the overt manipulations of Juliette, Hester's supposed best friend. Perhaps Southworth deflects the adultery from Minny to Juliette to avoid accusing the novel's hero—someone her reader must respect so proper order can be reasserted at the novel's end—of miscegenation. Juliette plans her strategy before meeting Colonel Dent, deciding to "*pique* his self-love first by indifference—to flatter it more effectually by an *after* admiration" (*R* 43). Her entire association with the Dents is characterized by this type of careful planning, from

7. Woodward, *Mary Chesnut's Civil War*, 29, 54.

deciding what to wear and say to deciding how to project herself—as competent woman or helpless maiden.

Though Ernest appreciates Juliette's physical attractions, it is her mental skill that finally renders him helpless. The trio journey to Washington, D.C., where Ernest is to make an important speech to the legislature. While Ernest is on the Senate floor, Juliette plants a seed of worry in Hester about the infant, suggesting she return to the house while Juliette completes some research Ernest had requested. Here, Juliette's skill as a writer first ensnares Ernest. As he reads her work, Ernest is impressed not only with Juliette's comprehension of the subject but also with the grace with which she presents her ideas: "She had accomplished the task admirably, bringing all her astute intellect and brilliant wit into the service of the subject; using here the acute comment, here the skillful comparison, and here the cutting sarcasm" (*R* 53). Southworth never shows the reader Juliette's writing, but the author offers high praise to a fellow writer. The bad belle is indeed the most artistic character in the novel, for she not only writes well, but she also sings, plays the piano beautifully, and adorns her form daily like a work of art. In fact, the independent and talented Juliette has far more in common with her creator than does the novel's mild and pure ostensible heroine, Hester. Also like her creator, Juliette so subtly challenges the patriarch and the society from which he derives his power that he does not at first realize it.

Conveniently for Juliette, as the young Marcus predicted on the eve of Hester's wedding, the wife soon withers in Ernest's shadow. In the fever that consumes Hester, both Ernest and Juliette see only opportunity for personal gain, Juliette for the wealth and position she covets and Ernest for a charming and beautiful wife who better fits his self-image. Here Southworth contrasts Juliette, the beautiful belle, with Minny Dozier, the slave girl. Though common prejudice of the time attributed seductive qualities to those of African descent and though many illicit liaisons occurred between master and slave, Southworth establishes no explicit link between Ernest and Minny.[8] Juliette, on the other hand, uses her best friend's illness as an opportunity to seduce Ernest. Feigning true devotion to the invalid wife upstairs, she deftly reels in the husband downstairs. These differences between Juliette's and Minny's conduct have a paradoxical dual effect on the reader. By assigning to the coquettish belle the behavior stereotypically

---

8. Wyatt-Brown, *Southern Honor*, 313.

attributed to the enchanting concubine, Southworth emphasizes the similarities between the two figures and implicitly challenges the social structure that prizes one while vilifying the other. But Hester no more suspects her treacherous friend than she did her beautiful servant, and the reader must wonder at the young wife's ingenuousness.

Juliette wins Ernest soon after Hester dies, but each grows to resent the other's presence. As ambassador, Ernest takes Juliette to France, where she becomes known as *La Circe Américaine* and enchants European men as successfully as she had enchanted Ernest. Like a succubus, Juliette grows stronger and more powerful after the marriage while her husband grows weaker. But Southworth warns the reader away from Juliette with one hand while enticing the reader toward her with the other. In "The Female Tradition," Showalter demonstrates that in women's fiction the secret room, the enclosed garden, or the attic hideaway often represents the separate world of women, the source of their individuality and strength.[9] Both Hester and the plantation are described through garden metaphors, linking them to each other and to the ideals of purity, fertility, and maternity. Southworth describes Juliette, who is at the height of her power in Europe, in a different enclosure, the boudoir, where her charms have their greatest effect:

> the last room of the suite, far removed from every sight and sound that could disturb the lulling dreamy languor of this vailed [*sic*] temple of beauty and repose. As you drew near, the light and splendor and glory of the scene became gradually obscured, darkened, and lost in the shadows stealing from the twilight—while your senses were overpowered by the delicious narcotic fragrance breathing from the flowers—and the low wailing of an Aeolian harp, sighing from the stillness of this soft retreat. You enter through parting folds of heavy velvet drapery, stepping upon a soft carpet, in whose deep-yielding, downy texture your foot sinks—the shadows scarcely disturbed by the warm, subdued light stealing through the draperied windows, filling the room with a still, amber-colored atmosphere—the silence and stillness of the air gently broken by the plaintive murmur of the invisible harp—the rich odor and sedative influence of the unseen shrubs and flowers—the absence of all that could disturb, and the presence of everything that could lull the faculties—the seductive languor of this scene, soothing the nerves, stealing on the brain, and weighing down the eyelids, overpower you, and you sink into a bathos of delicious repose. (*R* 97)

9. Showalter, "The Female Tradition" in *Feminisms,* 284.

The dark, fragrant, hidden room entered through folds of heavy velvet drapery, her vaginal sepulcher, is an image of the source of Juliette's power. It is here—literally in the boudoir and figuratively through her sexuality—that she plans strategy and charms suitors into a lotus-like intoxication. The language in this passage, hypnotic with alliteration and assonance, recreates the effects attributed to her magical room. The extended use of second person, unusual in the narrative, encourages the reader to participate in the synesthetic experience of Juliette's chamber. Far from warning the reader away or condemning the seductress, Southworth herself seems to be seduced, drawing the reader into the intensity and exhilaration of Juliette's potency with orgasmic dashes.

Southworth admits to the reader her extreme fascination with this character. After briefly reviewing what has happened to other characters who had been neglected for several chapters, Southworth apologetically and breathlessly returns to her villainess: "I am fevered and excited with this dark Juliette, with whom one can not even deal without danger of receiving and communicating evil. She comes upon me like a fiend, or a fit of insanity" (*R* 97). Like Juliette's victims, though Southworth outwardly condemns the seductress's manipulations, she cannot let her go. Juliette is the most interesting character in the novel to both the author and the reader, and her power, though evil, is awe inspiring. Even the mild Hester Grey feels the allure of Juliette; mesmerized by Juliette's beauty and seduced by her charm, Hester brings the bad belle into her home.

Hester, Southworth, and her women readers are fascinated with Juliette, not because of her feminine beauty, but because of her masculine strength of will. Jacques Lacan's psychoanalytic theories of gender roles and power help explain this attraction. According to Lacan, under society's usual gender roles, men "have" the phallus, meaning they occupy a position of authority, but women "are" the phallus, meaning they serve as the site and object of masculine power. As Judith Butler explains, women "signify the phallus through 'being' its Other, its absence, the dialectical confirmation of its identity." Lacan suggests the masculine subject needs the other to confirm his possession of the phallus, his power; so there is also power in the "feminine position of not-having."[10] But the femme fatale not only "is" the phallus because of her beauty and charm, which make men experience their own sense of power and virility more intensely, but she also "has" the

10. Butler, *Gender Trouble*, 44.

phallus because she exercises her own will and authority to overpower the men. Similarly, within the novel, the character of the femme fatale both "is" and "has" the phallus vicariously for the woman writer. She "is" the phallus for the woman writer because she reflects the power of the writer at its greatest intensity—Juliette is the embodiment of Southworth's creative talents at their height, and Southworth views her erotically as a man would view his sexual object. The femme fatale "has" the phallus the woman writer is denied in her society, because the character exercises her power against men, possibly acting out the author's repressed rage. The character combines beauty and coquetry with what society has deemed phallic power, forming a self-contained erotic pairing and an emblem of control many women of the time lacked, and perhaps secretly envied. The reader of the time could admire the bad belle's strength and freedom in part because her deeds are those a properly docile southern lady should never even dream of.

Lest the reader still be tempted to condemn Juliette's manipulations too whole-heartedly, her traumatic childhood is revealed. Born into the noble Italian Nozzalina family, the infant Juliette and her mother barely escape the Santo Domingo slave revolt with their lives; Juliette's father and siblings were killed. Her mother never recovers from the shock and spends the rest of her days in seclusion, much like Charlotte Brontë's Bertha Mason, in a wealthy Virginia family's upstairs bedroom, "walking the floor with her long black hair streaming down in strong relief against her white dress" (*R* 12). Here, the madwoman, with her more passive but still socially unacceptable way of dealing with society's abuse, is a direct antecedent of the dark seductress. Refusing to stifle her rage behind closed doors as her mother did, the daughter arranges her hair and clothing to go downstairs, where she can upset the system from within. Degraded in girlhood by the charity of a family less noble than her own and by the necessity of being trained as governess to earn her living, Juliette resolves to use her talents to reach a loftier position in society.

Given her background, Juliette's manic ambition, if not her methods, seems more justifiable. But though the reader may feel sympathy for Juliette's past and may be awed by her power, her deeds threaten the social structure; therefore she must be destroyed. In the final pages of the novel, Juliette elopes with a grand duke and their subsequent demoniac activity is too evil for Southworth to name. Her life ends in execution in Germany, where her head is displayed on a pole above the city gates until it is taken down for exhibition as a phrenological oddity. Southworth's separation from Juliette is as quick and harsh as the executioner's blade, the account of her life after she leaves Ernest taking less than a page. Her end is grotesquely brutal, but if Southworth had allowed Juliette to exit more nobly, she herself ran the risk of the community's moral censure. The hastiness and lack of attention to this section shows that the writer's heart is not in it. To protect her reputation as a writer, she must end her work with order restored, but so much of her energy has gone into creating Juliette, it is as if she does not know how, or does not want, to get rid of her.

In the final analysis, Juliette only succeeds as far as she does by skillfully manipulating a corrupt system. She preys on the characteristic traits of the self-sacrificing matron—kindness and innocence—and the strong patriarch—self-confidence and protectiveness—exposing these traits as potential weaknesses. As a parallel to the tragic mulatta, Juliette also challenges her society's assumptions about that character and about the character of the belle. Southworth can outwardly proclaim the nobility of Ernest and Hester and the villainy of Juliette, but the plot reveals that the system that created one created them all.

In a later novel employing the bad belle, *The Three Beauties* (1858), Southworth abandons her overt abolitionist stance, perhaps fearing the loss of southern readers as sectional tensions increased before the Civil War. There is no tragic mulatta in this story, only loyal and comical longtime family servants. By using a dark seductress, as she did in *Retribution,* however, Southworth still launches a veiled criticism of the patriarchal social structure. Also set on a southern plantation and in its surrounding towns, this novel describes the struggle of three young women, Winny, Harriet, and Imogene, to unite with the men of their dreams. An illustration opposite the title page in the first edition shows these three beauties of the title in antebellum splendor. The dark seductress of the story, Sinai Hinton, is not among them, though she is the most alluring woman in the novel.

Sinai, often shortened to Sina, is, like Juliette, a darkly exotic creature, who bears the name of the peninsula that separates Africa and Southwest Asia. Though she herself was not born in a distant country, there is mystery, if not outward doubt, associated with her parentage: her mother, a poor white woman of questionable morals married a brutish white man who deserted the family when Sinai was very young. But Sinai's name, for nineteenth-century readers, would conjure images of Cleopatra and Middle Eastern harems. As Roberts points out, in the nineteenth century, the harem has symbolic relation to the patriarchal household:

The harem was common cultural currency. In one of the most delicious ironies of slaveholding culture, Thomas Moore's *Lalla Rookh* was a favorite book in the South as well as a perennial subject for *tableaux vivants* performed by plantation ladies. Given the way many slaveholding women participated in Southern orientalizing by referring to the collection of slave women on the plantation as a harem, I have to wonder if they were not making a sly, subversive point in dressing up as members of the seraglio for their husbands' "entertainment" in these *tableaux vivants*. Perhaps in wearing the veils and kohl of oriental women they were subtly arraigning their husbands for sexual misconduct out in the *real* harem, the Quarters; or perhaps they were toying with a dangerous sexuality officially out of bounds for them: playing "black."[11]

In Southworth's novel, Sinai plays a one-woman harem, coming into the big house to emphasize that the lust associated with "darker regions," including the slave quarters, is not instantly purified at the front door.

Southworth's initial description of Sinai emphasizes her similarities to the Egyptian queen Cleopatra and to exotic harem girls: "If there be any truth in the old heathen idea of the transmigration of souls—Sinai or Sina Hinton's soul had ascended the scale of creation, first through the subtile narcotic poisons, then through the snake, the jay bird, the cat, and had at last reached its most powerful development—*Sina Hinton*. This fascinating, guileful, and intriguing girl was not strictly speaking handsome—she was below the middle size, her figure rather bony, her complexion dark, and her features strongly marked. Her hair and brows were black, and her eyes large, dark, and powerful in their force of attraction" (*TB* 41). Sinai is here linked to heathen religions, magical potions, evil beasts, deceit, darkness, and a mysterious physical allure despite her lack of classic beauty. All of these attributes were stereotypical of the jezebel figure, perhaps herself a descendant of African queens. As does Juliette's and the stereotypical femme fatale's, Sinai's power lies in her eyes, like "grappling-hooks," and her hair, like "nets and meshes" (*TB* 370), with which she entraps her prey.

Though her appearance (she is almost always described as "dark"), African name, association with magic and seduction, and questionable parentage could combine to lead the nineteenth-century southern reader to imagine that Sinai is part black, Southworth gives no definite indication that she is, and mixed blood is never something the other characters suspect. She is a poor girl, hired as a companion to a wealthy heiress, and her

11. Roberts, *Myth of Aunt Jemima*, 33–34.

aspirations overwhelm her. Coveting the estate of her wealthy cousin, she uses the flirtations and manipulations of the coquette for sinister aims. But by pointing out the similarities between this bad belle and the black concubine, Southworth again shows the similarity of their roles and subtly criticizes the patriarchy that created both, condemning one to a lifetime of sexual repression and worship and the other to a lifetime of sexual abuse and infamy. As Sanchez-Eppler points out, conventional nineteenth-century representations of the light-skinned mulatta serve not only to make the tragic heroines more sympathetic to white women readers, but "the less easily race can be read from his or her flesh, the more clearly the white man's repeated penetrations of the black body are imprinted there."[12] By using this dark figure of uncertain parentage who inspires uncontrollable lust to undermine the ideal patriarchal family, Southworth suggests that lust and miscegenation are the great sins that undermine the southern social structure in general.

This bad belle, herself a visual representation of unnameable patriarchal sins, exposes the weakness of the patriarchal system by attacking its supposed strengths. Soon after arriving at the plantation, Sinai discerns an innocent romance developing between her young companion Winny and Winny's tutor, Ardenne. Knowing that Winny's father would never approve a match between his only daughter and a tutor, Sinai preys on his need to control and protect, his defining traits as patriarch, to upset the family's tranquility. Then Sinai, preying in turn on the innocence and romantic notions of the carefully sheltered young maiden, convinces Winny that the only solution is to elope with Ardenne, at which time, Sinai says, her father will relent and all will be forgiven.

Southworth tells us that it is Winny's proper southern upbringing that makes her such an easy mark for Sinai and so unfit for life outside her father's protection. Winny is Sinai's physical and spiritual opposite. She has the pale golden ringlets and rosy complexion that were the white South's ideal of feminine beauty, and she has the innocence that was its ideal of feminine goodness. Surrounded by servants who arranged her possessions and her days "without a single volition of her own will in the matter," Winny is sheltered from "learning to think or act for herself, as she would have [been] shielded from war, pestilence, or famine" (*TB* 163). The poor tutor Ardenne, whom the father sees as the greatest threat to his patriarchal authority,

---

12. Sanchez-Eppler, "Bodily Bonds," 104.

points out the cruelty of her upbringing while advocating a more balanced alternative: "You have been told so [that she is incompetent], dear, until you believe it! . . . You must not set out by being persuaded that you have a poor judgment, and then let it grow really imbecile for want of exercise. In this march of life, I do not wish to go in advance alone, selfishly laying out the future and turning to consort with you only in hours of idleness and re-laxation" (*TB* 168–69). As described by the tutor, patriarchal control is a selfish whim of men that turns women into playthings (like harem girls) and makes them unfit for survival. Belle Kearney, a young southern woman of the planter class, expressed frustration at similar treatment as late as 1900: "If my life is to be spent on the plantation, and if living meant no more for me than it meant for the women around me, what was the use of reading, of trying to cultivate my mind when it would have the effect of making me more miserable." Significantly, Frederick Douglass experienced a compara-ble moment of doubt when he learned to read as a young slave.[13] South-worth shows that it is this sheltering of young women, touted by male southerners as one of the society's greatest achievements, that makes these women most vulnerable.

Contrary to what she tells Winny, Sinai knows that the patriarch's pride will never allow him to forgive his rebellious daughter and her new hus-band, and she hopes to use the family rift as an opportunity to usurp the prodigal daughter's place "in her father's home and heart" (*TB* 74). Un-fortunately for Sinai, she has learned her role as belle too well. Though she is only a few years older than his daughter, Squire Darling interprets the coyness intended as filial affection as something more mature: "'On my soul, Sina, you have got the sweetest, softest voice in the world! It—it's per-fect *music!*—it's—it's *cotton-wool!*—one could *sink down* into it!—it—it makes me feel *dizzy*—it—it—it is *oil!*—it *runs all over me!* Sina, I'm doomed! if I know what to do!' He caught both her hands in his. She raised her large dark eyes to his. 'And your eyes!—two large, soft, floating worlds, that make me sea-sick!—there!—go!—or I shall make a jackass of myself!'" (*TB* 96–97). The bizarre language he uses to describe her effect on him combines images of sensuality, danger, and intoxication. Without intending to, Sinai has entranced the squire. And in his declaration of enthrallment, Squire

13. Marjorie Spruill Wheeler, *New Women of the New South: The Leaders of the Woman Suffrage Movement in the Southern States* (New York: Oxford University Press, 1993), 85; Frederick Douglass, *Narrative of the Life of Frederick Douglass, an American Slave* (1845; reprint, New York: Penguin, 1982), 84.

Darling does just what he fears he will do: he makes a jackass of himself, to Sinai and to the reader. Though Southworth overtly condemns Sinai's manipulations and portrays her as a servant of Satan, as she did Juliette (*TB* 50), the reader's more visceral response is that of revulsion at this old man's lecherous passion. Sinai responds to the advances of this overweight, overwrought man with no enthusiasm: "Why that disgusting old soul! I do hope he has not taken it into his head to fancy me for a wife; that would horribly defeat my purpose to be his daughter!" (*TB* 97).

The comedy of the scene advances the author's intended parody of southern conventions and southern distributions of power. But as with all parody, the underlying reproach is altogether grave. Southworth creates in Squire Darling an image of the lusty patriarch, lasciviously preying on those he is bound to protect. Sinai mentions the two roles of wife and daughter, two types of dependent that seemed to have blurred for the squire. The suggestion of incest in this blurring calls to mind Mr. Dozier, who also suffered uncontrollable lust for the slave mistress his duty as patriarch bound him to protect. Mr. Dozier's lust, at least implicitly, was then transferred to the slave-daughter, whose right to protection as slave and offspring in an ideal patriarchal society would be doubly strong (though in an *ideal* patriarchal society, slave and offspring could never be one and the same). By pointing out Squire Darling's and Mr. Dozier's abuses of power, Southworth quietly challenges the whole patriarchal system, which placed unscrupulous and immoral men in charge of all aspects of women's lives.

But Sinai, a woman who refuses to be controlled, will not allow herself to become a victim of Squire Darling's repugnant advances. When Sinai responds to his marriage proposal with an offer to be his daughter, he becomes enraged. She refuses to be cowed by his threats, and he, with dire results, attempts to force himself on her bodily:

> "Oh! I'll tell him [Dangerfield, the man Sinai wants to marry]! Oh! I'll tell him! that—*thus!* and *thus!* and *thus!* I have suffocated her with kisses a hundred times!"
>
> "And that thus she finally punished with DEATH a violence she could not prevent!" said Sina, swiftly snatching a short dagger from her bosom, and driving it to the hilt in his chest.
>
> Suddenly, with a sharp cry, he bounded up, dropped her, pulled the blade from his bosom, and cast it down, exclaiming: "Serpent! so you really have fangs then!" A dark stream of blood trickled from the wound. (*TB* 385)

Sinai pulls out her own knife to defend against the patriarch's sexual assault (his verbal threats are accompanied by physical advances), thereby leveling the playing field. The bad belle wrests phallic power from her victim, symbolically deflowering him with the knife, as he would have deflowered her. Southworth clearly agrees that Sinai is a serpent in disguise—one of the plot twists involves Sinai using her satanic powers to blackmail a priest about whom she has learned a secret. But the instance of the attack points out the lack of legitimate options for powerful women in the society. Southworth paints an even starker portrait of the patriarchal male's lechery and obsessive need for control. With the attempted rape of dark-skinned Sinai, the writer hints at the sexual exploitation of slave women and the commodification and control of all women in the slave South.

As she did in *Retribution,* however, the author faithfully restores patriarchal order after suggesting its iniquities. Overwhelmed by her evil deeds, Sinai succumbs, immediately after her attempted murder of Squire Darling, to her hereditary malady, brain fever, and gives herself up to Satan in final madness. Again, the writer's hasty and implausible removal of this character adds to Sinai's parodic quality and reveals that Southworth's creative energies are focused elsewhere. Also as in *Retribution,* Southworth links the madwoman and the femme fatale as two possible feminine responses to society's abuses. The madwoman—irrational, emotionally unrestrained, and physically grotesque—protests the system by opting out. The femme fatale—cunning, reserved, and beautiful—is more threatening and more successful because she manipulates the system from within, co-opting it rather than opting out.

Though she constantly reminds the reader of Sinai's villainy and of her service to Satan, Southworth, as she did with Juliette, will not allow us to despise this bad belle completely. The confidence and power with which Sinai carries out her deeds are awe inspiring. As she explains her raison d'être to the priest, Sinai assumes the heroic stature of a fallen Lucifer: "The life that you see around you is not life, but a chaos of good and evil impulses, in which individuality—'myself'—is lost. Three destinies await the soul at the death of the body—angel-life, demon-life, or annihilation. Angel-life to those who have expelled the fiend, demon-life to those who have cast out the angel, annihilation to those weak souls lost in the struggle. . . . IMMORTALITY IS FOR THOSE ONLY WHO ARE STRONG ENOUGH TO GRASP IT!" (*TB* 116). By exerting her individual will against the patriarchal father, God's representative on earth, Sinai, like Lucifer himself, grasps her immortality in rebellion. As John Milton became fascinated by the seductive allure of his Lucifer's rebellious will in *Paradise Lost,* so Southworth and her readers are entranced by Sinai. Sinai is a creation of Southworth, just as Lucifer is a creation of Milton; both authors use their antiheroes as outlets for their own defiance, a defiance that probably is conscious on Southworth's part if not on Milton's. Sinai's masculine power, however, not only makes her beguiling to readers and the author alike but also makes her an excellent vehicle for social criticism of the power structure that silences other women. Sinai's main victim, Squire Darling, with his lechery and buffoonery, is a far less admirable patriarch than Colonel Dent of *Retribution,* and the reader rejoices in his victimization.

After Sinai's death, however, the patriarch recovers from his injury and reforms his ways, embracing his estranged daughter and son-in-law with paternal affection. The restoration of power at the end establishes the proper moral tone to gain the approval of Southworth's readers. But despite the author's assurance at this point that all is right with the world, her earlier ambivalence and the glimpses she provided behind the curtain of southern propriety cannot be forgotten. Like Juliette, Sinai succeeds by manipulating a corrupt system; she exposes the supposed strengths of the confident, domineering, protecting gentlemen and the sheltered, innocent, compliant ladies as actual weaknesses. Southworth finally destroys the bad belle, but the patriarchy and its institutions do not escape her offensive unscathed.

Southworth's novel *Self-Raised* (1863) provides an interesting contrast to *Retribution* and *Three Beauties.* Perhaps because the novel was written at the height of the Civil War, the novel's critique of southern social structure is more veiled, and it is shrouded in a Gothic romance. Southworth spent much of her life in the South, but she was a strong Union sympathizer during the war. Because of conflicting interests, she likely tried to ameliorate dissent between the two sides while keeping her readership on both.[14] Consequently, most of this novel's action takes place in an ancient Scottish castle, and the plot seems designed to distract readers from the troubles at home. Though a dark seductress appears in this work, Southworth does not offer her the same sympathy she offered Juliette and Sinai. Primarily, Southworth employs this seductress in the way male writers usually employed the figure, as a moral lesson to rebellious women. Still, the character's exaggerated qualities give her a parodic force similar to that of Juliette

14. Boyle, *Mrs. E.D.E.N. Southworth,* 15.

and Sinai, and her reform in the end is as unconvincing and halfhearted as the earlier villainess's deaths. Lord Vincent, the villain of the novel and the femme fatale's victim, is ostensibly the antithesis of the southern gentleman, but a harsh, if hidden, criticism of the southern social structure is revealed when the similarities of this European nobleman and the southern gentleman are examined.

The novel's heroine, Claudia, is the villainous Lord Vincent's chief victim and the object of the author's most overt criticism. Her fate reveals the unhappy results of willfulness and disobedience. Coveting a title, plantation heiress Claudia rejects the genuine love of a local man with humble background for a marriage of convenience to the Scottish lord. Refusing to allow her father to negotiate a marriage settlement securing her independent wealth, Claudia seals her fate: "She had always ruled her father and everyone else around her in every particular and she ruled in this matter also. The fact is, that she was determined to be a viscountess at any price, and she is one—for a little while!" (*SR* 117). Just as she uses Lord Vincent for social position, he uses her to shore up his dwindling finances. Without her father's protection, Claudia is prey to Vincent's sinister scheming. Another implied attack on the South comes through the character of Judge Merlin, Claudia's father. Gentlemanly and likeable, Judge Merlin is also elderly, frail, and ineffectual. His inability to control his daughter possibly suggests Southworth's estimation of a decaying southern aristocracy.

Faustina, the dark seductress, is the impetus for Vincent's plot. Her appearance is similar to that of Southworth's other dark seductresses: "The features were formed in the most perfect mold of Oriental beauty; the forehead was broad and low; the nose fine and straight; the lips plump and full; and the chin small and rounded. The eyebrows were black, arched, and tapering over half-closed, almond-shaped, dark eyes that seemed floating in liquid fire. The complexion was of the richest brown, ripening into the most brilliant crimson in the oval cheeks and dewy lips that, falling half open, revealed the little glistening white teeth within" (*SR* 109). Here, the orientalism common in the nineteenth century links Faustina to a forbidden sexuality. Because her victim is not a southern gentleman, however, the customs of the South seem, on the surface, to have escaped Southworth's censure in this novel. Faustina, with her siren's voice and hypnotic eyes, has dazzled Lord Vincent, and it is out of lust for her that he conducts his diabolic plan. As the source of evil in the novel, then, Faustina appears to exemplify the dangers that threaten unprotected women such as Claudia.

Because she did not listen to her father, Claudia is at the mercy of Vincent and "the fiend that rules [his] fate" (*SR* 221). In addition, Faustina's own fate seems to suggest a warning of what can become of willful, defiant women. Her character is utterly depraved; she plots with Vincent to destroy Claudia's reputation and even attempts to murder Claudia's mammy so the pair can possess the lady's fortune. She has no redeeming qualities, even betraying her lover when the two are arrested for their crimes. Southworth offers her no sympathy.

Like Juliette in *Retribution,* however, Faustina has something in common with her creator. Though she is not a writer, Faustina is an "artiste of the highest order" (*SR* 111), a well-respected professional opera singer. Instead of performing only to entertain relatives and close friends in the parlor as a proper lady should, Faustina, like Southworth herself, receives money for entertaining strangers. When Claudia discovers that she shares her husband's home with a professional artist, her indignation mounts, and she resolves to demand the singer's immediate dismissal, though she knows nothing of the improper liaison between Faustina and Lord Vincent. She assumes that the public performer has questionable morals, viewing her only slightly more favorably than she would a prostitute. Southworth also sold her work to entertain the public, and though writers were more respected than stage performers, her exposure to the public eye raised questions of impropriety. Faustina's power, beauty, and talent are larger-than-life, and through them, Southworth seems to mock (or capitalize on?) her society's fear and censure of the woman artist.

The author's major criticism of the South, however, is by no means overt in this novel. Southworth seems to have chosen a Scottish nobleman as her villain to distance him from her southern readership. Lord Vincent is quite different from the *ideal* southern gentleman, but how different is he from the real? The ideal southern gentleman's paternalistic duty to his household obliged him to protect every dependent, black and white. In this regard, Vincent is far from the ideal. He refers to the family servants Claudia brings to the castle as black gorillas; he locks Katie, Claudia's mammy, in a dungeon; and he sells the three slaves to a black marketeer from Havana. All of these deeds are presented as atrocities, distinguishing Vincent's values from those of the way of life Claudia abandoned. In reality, however, southern slave owners often compared blacks to gorillas as a way of justifying their enslavement. As George M. Fredrickson observes in *The Black Image in the White Mind,* in the antebellum period, a type of "hard" racism that characterized the "negro as beast" existed alongside the "soft" racism that depicted slaves as beloved children. If persons of African descent were not fully human, then they were not entitled to the same rights as humans.[15] Also, some southern men chained and imprisoned slaves, and the institution of slavery could not have existed without the sale of slaves by these same southern men. Vincent's lust for Faustina, which inspires all of his actions, echoes the constant accusation of unbridled lust and sexual corruption used by abolitionists against the South.

Vincent is similar to southern gentlemen in other ways, too. Southern plantation owners often compared themselves to European aristocrats, attempting to make their way of life appear more civilized than that of the industrial North. This southern pretense, and Southworth's novel itself, may have been influenced by the early-nineteenth-century works of Sir Walter Scott. Scott's romantic tales of Scottish lords and manors were wildly popular in the South, so much so that Mark Twain later satirized them, believing they were responsible for the foolish affectations of chivalry to which southerners were often prone. The light and dark symbolism Southworth invokes to delineate pure and depraved womanhood was also used frequently by Scott. In addition, southern concepts of extended family loyalty and family honor were influenced by the Scottish clan system, which later fueled the overtly racist creation of the Ku Klux Klan. Southworth no doubt chose a Scottish setting for its resonance in the southern imagination.

As was the case in many southern households, Vincent's dark mistress, by whom he is mysteriously enthralled, lives in the same house as his wife, causing his wife to feel outraged and dishonored while he pretends the relationship is innocent. Chesnut recorded the situation in her diary: "Like the patriarchs of old our men live all in one house with their wives and their concubines." As southern wives were for all intents and purposes the property of their husbands, holding no legal or property rights of their own, so Vincent treats his wife as property, marrying her strictly for her wealth. In fact, as Fitzhugh's 1854 work *Sociology for the South* assessed, "women, like children have but one right, and that is the right to protection. . . . The right to protection involves the obligation to obey."[16] Though Southworth

15. Fredrickson, *Black Image in the White Mind*, 58.

16. Woodward, *Mary Chesnut's Civil War*, 29; Amy Thompson McCandless, "Concepts of Patriarchy in the Popular Novels of Antebellum Southern Women" *Studies in Popular Culture* 10 (1987): 3.

does not criticize the South directly in *Self-Raised*, she makes Lord Vincent guilty of the same atrocities of which southern patriarchs were often accused.

In the three novels *Retribution, Three Beauties,* and *Self-Raised,* we can see how Southworth modified her outward stance on the southern social structure as the relationship between North and South became more precarious. Though she disapproved of slavery and all its related evils, she depended in part on a southern audience for her livelihood and she continued to live in the South. In each successive novel, therefore, though she used the dark seductress to point out the abuses inherent in the southern social structure, her criticism grew less direct as the southern hegemony grew more rigid.

CAROLINE LEE HENTZ

Though born in the North, Caroline Lee Hentz (1800–56) was on the opposite side of the slavery issue from Southworth. At age twenty-seven, Hentz moved from New England to North Carolina with her husband and spent most of the rest of her life in the South. Though she was never wealthy, many of her novels are set on Edenic southern plantations where the paternalistic slave system is ostensibly shown to be the best way of life for black and white southerners. But in "Caroline Lee Hentz's Alabama Diary," Rhoda Coleman Ellison suggests that this proslavery stance and idealization of the plantation may have been primarily (at least at first) a marketing strategy. Both Hentz and her husband taught school, and they depended on the income from her book sales to support their family. Though Hentz expressed fear and disgust toward "the children of Africa" and bitterness toward a system that treated ownership of slaves as the greatest wealth, she realized the best way to win an audience in her new homeland was to extol the virtues of its cherished institutions.[17] Her strongest defenses of slavery appear in two novels, *Marcus Warland* (1852) and *The Planter's Northern Bride* (1854), the latter written as a response to Harriet Beecher Stowe's *Uncle Tom's Cabin* (1852). Though her works strongly defend the social order, Hentz, like Southworth, employs the dark seductress figure in a way that hints indirectly at the wickedness of southern oppression of white women and blacks.

17. Rhoda Coleman Ellison, "Caroline Lee Hentz's Alabama Diary, 1836" *Alabama Review* October (1951): 255, 258.

In *Marcus Warland*, the heroine, Florence, though not a full-fledged femme fatale, is a prototype of the bad belle who emerges in *The Planter's Northern Bride*. But even this early novel does not represent Hentz's first treatment of the theme of interracial love. In a very early play, *De Lara; or, the Moorish Bride* (1843), a conquering Spanish nobleman falls in love with the daughter of a conquered Moorish nobleman. The young woman's vulnerability, "dusky tints," and jetty hair are sources of great attraction for the young Spaniard. The history of violence between the two races and the woman's divided loyalties, however, doom the romance. In *Marcus Warland*, Florence fits the typical physical description of the nineteenth-century dark seductress: flashing eyes, dark, massive ringlets, and "Egyption face" (*MW* 129). Willful, flirtatious, and demanding, she is a stereotypical southern belle who dominates the men in her family and refuses at first to submit to the hero, Marcus. To his first mention of marriage, she responds: "I have always dreaded the ideal of love . . . because I know, if I once yielded to its power, I should become far more of a vassal than any slave on this broad plantation" (*MW* 131). Here Florence practically reiterates Chesnut's lament that "there is no slave, after all, like a wife,"[18] but Hentz, at least outwardly, intends this as an example of the character's immaturity and lack of womanly sentiments. Florence is at heart a good person, and she does in the end learn to be trusting, forgiving, and self-sacrificing, all traits of the proper southern matron.

In many ways, however, Florence is not a typical heroine. Hentz constantly emphasizes her dark features, sometimes describing her as Egyptian and sometimes as Creole, alluding to the population of New Orleans, which was notorious in the South for its formal system of concubinage that paired wealthy white gentlemen with mixed-race women. In the description of the features of the heroine, there is a subtle jab, never acknowledged by the author, at the southern practice of miscegenation, along with the exploitation and hypocrisy it usually entailed. Clark points out that, though racial mixing was acceptable in some small areas of the South, such as New Orleans, it was viewed by most people as the greatest evil of slavery and it was the charge southerners were least able to refute.[19] The link to concubinage, however, could also emphasize the similarities between the lives of married women and the lives of slave women, both of whom were treated

18. Woodward, *Mary Chesnut's Civil War*, 59.
19. Clark, "Serpent of Lust," 814.

as the property of the "Lord and Master." But Hentz does make it clear that Florence's fiery, dark blood makes her strong, powerful, and fascinating, and that it is this fiery blood that must be tamed.

In that taming process, however, Florence darkens her features even more. When, before their marriage, Marcus is seriously injured in a fight, she disguises herself as a mulatta slave so she can sit by his bedside and nurse him back to health. In assuming this disguise, Florence does what nineteenth-century women authors do with their bad belle characters: she takes on a dark double who is at once more free and more confined than she normally would be. In *Playing in the Dark,* Morrison explores the white men's use of the "Africanist persona" in American literature as "an extraordinary meditation on the self; a powerful exploration of the fears and desires that reside in the writerly conscious." The slave population, she posits, was used by the white imagination as "surrogate selves" to explore hidden fears and forbidden desires. And as Sander Gilman points out in "Black Bodies, White Bodies: Toward an Iconography of Female Sexuality in Late Nineteenth-Century Art, Medicine, and Literature," from the time of the Middle Ages, images of blacks in paintings were used to indicate illicit sexual activity. Often a sexualized white woman was shown with a black servant to emphasize their similarities, the "overt sexuality" of the black woman indicating "the covert sexuality of the white woman."[20]

In taking on a black disguise, Florence becomes at once more sexually free and more physically subservient. As a mulatto girl, she is allowed a proximity to her lover no unmarried white girl would be permitted, sitting alone with him through the night, wiping his brow, administering his medicine, and waving a peacock feather fan over his bed. Florence wears a green shade over her eyes to conceal her identity, resembling in her demeanor and action a veiled harem girl. She glides noiselessly about the room, speaks only when spoken to, and strews rose petals about the sick chamber, even on the patient's pillow. In her hours of servitude, Florence realizes the strength of her love for Marcus, and the devotion he senses in his nurse flatters and slightly embarrasses the young gentleman, who does not recognize her as his lover.

In this scene, Hentz obliquely critiques the southern social system. Mor-

20. Morrison, *Playing in the Dark,* 17; Sander Gilman, "Black Bodies, White Bodies: Toward an Iconography of Female Sexuality in Late Nineteenth-Century Art, Medicine, and Literature," in *"Race," Writing, and Difference,* Henry Louis Gates Jr., ed. (Chicago: University of Chicago Press, 1986), 227–28, 231.

rison's argument about the role of blacks in texts by white authors comments on the complex and sometimes hidden levels of meaning these characters often bring to the works: "Encoded or explicit, indirect or overt, the linguistic responses to an Africanist presence complicate texts, sometimes contradicting them entirely. A writer's response to American Africanism often provides a subtext that either sabotages the surface text's expressed intentions or escapes them through a language that mystifies what it cannot bring itself to articulate but still attempts to register."[21] Though Hentz deals ostensibly with a traditional marriage plot in a proslavery novel, the use of an Africanist persona allows her to create (perhaps unconsciously) an encoded subtext that subverts the conventions she outwardly supports. The very existence of the beautiful mulatta, suggestively dressed and behaving as a harem girl, indicates that the forbidden liaisons between black and white—of which abolitionists accused the South and which proper defenders of the South tried to deny—actually occurred, whether by mutual consent or not. Hentz also indicts the arbitrary distinctions in status and protection afforded to slave women and white women. Though it would be improper for a white girl to spend the night alone with a man to whom she was unrelated, by only slightly darkening her skin and pretending to be a stranger, Florence eliminates the need for protection. The rationale for this difference might be the pretense that no southern gentleman would lower himself by seducing a slave, but again, the mulatta's existence tells us that some southern men, who may or may not have been considered gentlemen, would and did. Another possible rationale is that the slave woman's supposed natural promiscuity made protecting her virtue an irrelevancy. But by putting Florence in a slave woman's place, Hentz forces her readers to see the hypocrisy of the double standard that assigned obverse sexual roles to black and white women based on a few drops of blood. Finally, Hentz silently compares slavery to marriage. Florence becomes most womanly and most prepared to be a wife while acting as a slave, showing that the two roles are in fact very similar. Though neither Florence nor her alter ego has the destructive attributes of the traditional bad belle, their presence in the novel provides a similar function to that of the dark seductresses in other nineteenth-century women's works—a veiled attack on an oppressive system.

Unlike Florence, Claudia, the dark seductress of *The Planter's Northern*

---

21. Morrison, *Playing in the Dark*, 66.

Bride, will not be tamed. She is the rebellious first wife of Moreland, the plantation master, Lilith to his prelapsarian Adam. When Claudia refuses to submit to her husband's authority, she is cast out of the plantation Eden to make way for a new, more compliant wife, Eulalia, also known as Eula. Once happily married, the couple preside over a perfect setting in a hierarchical order that descends directly from God to Moreland-Adam, to Eulalia-Eve, and finally to the slaves and animals they control. Claudia, true to character, refuses to submit even to her banishment. She continues to torment the master, appearing like the biblical serpent to disturb his newfound domestic bliss. But the fact that she haunts Moreland and Eulalia even after her death—pricking their pride, sympathy, and conscience—indicates their complicity, like Adam and Eve's with the serpent, in the evil she represents.

Claudia's appearance is similar to that of the dark seductresses discussed already in the works of Southworth and Hentz. When she first meets Eulalia, the new mistress of the plantation, her dark features and haughty manners form a bold contrast to Eula's pale features and mild demeanor:

> There were the large, black, resplendent, yet repelling eyes, that were for ever haunting her,—the red lips of scorn, the pale olive cheek, the bold, yet classic brow—all the features daguerreotyped on her memory. . . .
> Claudia threw herself on a sofa, in an attitude of careless independence. The crimson velvet of the covering brought out, in strong relief, the handsome, but bold outlines of her figure, which swelled through the dark mistiness of a black lace drapery. She sat, wrapping this drapery round her exquisitely white hands, all glittering with rings, then suddenly untying the strings of her bonnet, she tossed it down by her side, and shook her raven black hair from her brow. (*PNB* 362–63)

The two wives of Moreland are literally as different as black and white, a difference coded with moral symbolism for Hentz's readers. The bad wife is dark, as immoral and uncivilized Africans are dark, as sin itself is dark. In contrast, Eulalia, the good wife, is fair and blond. In this first detailed description of Claudia—before she is referred to in conversation and only momentarily introduced—we see the characteristic dark features that suggest mixed blood. Coupled with these dark features are her handsomely swelling figure and exquisite lace draperies, which insinuate a sexuality barely controlled. The focus on Claudia's body, here, is unusual in nineteenth-century women's fiction. According to Baym, "Victorian-American women and men interpreted women's weaker body as signifying less body, a different kind of body, and that they translated this different, lesser body into a sign of more spirit. . . . Accordingly the protagonist's appearance is dwelt on extensively. But the appearance testifies to a spiritual body, a non-body. Accordingly, the body was ignored." The villainess, however, is not as pure a spiritual being as the protagonist: "Sexually appetitive women were man-like women, and a certain masculinity informs the representations of the occasional melodramatic villainess who appears in women's fictions."[22] Though Claudia is not physically masculine, her presence is certainly more corporeal than Eulalia's, perhaps indicating her more masculine willfulness.

As did Southworth, Hentz seems to gaze longingly at her seductive creation and to transfer her desire to her readers. In "Visual Pleasure and Narrative Cinema," Mulvey describes two types of visual pleasure that expand on Lacan's division of phallic power into those who "have" and those who "are" the phallus. Mulvey's explanation seems relevant to this visual description of the beautiful Claudia: "The first [form of visual pleasure], scopophilic, arises from pleasure in using another person as an object of sexual stimulation through sight. The second, developed through narcissism and the constitution of the ego, comes from identification with the image seen." According to Mulvey, viewers normally derive narcissistic pleasure from the active male hero and scopophilic pleasure from his passive female counterpart.[23] Femme fatale characters disrupt this neat dichotomy, because, though they are beautiful to look at, they are also active agents who fulfill their own desires. They provide both scopophilic and narcissistic pleasure, but they also disrupt normal power structures and create a sense of fascinated uneasiness in readers that advances the author's social critique.

The social critique is furthered by the exotic and obscure parentage Hentz assigns to Claudia. Born to Italian parents, Claudia wanders the southern countryside with her family as a performing Gypsy until a wealthy matron buys her (as one would buy a slave) from her parents, taking the beautiful child to raise as her daughter (*PNB* 373–74). Like Claudia's ancestry, the racial connotation of the label Gypsy is somewhat ambiguous. Though Gypsies are actually a tribe of nomads originally emigrating from an area between Iran and India, the term also has been used to mean Egyptians. Like Southworth, Hentz draws on racist assumptions about Italians, similar to American assumptions about blacks, to hint at miscegenation

22. Baym, *Woman's Fiction,* xxxvi–xxxvii.
23. Mulvey, "Visual Pleasure," 18, 20.

without actually presenting it in the narrative. Hentz never suggests overtly that Claudia is part black—the novel would be less likely to sell—but the author does give her the conventional traits of the mulatto, making her similar to but even more seductive and exotic than the pretend mulatto portrayed in *Marcus Warland*. Though Claudia's dark features link her to a long tradition of dark seductresses, in the slave South her darkness takes on a more concrete racial meaning.

As the dark seductress was reputed to do, Claudia enchants Moreland when they first meet. Under the patronage of the adopted mother who earlier purchased her, Claudia is educated and introduced into the best society, where she soon becomes the most fashionable belle in the area. Moreland meets her in the ballroom, where "the airy graces she had cultivated in childhood hung round her . . . giving a wild charm to her beauty that rendered it irresistible" (*PNB* 374). Though he later labels this infatuation a "boyish passion, caused by a fascination such as the serpent exercises on its victim" (*PNB* 372), Moreland falls deeply in love with Claudia and they soon marry. As Clinton tells us, young southern gentleman were often subject to another type of unacceptable and dangerous infatuation: "The plantation mistress was especially sensitive to what she had been taught to see as the debauching influence of slave women on sons who had reached puberty. 'Lewd and promiscuous' behavior was always blamed on the slaves in the case of planter-concubine liaisons." And Wyatt-Brown observes that southerners sometimes worried that unsuspecting white men would marry "bewitching" girls of mixed race, thinking them white.[24] Though Claudia is not described as a woman of slave descent, Hentz, like Southworth, in her various descriptions of Claudia's appearance and actions blurs the lines between the typical belle and the slave seductress. Both are creations of male patriarchal society who exploit women in service of a male-dominated sexual economy. This elliptical association quietly implicates these unacceptable liaisons as a destructive influence on southern domestic harmony, placing the blame for them, for the time being, where it normally is placed, on the woman.

Though Claudia's magical allure is too powerful to resist, the fault lies not in this power, which any belle would exercise, but in her refusal to submit this power to her husband's will after marriage, as any proper belle was required to do. After comparing the concubine to the belle, Hentz alludes to the similarity between the dutiful slave and the proper wife. Soon after their marriage, Moreland realizes he cannot control Claudia: "The slightest

---

24. Clinton, *Plantation Mistress,* 49; Wyatt-Brown, *Southern Honor,* 311.

opposition to her wishes, the mildest admonition or reproof, created such a storm of passion in her, he often turned from her in consternation and dismay, almost believing he had been the victim of an evil spirit, who, assuming the form of a beautiful woman, had ensnared his heart, and was seeking the destruction of his soul" (*PNB* 375). Disobedience is portrayed as the greatest sin a wife could commit, as it was for a slave. In either, it threatens the "soul" of the patriarch and the very foundations of southern culture. Because of her disobedience, Claudia becomes unwomanly—an evil spirit. She is a negligent mother and pursues an association with "one of her countrymen," meeting him clandestinely when Moreland is away from home and bringing dishonor on the household by disregarding the greatest duties of a matron: subservience, motherhood, and self-sacrifice.

Because the primary duties of a patriarch are to command and control, Moreland does the same with Claudia as he does with his rebellious slave Vulcan: he drives her from his household. Still, for a time after the divorce, it appears Claudia has done exactly what Moreland feared she would do—capture his soul. At the novel's beginning, Moreland is depicted as an exile from Eden, wandering downhearted and lonely through the North. He is redeemed by a woman who is Claudia's opposite in every way: northern rather than southern, meek and self-deprecating rather than proud and willful, and fair rather than dark. Hentz's ostensible objective in *The Planter's Northern Bride* was to ease the sectional tensions inflamed by *Uncle Tom's Cabin*. By choosing a northern Eve to marry her southern Adam, she effected a symbolic union between North and South, in addition to securing readers both sides of the Mason-Dixon Line. This northern bride would indeed have appeal to Hentz's southern women readers. Golden-haired, with pale, translucent skin, she is the white ideal of angelic beauty. Many of Hentz's southern readers possibly saw themselves, or the perfection to which they aspired, in Eulalia. Hentz presents Eulalia and Moreland's relationship as an ideal, and they exist together in the southern garden like Milton's Adam and Eve, Eve worshiping and depending on Adam as Adam worships and depends on God.[25]

25. As Nina Silber points out in *The Romance of Reunion* (Chapel Hill: University of North Carolina Press, 1993), the use of marriage as a metaphor for reconciliation was a conventional plot device of novels written in the years surrounding the Civil War. In novels written by northerners, the South is represented by a woman, to indicate the weakness and irrationality believed to be characteristic of southerners. Hentz reverses this pattern, making the North female and the South male, but she still suggests weakness in her southern gentleman through his interactions with women.

But contemporary diaries and other literature show that many nineteenth-century white women were aware of the less pleasant correspondences between their own situations and Eulalia's. Shirley Samuels cites one contemporary allegorical piece, "Slavery and Marriage: A Dialogue" (1850), attributed to John Humphrey Noyes, that applies antislavery arguments to the institution of marriage and compares the abuses suffered by slaves to those suffered by married women. Evidence suggests that Hentz did not have this type of submissive relationship to her own husband. She worked as a teacher and writer, sometimes as the family's sole financial supporter.[26] The depiction of Eulalia is as unrealistic as that of Claudia, and perhaps both are parodies of differing southern conceptions of womanhood. Though Hentz outwardly praises Moreland and Eulalia's hierarchical relationship, many women of the time resented this type of domination and would have noticed the similarities between Moreland's treatment of his slaves and his treatment of his wives. Many readers no doubt saw themselves in Eulalia in more ways than one.

Even in the ostensibly blissful marriage Hentz presents, the serpent intrudes to unsettle Moreland and Eulalia's peace of mind. Not long after the wedding, when Moreland is away from the plantation, Claudia visits her former home to meet the new mistress and to reclaim her daughter. Eulalia haughtily repels her, saying she is unworthy to care for the child Eulalia has adopted as her own. The heroine is understandably offended at the fallen woman's intrusion and attempt to usurp the limited authority as mistress she now commands. But her reaction to her husband's past association with Claudia is more emotional than one might expect: "She was humiliated by the knowledge of such deep depravity in one of womankind. It was exquisitely painful to her to think that Moreland had ever loved such a being. It seemed to detract from the purity, the dignity of his love for her" (*PNB* 372). Her sensibilities seem overly offended, especially because the only new evidence she has received of Claudia's depravity is her appearance. During their interview, Claudia even denies her former husband's accusations. But Eulalia nonetheless blushes with shame when she must later reveal to an itinerant preacher that her husband was married before and divorced. As Wyatt-Brown notes, though, men in the nineteenth-century South had a far easier time obtaining a divorce than did women, the pro-

26. Shirley Samuels, "The Identity of Slavery" in *Culture of Sentiment,* 166; Jamie Stanesa, "Caroline Lee Whiting Hentz" *Legacy* 13 (1996): 132.

tection of male honor being the primary objective in most divorce settlements. Regardless of the facts, a divorced woman's honor was always suspect, and because the duty to make a marriage happy rested solely on her, the disgrace associated with a failed marriage was far greater for the woman.[27] The society, therefore, would not have heaped as much shame on Moreland for his failed marriage as Eulalia does.

There was another type of male liaison, which, though not often publicly acknowledged, was a severe source of shame to white women. Many southern women considered association between black women and white men not only disgraceful to the white man but also an insult to the white women to whom he was related. Gertrude Thomas opposes slavery's "terribly demoralizing influence on our men and boys"; Chesnut writes of philandering southern men, "the lower the mistress, the more degraded they must be"; and Keziah Goodwyn Hopkins Brevard extends this dishonor to herself in her antebellum diary: "I thank Heavenly Father I have never had a son to mix my blood with negro blood."[28] Eulalia feels that the purity and dignity of her own marriage has been somehow tainted by Moreland's past association to Claudia, a being who appears not only morally stained but physically stained as well. Though antebellum morals do not permit Hentz openly to suggest miscegenation with a patriarch of Moreland's standing, she may use Eulalia's mortification upon seeing the dark seductress to remind her women readers of their shame and indignities over male liaisons with dark mistresses.

Through the contrasting female characters Claudia and Eulalia, Hentz also spotlights other southern conventions for inspection. Both of these women were artists in their youth. Claudia's supporting her family by dancing publicly for money that strangers throw to her foreshadows the moral laxity that will ruin her marriage, as Faustina's professional artistry suggests her loose morals. Eulalia, on the other hand, reaps praise for her beautiful singing, which she performs in church while standing modestly behind a curtain. Hentz, similar to Claudia, supported her family by writing and selling novels, and Ellison relates that Hentz's own marriage was often threatened by her husband's irrationally jealous tantrums. One wonders if this

27. Wyatt-Brown, *Southern Honor*, 283–92.

28. Whites, *The Civil War as Crisis in Gender,* 100; Woodward, *Mary Chesnut's Civil War,* 31; John Hammond Moore, ed., *A Plantation Mistress on the Eve of the Civil War: The Diary of Keziah Goodwyn Hopkins Brevard, 1803–1886* (Columbia: University of South Carolina Press, 1993), 95.

woman who depended on her craft for survival was not derisively calling attention to this double standard, which honored artistic accomplishments but only when they were of no practical value. In a later novel, *Ernest Linwood* (1856), however, Hentz refers to her craft with seeming dismissal and chagrin: "Book! Am I writing a book? No indeed! This is only a record of my heart's life, written at random and carelessly thrown aside, sheet after sheet, sibylline leaves from the great book of fate." Is her false modesty a ploy to prevent the cultured reader's distaste at reading women's fiction? Or is she genuinely ashamed of her profession?[29] More likely, the quotation is another example of her artistic skill, her ability to create a persona that would charm her reader. It is doubtful she would have written as many novels and fared as well with them if she had really had such distaste for her work.

Hentz further soothes southern sensibilities that may have been provoked by the implied social criticism delivered through the femme fatale by destroying, as did Southworth, the bad belle to restore patriarchal order. As a result of her dissipation after leaving the control of her husband, Claudia suffers an incurable malady, which leads to her death. At the final hour, she summons Moreland to reclaim the daughter she had managed to kidnap. In a Gothic scene resembling the ending of Poe's "The Fall of the House of Usher," Claudia meets her end at her crumbling family estate:

> "Oh! thou who ridest upon the wings of the wind, who makest darkness thy pavilion," cried Moreland, turning from the dim-lighted couch to the darkened heavens, "come not in judgment, but mercy! Have pity on the frail and erring creatures thou has made! Thou knowest our frames: thou rememberest that we are but dust! Oh! it is a fearful thing, this rending of the immortal from the mortal—fearful to witness, but alas! more dread to bear!"
>
> At this moment, a large branch of the live oak came tumbling, crashing against the house, bursting in the casement, and shivering into splinters the crystal panes. The house rocked, and every article of furniture vibrated with the concussion. (*PNB* 475–76)

Nature appears to participate in Claudia's destruction, and Moreland's prayer suggests his fear that he will share in her punishment. His pleas for mercy are more desperate than one would expect from a man who merely

29. Rhoda Coleman Ellison, "Mrs. Hentz and the Green-Eyed Monster" *American Literature* 22 (1950): 345; Susan Phinney Conrad, *Perish the Thought: Intellectual Women in Romantic America, 1830–1860* (New York: Oxford University Press, 1976), 27.

intercedes on behalf of a dying sinner, especially one from whom he has been so long estranged. At the end of "House of Usher" a similar storm takes place, rending the decayed house in two and dissolving it into the misty tarn. Lewis P. Simpson interprets this story allegorically, saying that the house represents the South itself, and the rift is the sin of slavery that tears the South apart.[30] Hentz probably would have read Poe's story, and perhaps she modeled this scene on his ending. At any rate, the storm's rage and Moreland's fear of it seem to implicate him in Claudia's fall. Through Moreland, the patriarchal Adam in the southern Eden, Hentz implicates the entire social structure for its sins against women.

Before Claudia's death, though, Hentz offers sympathy to the bad belle, lest the reader dismiss her messages too hastily. On her first meeting with Eulalia, Claudia denied the charges of adultery for which her husband sought a divorce. Eulalia haughtily and indignantly refused to listen, choosing to believe only what she heard from Moreland. On her deathbed, however, Claudia again denies the charges. She says that she had not refuted them when she was married "because they reflected shame and misery" on her husband (*PNB* 468). Moreland and the reader believe this deathbed confession, but only the reader wonders what Moreland did to cause such bitter feelings. Claudia's vindication also raises concerns about Eulalia's lack of Christian charity and forgiveness in their earlier encounter. But despite her absolution, Claudia maintains the same awe-inspiring defiance that characterized Juliette and Sinai in Southworth's novels. Just before Claudia dies, Moreland begs her to give him a look indicating she has made her peace with God, but instead she meets his gaze with a final rebellion: "She could not speak, but she lifted her eyes, where all that remained of vitality was concentrated in one burning spark, and fixed them steadfastly on his. Never, never did he forget that glance. It haunted him years afterwards. He saw it in the blaze of noonday—the darkness of midnight. It haunted him till his dying day" (*PNB* 477). She refuses in the end to submit to the ultimate patriarchal authority. Moreland reads in her eyes a rejection of all he represents, perhaps accusation for past wrongs as well. Though Moreland remains secure in his patriarchal authority, his interactions with Claudia and with Eulalia, the bad wife and the good wife, show that his authority is not always benevolent.

30. Lewis P. Simpson, *The Brazen Face of History: Studies in the Literary Consciousness in America* (Baton Rouge: Louisiana State University Press, 1980), 101–2.

Hentz's use of the belle gone bad differs from Southworth's, and these differences emphasize the seditious nature of southern women writers' use of the character. While Southworth uses the belle gone bad repeatedly in her works, there is only one example in Hentz. And while Southworth overtly shows her fascination with the character—in *Retribution* and *Three Beauties* at least—Hentz outwardly condemns everything about Claudia, though her descriptions of her are lingering and sexually charged. Hentz's reserve toward her character may be due to the climate in which she wrote, which made dissent more dangerous, and also due to her own greater investment in the southern establishment. Southworth lived on the northern fringes of the South, and her political allegiances lay north of the Mason-Dixon Line. Hentz, however, spent her adult life in the South and made her reputation defending its institutions. But Hentz evidently felt some reservations about this society, and these reservations creep, though in a more circumspect way than those of Southworth, into her portrayal of the belle gone bad.

AUGUSTA JANE EVANS

Augusta Jane Evans (1835–1909), unlike Southworth and Hentz, was born in the Deep South and lived there her entire life. Like them, however, she wrote popular novels about southern culture. Evans strongly supported the Confederacy, and her novel *Macaria* (1863) was a piece of wartime propaganda that idealized the South and the cause for which it fought. According to Evans's biographer, *Macaria*'s "value as propaganda was recognized immediately by the enemy, for General G. H. Thomas, who commanded a Federal army in Tennessee, pronounced it 'contraband and dangerous,' banned it among the Yankee troops, and burned all copies which he found."[31]

As did Southworth and Hentz, however, Evans uses the bad belle as a vehicle to critique her cherished region in *Beulah* (1859). In this early novel, her most autobiographical, Evans details the life of an intellectual young woman writer who learns the value of love over individual ambition. Evans herself did not marry until she was thirty-three (the average age of marriage for women in the South was about twenty), and though her nov-

31. William Perry Fidler, *Augusta Evans Wilson, 1835–1909: A Biography* (University: University of Alabama Press, 1951), 107.

els praise the necessity of love and self-sacrifice for women, she knew what it was like to pursue her intellectual interests and support herself.[32] Another inconsistency between Evans's life and the one she portrays for her heroine is that, though Evans owned slaves, in *Beulah* especially she studiously masks the presence of slaves, referring to them only occasionally as "the servants," never indicating that they are of another race. Perhaps she omits slaves from her narrative because their presence would detract from an already complex story of the incompatible quests for love and self-fulfillment or perhaps because their presence would detract from the domestic ideal she was trying to create for her heroine. But southern reality as Evans lived it becomes more visible in the novel when we examine her treatment of Beulah's artistic career and her treatment of the bad belle character, Creola.

The dark seductress in *Beulah* is not really a character, because she appears only as a memory from another character's past. She serves as a foil for the heroine, Beulah, a proud orphan who supports herself by teaching and writing for a southern magazine. Beulah is happily independent and rejects two marriage proposals, one from her much older, wealthy guardian, Guy Hartwell. But intellectual endeavors take a toll on Beulah's health. Sometimes staying up all night to read or write, she grows more and more sickly, until her friends fear she will study to her death. Not only her physical being is in jeopardy. The philosophical texts Beulah reads so shake her faith in God that she becomes a religious skeptic and spends long hours trying to regain spiritual peace. Though Beulah is at first contented and proud of her independence, her heavy burdens, Evans suggests, will lead to an early grave followed by eternal damnation.

Unlike Southworth and Hentz, Evans makes her heroine rather than her villainess an artist figure. Like Southworth and Hentz, however, Evans recognizes that her culture's fear of powerful, independent women threatens to silence the woman artist, and she uses the bad belle to dramatize this threat. Evans herself felt compelled to silence her artistic aspirations when they competed with those of a male contemporary. According to Faust, "Evans abandoned her intention to write a Confederate history in deference to former vice-president of the Confederacy Alexander Stephens, who planned one of his own. 'I humbly put my fingers on the throat of my ambitious daring design of becoming the Confederate Xenophon and strangled it. . . . I confess it cost me a severe struggle to relinquish the fond

32. Clinton, *Plantation Mistress,* 233.

dream . . . but abler hands snatched it from my weak womanly fingers and waved me to humbler paths of labor.' "[33] A similar violence to that with which she strangled her own ambitions is projected outward in her earlier novel through the dark double.

Beulah's artistic endeavors closely resemble those of her creator. Like Evans, Beulah is a talented writer, and also like Evans, she manages to sell her manuscripts to southern magazines, which at the time rarely paid their contributors. Evans even uses Beulah as a mouthpiece for her views on the deplorable state of southern letters (*B* 293–94). But the novel reveals that Beulah is uncomfortable with her professional career. The character wears heavy veils when walking to her publishers; she uses a pseudonym for her published works, as if her artistic endeavors were somehow shameful; and at one point she says prophetically that poetry is "the highest and purest phase of insanity" (*B* 217). Other characters warn Beulah that her life of the mind is an improper one for a woman. Hartwell tells Beulah that her "woman's heart will not be satisfied long with dim abstractions" (*B* 324), and she is also told, "Man may content himself with the applause of the world, and the homage paid to his intellect; but woman's heart has holier idols" (*B* 401). The holier idols that rule a woman's heart, as it turns out in *Beulah,* are God and his patriarchal representative, man. Evans was no doubt offered similar words of warning that she managed, up to a point, to resist. But as William Perry Fidler tells us, she wrote much less after her marriage in 1867.

A similar fate, marriage and professional silence, awaits Beulah, though this work was written eight years and many novels prior to Evans's own wedding. Jones notes the incongruity between Beulah's quest for self-awareness and independence throughout most of the novel and her eventual capitulation to Hartwell in marriage at the novel's end:

> Augusta Jane Evans found herself split between an inner vision and a desire to conform. That inner vision develops a female *Bildungsroman,* promising psychic integration and an interdependent relationship with one's community. But Evans's mask was that of the southern woman writer; the actual community for which and within which she wrote held strongly patriarchal values concerning religion, women, and the structure of society itself. Thus when Evans forces her *Bildungsroman* to fit the social expectation that it must, she has to convert her speculative protagonist to an All-Father God and shape her

33. Faust, *Mothers of Invention,* 178.

character into that of the child-wife who can serve as idol for southern gentleman.[34]

Though this reversal of goals seems sudden, Evans does prepare a way for it through the introduction of the bad belle, who reveals the madness and depravity that may lie at the end of the path Beulah has chosen. Through this character, Evans invokes an image of strong womanhood—a perception that equated female physical and mental independence with moral corruption—that shames the woman artist into wearing veils when delivering her manuscripts.

Guy Hartwell's first wife, described only in a memory, provides an example of the ill fate that befalls women who refuse to submit to male authority; the example convinces Beulah to marry her guardian. Creola is a complex figure, who, like similar manifestations in the works of Southworth and Hentz, calls attention to the sins of the patriarchy while simultaneously emphasizing that there is no escape from its control. Gazing at a portrait of the deceased wife, Beulah notes the enchanting eyes, frequently associated with the dark seductress's power: "It was a young, girlish face sparking with joyousness, bewitching in its wonderful loveliness. The eloquent eyes were strangely, almost wildly brilliant, the full crimson lips possessed that rare outline one sees in old pictures, and the cheek, tinted like a sea-shell, rested on one, delicate dimpled hand" (*B* 465–67). For the first time, Evans hints, perhaps unconsciously, at the problems of southern race relations and the similarities between wives and slaves in the Old South. Creola's name, her New Orleans origin, "tinted" features, and humble background (Hartwell took her from a poor, fatherless home) all subtly hint at mixed blood and the formal concubinage for which her birthplace was notorious. Her ability to fascinate Guy Hartwell despite his family's objections reminds us of the magical powers of seduction attributed to the African slave woman, who was often accused by southern matrons of enchanting young white gentlemen. But as was the case in most actual instances of mixed-race liaisons, Evans makes it clear that the planter took an active role in the courtship.

Because Creola is a "mere child" without money when she meets Hartwell, he takes charge of her education, placing her in a fine school to cultivate her as a suitable bride. Here, as the male guardians do with Sinai in *Three Beauties* and Minny and Hester in *Retribution,* the planter blurs the lines between his duty as protector and his role as lover, a problem that

---

34. Jones, *Tomorrow Is Another Day,* 91.

seems endemic to the patriarchal structure. Like Beulah herself when she first meets Hartwell, Creola is a child, for whom he assumes the role of guardian and protector. And as with Beulah, he seems to rear Creola for his own use. Here, though Evans never overtly refers to slavery in the novel, the parallel drawn by the author seems to implicate the southern institution. Planters often stated they had benevolent motives in keeping slaves because the slaves were unfit to care for themselves, but these slaves were always used for the benefit of the master, too often for his sexual pleasure. The lady of the house, though she shared the master's proper bed, was, like his slaves, subject to the authority of the master. Once again, we see the patriarch in the dual role of father-lover, even with his wife.

But Hartwell soon discovers that he has not fully trained his first young bride. When he discovers that she has clandestine meetings with a former young suitor, he confronts her. She responds by raving and refusing to submit to his control. Her duplicity destroys Hartwell, and the friend who relays the story to Beulah says that Hartwell was never the same afterward: "Ah, Beulah! it makes my heart ache to think of the change this discovery wrought in Guy's nature. He was a proud man, naturally; but now he became repulsive, cold and austere. The revolution in his deportment and appearance was almost incredible" (*B* 467). The dark seductress has consumed the once strong man. But Creola, as a result of the conflict, is also destroyed, like Southworth's Sinai, in sudden madness. Creola returns to her mother and dies a few weeks later. Once again, the dark seductress and the madwoman are shown as associated options for protest against male control, but neither permits survival in the male-dominated culture.

Significantly, the revelation of the first wife's fate occurs in an attic room when Beulah is struggling to find some peace of mind in a moment of extreme personal loneliness and spiritual distress. This scene calls to mind similar ones in Charlotte Brontë's *Jane Eyre,* published twelve years earlier in England. Jane discovers Bertha Mason, the mad first wife of her much older emotionally debilitated employer and future husband, imprisoned in an attic room on his estate. Gilbert and Gubar have suggested that Bertha serves as a dark double for Jane and for Brontë herself, a manifestation of desires society considered unacceptable. In *Jane Eyre,* they argue, the madwoman is destroyed as an exorcism of the author's inappropriate drives and as a warning about the fate of women who do not conform.[35] Perhaps, in-

35. Gilbert and Gubar, *Madwoman.*

stead, it is an angry commentary on the society that imposes this fate. In *Beulah,* the heroine appears chastened by Creola's negative example, rediscovering in the next chapter her faith in God, the ultimate patriarch, and surrendering to her love for her guardian, Hartwell, God's delegate in a patriarchal southern society. She accepts her duty as a woman to sacrifice herself for her husband, giving up her intellectual pursuits to restore his former happiness and to help him find his faith in God. Ironically, Beulah rationalizes her decision to give up her independence by convincing herself that she must save Hartwell from the life and death of a nonbeliever. In reality, she sacrifices herself to a patriarchal system designed to keep her subservient, and as Creola's fate reveals, she really had little choice in the first place.

The question of whether Evans unconsciously punishes her own creative independence through the character of Creola and Creola's impact on Beulah or consciously calls attention to her culture's abuse and destruction of strong-willed, independent women remains open. Another possibility is that the author may simply be capitalizing on a conventional attitude of her culture, which she rejected for herself. But the productivity and popularity of her career suggests that she did not feel as much shame as did her character, Beulah, when she turned in a manuscript for publication. Perhaps instead of advocating submission to patriarchal authority, through Creola's effect on Beulah, Evans records a warning message for herself and others like her that would help her to postpone the inevitable stifling of her creative voice in marriage.

As did Southworth and Hentz, Evans restores patriarchal order by destroying the femme fatale and returning the patriarch to a position of authority. Evans's heroine Beulah learns from the negative example of Hartwell's first wife that there is no alternative to marriage and submission to patriarchal authority. On her own, Beulah faces physical and spiritual decline; through Creola she sees that the price of independence is depravity, madness, and death. Though Evans offers no alternative to male control, she still points out the flaws of the social structure by describing Creola's background and allowing us to feel sympathy for this bad belle. The reader does not condemn Creola for enchanting and consuming the hero because she is described as a beautiful and spoiled child deprived of her true love by a rich older man and by her mother, who coveted the man's fortune. Though Creola makes the patriarch her victim, she is herself a victim of the patriarchy.

*   *   *

Through the character of the bad belle, then, these antebellum women writers reproach southern attitudes about race, gender, and writing itself. Their novels resemble one of the nineteenth-century South's favorite narrative types, the plantation novel. But these women rewrite the form to show the follies of the typical characters—the matron, the master, the belle, and the slave. By making the dark seductress a bad belle, the authors involve two southern types created by southern men, the coquette and the jezebel. Linking these seemingly opposite figures allows the writers to show the arbitrariness of the distinctions made between them, emphasizing the abuse each is subject to as well as pointing out the vulnerabilities of good women and the males who are charged with protecting them. But because these women write in a male-dominated society, their challenge to it may go only so far. The authors' capitulation to their market manifests itself when, after hinting at the bad belle's victimization and using the character to expose the weaknesses of those in charge, the authors destroy the dangerous woman, usually the character who most closely resembles the authors themselves, and restore the proper order.

A regression in the use of the dark belle gone bad from Southworth to Hentz to Evans can be seen. As the South became more defensive, the authors' critiques became more constrained, and because the bad belle seems inevitably, though enigmatically, to convey critique, her role diminishes in the works. In Evans's *Beulah,* the only work in which she employs this type, the bad belle is only a memory. Evans does create a similar character in *Vashti; or Until Death Us Do Part* (1869), but in this work the bad belle is reformed before the novel's end. Because Evans began writing only on the brink of the Civil War, she had less freedom than the other two authors to engage in censure without suffering social repercussions. Though the younger author appears to have had her own latent dissatisfaction with the southern social structure, especially with its gender roles, she outwardly endorses its institutions and mutes her powerful voice.

2　WOMEN WITH MOVEABLE WAYS
The Bad Belle as Survivor

Though much local-color literature was written in the South between the Civil War and World War I and though Kate Chopin, Mary Johnston, Ellen Glasgow, and others wrote respected novels about women's roles during that period, the willful manipulation and destructiveness characteristic of the belle gone bad seems temporarily to have dropped from these writers' repertoires. Amélie Rieves, for example, employs a beautiful female character who drives a man to distraction in *The Quick or the Dead* (1888), but rather than being corrupt and manipulative as the belle gone bad would be, this woman is merely indecisive. Chopin's Edna Pontellier (*The Awakening,* 1899) is an unconventional, sexual woman, but she does not use her sexuality to manipulate and control men as do the bad belles already examined. The coy strategies of Calixta and Clarisse in "At the 'Cadian Ball" and the shameless adultery of Calixta in "The Storm" come closer to the manipulations of the dark seductress. Like later women writers of the Southern Renascence, Chopin refuses to condemn the women's transgressions of social norms, but unlike those writers, she does not explore the characters' motivations or the repercussions of their actions in depth. On the other hand, Johnston often wrote in depth about women's struggle for independence, and she linked that struggle to their use of language. In *Hagar* (1913), for example, a southern gentleman laments that his independent daughter can support herself by writing: "If you couldn't write—couldn't earn, you'd trot along quietly enough! The pivotal mistake was letting women learn the alphabet." As Johnston knew, many slaveholders said the same of their slaves. But in a 1910 suffrage speech, Johnston stated that "the 'gravest fault' of women was still the 'sinuous, indirect way of approaching and of obtaining the object or the end which they desire.' 'Beg: and if you are refused manoeuvre!'" Her characters approach their goals and respond to opposition more directly. Though she was familiar with the methods of the bad belle, as well as the oppression that inspired those methods, she did not often have her characters make use of them.[1] And though Glasgow employs the bad belle in her later novels, in her early works, women are dangerous because of their ignorance of sexuality and the ways of the world, not because of any willful desire to command.

Perhaps we can attribute this character's temporary disappearance to the turmoil of the times. As LeeAnn Whites in *The Civil War as a Crisis in Gender* and Nina Silber in *The Romance of Reunion* argue, the war called into question many of the assumptions southerners had made about the roles of men and women. The gentleman's role was defined by his ability to control and protect a household of dependents, and the lady's role was defined by her need for protection and by her freedom from labor. The Civil War made these roles nearly impossible because it freed slaves and forced the men away from the plantations, necessitating that women take over the duties of overseer and manager. One southern woman whose exploits clearly manifest the confused gender roles during the war is Belle Boyd. According to her memoir, published in England at the close of the war, Belle's first act of heroism, at age seventeen, was to shoot and kill a Yankee soldier who had insulted her mother. Fiercely devoted to the Confederate cause, she soon becomes a spy, carrying communications to and from southern officers, charming military secrets from Yankee officers, and smuggling contraband materials across the lines. At times, she disguised herself in men's clothing to accomplish her goals, but more often she relied on her feminine charms to lull her victims and disguise her true intent. Her nicknames included "the Siren of the Shenandoah" and "the Secesh Cleopatra," and some northern newspapers labeled her an "accomplished prostitute." She was a living example of the belle gone bad. As Faust explains, "Her extraordinary ex-

1. Mary Johnston, *Hagar* (New York: Houghton Mifflin, 1913), 261; Wheeler, *New Women of the New South*, 96.

ploits . . . represent the most extreme manifestations of ambitions and strategies embraced by hundreds of Confederate females who used women's weapons but did not play by women's rules. . . . Feminine 'weakness' served as the foundation of female strength. Perhaps most significantly, however, Boyd's story marks a destabilization of the fixed assumptions that permitted her in some sense to live in two genders and two worlds of gender relations simultaneously. Belle Boyd maintained the dress and demeanor of a lady, but her actions and purposes were those of a man." The freedom with which Belle Boyd violated decorum was mainly attributable to the desperate times in which she lived. And though Belle's case was extreme, other women experienced similar freedoms, at least for a time.[2] Perhaps it seemed less urgent to undermine in fiction gender roles that were growing uncertain in reality.

The upheavals of war also brought women a new sense of their own interests. As Faust points out, women wrote personal letters to friends and loved ones during the war, bringing them new self-awareness and a new focus on their feelings. The war also necessitated that women write business letters, and many began this unaccustomed chore with "apologies and disclaimers for the unseemly assertiveness the composition of a letter represented," but their words were read and answered. The war seemed to herald an era of greater independence for women in both the public and private arenas.[3]

In the early twentieth century, the South changed further, largely because of the efforts of its women. In her landmark study *The Southern Lady: From Pedestal to Politics,* Anne Firor Scott traces the movement of the southern lady down from the pedestal on which she had been marooned in the nineteenth century to the socially active role she played in the early twentieth century. Before women had the right to vote, their activism was directed at the rights of blacks through antilynching leagues and at the plight of the poor through women's charitable organizations, or "clubs." As Scott points out, these early-twentieth-century women's clubs played an important role in the South's modernization after the trauma of Reconstruction: "Southern clubwomen undertook a formidable list of civic pro-

2. Belle Boyd, *Belle Boyd in Camp and Prison, Written by Herself,* new ed., prepared from material by Curtis Carrol Davis (South Brunswick, N.J.: T. Yoseloff, 1968), 64, 66; Faust, *Mothers of Invention,* 218–19.

3. Faust, *Mothers of Invention,* 163.

jects, from planting trees and improving garbage collection in some small towns to the ambitious undertaking of the Rome, Georgia club, which built a hospital, and the work of the North Carolina Federation of Women's Clubs in helping to build a women's college and to develop university extension courses." Later, with the right to vote, women were able to focus their attention on such legislation as child labor laws and prohibition.[4]

Paradoxically, however, though women's greater public roles continued after the war through clubs and charities, male control was reasserted and strengthened in the home. In *Gendered Strife and Confusion,* Edwards points out that, because slavery had been viewed by southerners as a domestic relation with white men at the head of the household, the abolition of slavery made all other domestic relations less secure. The society's reaction was to reinforce white male power over wives and children. The landmark court case *State v. A. B. Rhodes* reaffirmed this power. When Elizabeth Rhodes pressed charges against her husband for beating her without provocation, Justice Edwin G. Reade ruled that "the sanctity of the private sphere shielded the husband's actions from the scrutiny of the public." In addition, many women dutifully reaffirmed the dominance of their men in an effort to soothe the wounded pride resulting from the region's military defeat. In the home, at least, the white man was still lord and master. More women worked and went to college in the early decades of the twentieth century than ever before; nevertheless, the family was still the "center of most women's lives" and, even beyond World War II, their primary role was homemaker.[5]

The unstable gender roles of the period are also reflected in the literature. In her essay "Reconstructing Southern Manhood: Race, Sentimentality, and Camp in the Plantation Myth," Caroline Gebhard identifies a change in the portrayal of male characters in southern literature from 1880 to World War I. Most notably in the popular works of Thomas Nelson Page and James Lane Allen, "men take the place of women and slaves as objects of sentimental identification." This sentimental male character "embodies for an audience that both desires and cathartically identifies with him, a struggle of masculine identity with emotions or physical stigmata stereotyped as feminine." This new character, as Gebhard argues, manifests the

4. Scott, *Southern Lady,* 159.
5. Edwards, *Gendered Strife,* 30, 29; Wheeler, *New Women of the New South,* 7; Numan V. Bartley, *The New South, 1945–1980* (Baton Rouge: Louisiana State University Press, 1995), 114.

white man's emotional and physical defeat by the North and also conveys, through his relationship with loyal, *paternal* slaves, a message of racial harmony in the South. According to Silber, northern writers routinely represented the South as feminine to portray the North's dominance over a region they saw as weak, emotional, and willful.[6] At the same time, southern women writers suspended their protest via the bad belle against a society that appeared to be waning fast.

Though woman's rights and roles were changing, the images and ideals of the southern past, made more powerful by the nostalgic backward gaze of the Reconstruction era, still lingered. Social changes that seemed immanent from the upheavals during and after the war did not fully materialize. As Kenneth O'Brien observes in "Race, Romance, and the Southern Literary Tradition," the white lady became an even weightier symbol of the southern way of life after the Civil War. White women in plantation fiction, he states, are characterized by "sexual purity, religious piety, devoted domesticity, and submissiveness to both God and man. In Reconstruction literature, however, they play a further part, for they are the objects of black lust."[7] Though the changes Gebhard observes in male characters reflected a change in society's attitudes about masculine roles, the relative consistency in female characters reveals that a corresponding change did not occur in society's attitudes toward feminine roles.

Court cases of the Reconstruction era reveal a view of women similar to that expressed in the literature. In 1864, a poor white North Carolina woman, Susan Daniel, accused two slaves, William and Henderson Cooper, of rape. Both men were sentenced to death, and William Cooper was hanged. But before Henderson Cooper could be executed, he escaped and was later taken into custody by the Freedmen's Bureau to await a more objective trial. An outraged Governor Worth equated the rape of Susan Daniel with the North's rape of Southern power during and after the Civil War: "This was a rape of peculiar atrocity. Two strong negroes enter the house of a poor but worthy woman and in the presence of her little daughter each of them commits a rape upon her. . . . [The federal government] interposes its shield and allows one of the monsters to go unpunished. . . . If alienation to

6. Caroline Gebhard, "Reconstructing Southern Manhood: Race, Sentimentality, and Camp in the Plantation Myth," in *Haunted Bodies,* 136, 134; Silber, *Romance of Reunion,* 6.

7. Kenneth O'Brien, "Race, Romance, and the Southern Literary Tradition" in *Recasting: "Gone with the Wind" in American Culture,* Darden Asbury Pyron, ed. (Miami: University Presses of Florida, 1983), 156.

the government in this state is on the increase, as is often alleged to our prejudice, is it to be wondered at?" After the war, the white lady became a symbol for all that had been taken away and all that was yet to be lost. Rather than transforming as the old way of life passed, the image of the southern lady was held up as the last remnant of an idealized past. To claim her legal and social rights, the new woman had to flout the expectations of a society that wanted her to be a passive exemplar of moral purity or carefully balance both roles by choosing only acceptable causes for her activism and going through properly modest channels. According to Sims, "As long as women worked for others rather than for themselves, they remained within the boundaries of proper feminine behavior."[8] Some southern women did of course defy expectations, participating in the flapper movement, which radically overturned the conventions for proper behavior. These rebels, however, had to contend with the judgments of a community that refused to abandon its idealized past.

As had the Civil War, World War I gave women an opportunity for increased independence, an independence they would not so easily relinquish again. Southern Agrarian Allen Tate posited that this tension between the old and new ways of life was responsible for a period of literary flowering in the South: "With the war of 1914–1918, the South re-entered the world— but gave a backward glance as it stepped over the border: that backward glance gave us the Southern renascence, a literature conscious of the past in the present." Writers of this period, of whom William Faulkner is the best-known representative, explored the transformation of southern ideals and southern people as the South joined the rest of the nation in the twentieth century. But it was not simply the new century and the passage of time that inspired the Southern Renascence. Prenshaw argues that this literary movement was primarily focused around a particular image: "the profound historical consciousness that distinguishes the Southern writers who ushered in a literary renaissance in the first half of the twentieth century has been significantly formed by their effort to understand and come to terms with the dominating image of the 'lady.'" Prenshaw goes on to argue that "the image of the Southern Lady, no less than that of the black and the Confederate dead, has pervaded the mind of the South, powerfully evoking its literary imagination." We find evidence to support these claims in a toast given at a 1930s celebration of Georgia's one hundredth anniversary, which captures the centrality and emotional import of the southern lady to her re-

8. Edwards, *Gendered Strife*, 4–5; Sims, *The Power of Femininity*, 15.

gion: "Woman!!! The center and circumference, diameter and periphery, sine, tangent, and secant of all our affections!" Marjorie Spruill Wheeler suggests that the ideal of the lady spread beyond the upper classes after the war and was "increasingly expected of all southern white women who wished to be considered 'respectable.'"[9]

Many novels of the Southern Renascence also focus on the southern lady, treating her as an anachronism—no longer viable yet refusing to die. Faulkner's Ellen Coldfield and Mrs. Compson, for instance, both sit atop pedestals, where they either distance themselves from their children's actual needs or make impossible demands that ruin their children's lives. And his Temple Drake plays the belle, a younger version of the lady, at a time and place in which the men who surround her are no longer gentlemen, thereby inviting violation.

But for women writers in the Southern Renascence, the figure of the lady—of whatever age—was doubly problematic. Not only was it a symbolic emblem of their region's defeated past, but it was an emblem, to a large extent, these women were still expected to embody. As Jones points out in her study of the woman writer in the South, all of the writers on whom she focuses—Augusta Evans, Grace King, Kate Chopin, Mary Johnston, Ellen Glasgow, Frances Newman, and Margaret Mitchell— "were raised to be southern ladies, physically pure, fragile, and beautiful, socially dignified, cultured, and gracious, within the family sacrificial and submissive, yet, if the occasion required, intelligent and brave." That the birth dates of these writers span almost seventy years seems to have made no difference in their upbringing or in the roles society expected them to play. During this period, the bad belle reappears in the works of southern women writers as a parody of their society's negative conception of independent and powerful women and as a vehicle through which to protest the limiting and outmoded social conventions that still confined those writers.[10]

Like those of Southworth, Hentz, and Evans, the bad belles employed

9. Allen Tate, *Collected Essays* (Denver: A. Swallow, 1959), 292; Prenshaw, "Southern Ladies and the Southern Literary Renaissance," in *The Female Tradition in Southern Literature*, 74, 78; Cash, *Mind of the South*, 89; Wheeler, *New Women of the New South*, 7.

10. Jones, *Tomorrow Is Another Day*, xi. In *The Southern Belle in the American Novel*, Seidel asserts that the tension created by this conflict of past and present created many corrupt belles in the works of Southern Renascence women writers. See Seidel's discussion of Glasgow's *Romantic Comedians*, Scott's *Narcissus*, and Mitchell's *Gone with the Wind*. Seidel's treatment of bad belles focuses more on their self-destructive qualities than on their destruction of others. Her broader study also contains many other types of belles and many other authors, male and female.

by Southern Renascence women writers exploit men and women who cling to old power structures by using their supposed strengths against them. Unlike their nineteenth-century predecessors, though, the Renascence women writers assert their protest more clearly by not destroying the dangerous woman to restore patriarchal authority. This more overt self-examination and critique was no doubt fostered by the literary climate of the Southern Renascence, which encouraged comparison between the South and the outside world and between the past and the present. It is hard to say to what extent these modern women writers consciously revised the image of the bad belle found in antebellum women's works. Augusta Jane Evans's most popular works, *Macaria* and *St. Elmo,* were still read, and Glasgow at least was familiar with Southworth—she has the husband Oliver refer to the works of Mrs. Southworth with derision in her novel *Virginia* (1913). Though Oliver's words are not necessarily a reflection of the author's opinion, his contempt for the popular women writers of the nineteenth century was shared by many readers of his time. These writers had been largely denigrated by the 1930s as a result of the canonization of modernist literature. Southern Renascence women writers may have responded to the image of the bad belle in these soon-forgotten ladies' books, or more likely, they responded to the more conventional image of the femme fatale in "real literature" written by men, as well as to examples of actual southern belles who still surrounded them.

In these women writers' novels, the old order languishes but the bad belle survives to profit from its decline. In works that cover the scope of the Southern Renascence, writers Ellen Glasgow, Evelyn Scott, Margaret Mitchell, and Caroline Gordon protest the lingering image of the belle by using her worst traits—coquetry, willfulness, moral weakness, vanity—as weapons against a patriarchy that refused to let her die. The lady's so-called good traits—passivity, innocence, courage, obedience—are not wholly absent from these works, but they rest in a separate character. As Prenshaw observes, "The Southern writer repeatedly 'divides' the heroine in a doppelganger motif to create a parade of Scarletts and Melanies, or variants of the pair." A variant of the pair Prenshaw mentions is Faulkner's Lena Grove and Joanna Burden in *Light in August*. Predictably, though, in this male author's work the strong, assertive woman is destroyed and the passive woman triumphs.[11] The women writers of the Southern Renascence reverse

11. Prenshaw, "Southern Ladies," 81.

this pattern used by male writers and by nineteenth-century women writers; they destroy the "good" (or passive) woman to show that she no longer has a place in the modern world but allow the "bad" (or powerful) woman to manipulate her way to success. These modern women writers do not condemn only the southern past. Their work reflects a complex blend of moving forward while keeping an eye on the past that characterized the entire Southern Renascence. The fact that the bad belle succeeds is an indictment of both the old way of life, whose decayed remnants she exploits, and the new way of life, whose superficiality and materiality inspire and support her.

Unlike Southworth and Hentz, the Renascence women writers no longer identify themselves with the bad belle by making the character an artist figure. Instead, the artist figure is usually the bad belle's male or female victim. This connection seems to indicate that Southern Renascence writers were beginning to recognize what later twentieth-century writers directly assert: that the image of the femme fatale, which portrays any strong, creative woman as wicked and dangerous, also threatens the woman artist.

The bad belle used by Southern Renascence women also differs physically from that used by nineteenth-century women writers. No longer the dark, exotic Creole or Italian, the modern belle gone bad is someone with whom the intended audience—white women—can more easily identify. Often she has fair hair instead of black, green eyes instead of brown. Fiedler links the femme fatale's changing countenance in American literature to the country's general loss of innocence in the early twentieth century, a time when the American Girl ceases to embody goodness and purity. He uses F. Scott Fitzgerald's Daisy Buchanan as a prime example: "To Fitzgerald . . . the fairy glamour is illusory, and once approached the White Maiden is revealed as a White Witch, the golden girl as a golden idol. On his palette, white and gold make a dirty color; for wealth is no longer innocent, America no longer innocent, the Girl who is the soul of both turned destructive and corrupt."[12] Fitzgerald allows the manipulative golden girl to survive, but doesn't, as do his southern female contemporaries, offer a "pure" analogue that must be sacrificed to the modern age. With Daisy, Fitzgerald uses the femme fatale as a vehicle for social commentary, but doesn't, as do his southern female contemporaries, allow his reader to celebrate this character's manipulations of a corrupt society.

12. Fiedler, *Love and Death,* 300–1.

In addition to the bad belle, Southern Renascence women writers employ other characters differently than do their nineteenth-century predecessors. The conventional woman does not grow darker as the bad belle grows lighter. Rather, she is a slightly washed-out, less vital version of her counterpart. The two women usually are closely related (Scarlett and Melanie are sisters by marriage), perhaps to indicate that characteristics of each exist in every woman but that only one type is viable in the modern world. Men are also weaker in these writers' versions of the New South. Men no longer command—not even poorly—and they often seek protective mothering from the very women who would destroy them, women who are incapable, like Daisy Buchanan, of even successfully mothering their own children. Though the modern belle skillfully uses sex to achieve her goals, she seems to lack the passion of the nineteenth-century belle. Instead, passion is often projected onto a darker character. The modern bad belle often fixates on a black shadow figure who serves as a projection of the belle's passion that the author or her society did not wish to confront directly. The shadow figure forms a visual marker of the bad belle's (repressed) guilt or of the vulnerability to passion that she cannot afford. In most of these works by twentieth-century women writers, therefore, race—a central element of the southern past—still plays a role linked to the dangerous sexuality of the belle gone bad.

ELLEN GLASGOW

Born in a large well-to-do Virginia family, Ellen Glasgow (1873–1945) learned at an early age the southern lady's proper role. Her family was a traditional one, her father stern and authoritarian, her mother submissive and frail. In her autobiography, *The Woman Within* (1954), Glasgow says of her father, "Not once in my knowledge of him had he ever changed his mind or admitted that he was wrong—or even mistaken" (*WW* 70), and in her collection of essays, *A Certain Measure,* she comments on the "top heavy patriarchal system" that dominated the South, Virginia in particular. Glasgow resented her harsh father and identified with her downtrodden mother, but this weak woman was, for obvious reasons, not a good role model for her creative and independent-minded daughter.[13]

In Richmond, Virginia, at the turn of the century, Glasgow did not meet

---

13. Ellen Glasgow, *A Certain Measure: An Interpretation of Prose Fiction* (New York: Harcourt, Brace, 1943), 134.

many encouraging role models outside the home, either. As Pamela R. Matthews puts it, "Glasgow learned to disguise her anger, her problems, her despair in order to be the jovial and carefree Richmond hostess that many of her admirers . . . have remarked." And Linda W. Wagner states, "Fifty years too early, Glasgow was an American woman writer. . . . [S]imply because she was female—and subject to the stereotypes inflicted on women writers—she had to mask what should have been obvious correlations. What should have been strength became a liability, and even at her most assertive—at the end of her life—she had to title her autobiography *The Woman Within*. Glasgow the writer was—or should have been—somehow unsexed. Only under the mask, inside the writerly disguise, could a woman exist."[14] The world in which Glasgow lived forced her to disguise her voice, to project her artistic vision into male characters, and to challenge that world with dangerous women in her novels. Even in New York, supposed haven for artists, Price Collier of MacMillan told the young writer, "The best advice I can give you . . . is to stop writing, and go back to the South and have some babies" (*WW* 108). Glasgow did go back to the South, but instead of having babies she continued to write and continued to struggle, through outward oppression and inner conflict, to change the society that tried to silence her.

In her novels, Glasgow repeatedly works through tensions caused by her relationship to her parents and the suffocating conventions of her day, exploring the roles and expectations for women. Her first two novels, set in New York, feature independent, artistic female protagonists. In her later and better-known novels, she returns to her native Virginia, where she examines the contrast between old, lingering southern values and the modern values of the twentieth century. In these works, the paired opposites of the ideal antebellum lady and the modern woman figure prominently, revealing Glasgow's ambivalence about her heritage as well as the era in which she lived. Though she portrays the grace and dignity of the traditional southern lady, she also shows the oppression and limited resources with which they live; and though she reveals the self-assertiveness and greater liberty of the twentieth-century woman, beside her counterpart this new woman seems vulgar and shallow.

14. Pamela R. Matthews, Introduction to *The Woman Within*, Ellen Glasgow (Charlottesville: University of Virginia Press, 1954), x; Linda W. Wagner, *Ellen Glasgow: Beyond Convention* (Austin: University of Texas Press, 1982), 117.

One of Glasgow's major concerns, in her art and in her life, is women's sexuality. In *Virginia* she shows that the traditional lady's sexual repression is part of her general policy of self-denial, which can eventually lead to isolation and emptiness. But in general, Glasgow's attitude toward sex seems to be one of suspicion. Her autobiographical character Rachel in *The Descendant* (1897) rejects physical love, and after an early disillusioning experience of passion and pregnancy, so does her strongest female character, Dorinda Oakley, in *Barren Ground* (1925). More than once in her autobiography, Glasgow denies her own sexuality. In her memory of childhood, she protests that, despite what Freudian theorists may say, she "cannot recall that [she] speculated about sex, or singled out this instinct as a special province of wonder" (*WW* 54); but, separating the physical from the emotional aspects of love, she refers to the "illusion of romantic love" as her "ancient antagonist" (*WW* 57). And in the chapter "Rootless Years," she refers to flappers as "nymphomaniacs in green hats" (*WW* 268). Glasgow never married, though she was engaged twice and had a long-term involvement with a married man, and she seems to say that she never experienced sex: "The modern adventurers who imagine they know love because they have known sex may be wiser than our less enlightened generation. But I am not of their period. I should have found wholly inadequate the mere physical sensation, which the youth today seek so blithely. If I were young, now, I might feel differently. It is possible that I may have been only another victim of the world's superstitions about women" (*WW* 163). Her choice of wording, referring to the "illusion" of love as an "antagonist" and describing herself as a "victim," indicates her conflicted and fearful attitude toward love and sex, which she seems to view as a trap. Because of her suspicion of sex, Glasgow has her most sympathetic female characters reject it altogether.

Perhaps, however, Glasgow protests too much about her lack of knowledge of or interest in sexuality. Perhaps, sensitive to her conservative society's association of feminine public exposure and creativity with promiscuity, she attempted to mask her sexuality in her memoir, just as Wagner perceives her masking her femininity in her art. Glasgow shows that she is aware of the precarious position of the woman artist when she has poet Laura Wilde, a character in her 1906 novel *The Wheel of Life,* observe that "men have 'ruled the world' by making both the laws and the jokes that obscure women's voices." Judith Allsup links this masculine dominance to feminine sexual strategies in other Glasgow novels: "While Miss Glasgow does depict many selfish women who use their femininity for exploitive purposes, her feeling about them is more ambivalent. They were, after all, exploiting myths made by man. . . . These are the ones who use the domestic, educational, and professional prejudices against their sex by turning these stereotypes to their own advantage."[15] One creation of men that obscures women's voices is the femme fatale, used in traditional literature by men to portray negatively the woman who refuses to submit to male power. But Glasgow and other Southern Renascence women use this frightening female figure as a parody of the "myths made by man," a means of turning society's stereotypes back against it. The character mocks society's conflation of feminine independence with immorality by using the victim's prejudices to destroy him and allowing the seductress to survive and prosper.

In most of Glasgow's novels, the free, sexually manipulative women, although not very sympathetic for the reader, seem to lead charmed lives in which they cause others pain, including conventional older women, but never suffer the consequences of their actions. Through these female characters' interactions with men, who invariably make the rules and decide whom to hold accountable, Glasgow wields her social criticism. The two Glasgow novels *The Romantic Comedians* (1926) and *In This Our Life* (1941) best exemplify the bad belle as survivor, because in them the young, sexualized woman has more agency than would a simple, misguided free spirit (as she is in *Virginia, Life and Gabriella* [1916], and *The Sheltered Life* [1932]) and because these novels highlight the bad belle's interaction with men and with her opposite, the conventional woman. In Glasgow's late work especially, however, we see the damage done to artistic voices by the stereotype of the femme fatale, even when it is used for feminist aims.

The Romantic Comedians is a comedy of manners that criticizes the present as well as the past. The plot concerns the ill-advised and ill-fated marriage of a sixty-five-year-old widower, Judge Gamaliel Bland Honeywell, to a twenty-three-year-old beauty who claims to be through with love. True to the pattern Fiedler describes, Annabel presents a fairer version of the femme fatale. With fragile body, "nut-brown hair," and eyes "grey-green as an April mist," Annabel appears to the Judge more charming than beautiful, but she diffuses a "subtle fascination—was it only glorified sex-magnetism?" like a fragrance (*RC* 18). This well-dressed, elegant twentieth-century bad belle

---

15. Matthews, Introduction, xvi; Judith Allsup, "Feminism in the Novels of Ellen Glasgow" (Ph.D. diss., Southern Illinois University, 1973), 71.

physically resembles the ideal beauty held up to Glasgow's intended audience—middle-class, young white women. By creating a bad belle with whom her audience can identify, Glasgow presents her manipulations as reasonable alternatives for women who wish to resist control. She is an exaggerated representative of the modern woman and her beauty and brains combine to take advantage of a decaying southern gentility. That her victim falls for wiles so lacking in subtlety as hers calls attention to the man's ineptness and to the absurdity of the stereotype Annabel embodies. Glasgow ridicules Annabel, she ridicules the Judge, and she ridicules the society in which the two could exist.

Given the novel's comic tone and the young Annabel's often naively hyperbolic declarations about life and love, the reader tends at first to view Annabel, as does her elderly admirer, with amused indulgence. But Glasgow also shows us Annabel's coldly calculating side. As Annabel tells the Judge, displaying her first real spark of passion, "I'd rather have money than anything in the world!" (*RC* 69). Recovering from a broken heart, Annabel plays on the Judge's pity and protectiveness, flattering his ego to gain material advantages. Because she hopes he will buy her a flower shop, Annabel visits the Judge in the afternoons and cries about her lover's betrayal. To the Judge's gifts she responds with girlish delight and grateful kisses, and to his inquiry about their difference in age: "'Oh, you're not old. You don't look old and you don't act old,' she replied with encouraging alacrity, 'and, besides, I despise young men!'" (*RC* 104). Though she is bewildered by his proposal of marriage, she accepts because of his material generosity. She tells her mother, "Of course I am fond of him . . . . He gives such nice presents" (*RC* 125), and she tells the Judge, while fondly gazing at his latest gift, that she cares for him (*RC* 156). Annabel's motivations for marrying the Judge amplify Charlotte Perkins Gilman's comparison in *Women and Economics* (1898) of wives to prostitutes: each must please men in return for financial support. As Julius Rowan Raper succinctly puts it, "Annabel is a gold digger, not a Lolita—a serious-minded, even philosophic gold digger."[16] Annabel has learned to take advantage of both old and new. She embraces the coquettish form of the past and the morality of the present, forming a near-deadly combination for the Judge. Through Annabel, Glasgow portrays the modern age, which appears, like its representative, to be self-centered, uncommitted, undignified, materialistic, and shallow.

16. Julius Rowan Raper, *From the Sunken Garden: The Fiction of Ellen Glasgow, 1916–1945* (Baton Rouge: Louisiana State University Press, 1980), 109.

Through the Judge's reactions to Annabel, however, we see the author's indictment of the past. Though he is a likeable character with the best of intentions, the Judge is still made ridiculous by his masculine pride, possessiveness, and outdated assumptions about womanhood. His first instinct toward Annabel, a woman young enough to be his granddaughter, is one of protectiveness: "She was . . . a badly treated little thing; and since he was the pattern of chivalry, it incensed him that any man in the world should have been capable of such conduct to a woman who combined the merits of being both little and pretty. He felt as if she were his daughter, and yet in some profound sense, which he prudently refrained from analyzing, as if she were not his daughter" (*RC* 39). Being little and pretty are merits enough in the Judge's eyes to excite all his manly instincts. Being a southern gentleman, constrained by a code of behavior, he assumes that Annabel, as a well-brought-up southern woman, adheres to that code as well. But the Judge confuses appearance with reality. Behind her physical attraction, he believes, must lie the traditional spiritual attractions—womanly affection, modesty, decorum, and a sense of duty—and he ignores all evidence to the contrary.

As the Judge observes, he feels toward Annabel as if she were his daughter, also as if she were not his daughter. He combines conflicting paternal and amorous desires, indicted by nineteenth-century women writers as one of the flaws of the patriarchal system: father-protector and husband-lover seem to merge. At once the doting father and the fearful lover, like Squire Darling in Southworth's *Three Beauties,* the Judge is doubly vulnerable to Annabel's demands. On their wedding trip, she spends his money improvidently on clothes, gifts, and rich meals, extravagant behavior similar to Southworth's Juliette in Europe. Though the purchases tax his bank account and the meals tax his digestive system, the Judge, like Juliette's smitten husband Colonel Dent, restrains his criticism for fear of losing the few caresses with which Annabel repays his generosity.

But what the Judge really longs for, and what he waits impatiently for, is Annabel's transformation from willful, flirtatious, young belle to self-sacrificing, submissive matron. Here, the Judge's role seems to shift and a side of traditional southern marriage appears that was not shown by nineteenth-century women writers. Instead of combining the roles of father and lover, in his physical desire for Annabel, the Judge seems to combine the roles of son and lover. Perhaps the mothering he craves and the comparisons he draws between ideal womanhood and his own mother show the yearning of a displaced gentleman to return to a more secure past (the Old

South of his youth) and he clings to the image of the southern lady as the vehicle to transport him. Suffering from dyspepsia on the honeymoon and frustrated by Annabel's apparent lack of concern, the Judge thinks with longing of his late wife, whom he wishes could have accompanied them "in the capacity of a ministering angel" (*RC* 176). Later, he feels closest to Annabel when, after catching a cold from the fatigue of attending too many dances with his young wife, she stays home to nurse him.

Finally, after Annabel's ultimate rejection of him for a younger man, as he lies on what appears to be his deathbed, he dreams of his mother but wakes to find instead a young nurse: "Fresh, spotless, and womanly, in her white uniform, with the competent hands of a physician and the wise and tender touch of a mother. Those beneficent hands and that infallible touch, he supposed, had made him dream that he was a child again. . . . Swifter than light, swifter than inspiration, while he followed her with his eyes, the thought darted into his mind: 'There is the woman I ought to have married!' There, sympathetic and young, obeying her feminine instinct in every exquisite gesture, was the woman he ought to have married" (*RC* 345). The embodiment of the ideal woman is just like his mother, a woman whose time came and went in the last century. Having learned nothing from his experience with Annabel, unable to see that his outdated ideals make him vulnerable to the modern coquette who refuses to be a lady, he is foolishly inspired by his vision. For the nurse, like Annabel, is a woman who spends time with him only for the monetary compensation she will receive. Glasgow gives us a metaphorical portrait of the weak and ailing patriarchy in its dotage, which, though it pretends to the strength and vigor it once had, is now (and perhaps secretly always was) dependent for its survival on the coddling affection of those it once dominated.

The one woman in the novel who truly does embody the old ideal the Judge seeks does not fare as well as the Judge himself. Having waited patiently for her true love through his first marriage and having sacrificed any hope of happiness, Amanda Lightfoot is too much of a lady to make her feelings known once he is free. The Judge, operating under a traditional double standard, convinces himself that Amanda would not allow herself to think of love at her age, though he still thinks of it at his—and she is seven years his junior. More important, she is no longer young enough to serve as an echo of his young mother, no matter how motherly she may be, and so she cannot fulfill his desires to return to the past. Despite what she may feel, Amanda plays her role as lady to the end, refusing to admit her love even when Annabel, in a rare moment of compassion, asks for her leave before agreeing to marry the Judge. After the marriage, Amanda's last hope of womanly fulfilment having vanished forever, her queenly appearance fades and she becomes an eccentric old maid with canaries as her only companions. The rules of the old order were established by men, and women who follow those rules are subject to the inconsistencies of men's enforcement of them.

Glasgow's last novel published during her lifetime, *In This Our Life*, won the Pulitzer Prize in 1942. The author said this novel was close to her heart and that she "weld[ed] together, in this one symbolic expression, all the varied themes in my earlier and later interpretation of life" (*WW* 286). These varied and interrelated themes include the nature of southern society, family, love, and sexuality. In the southern society Glasgow portrays, feminine sexuality makes one vulnerable, as it does Roy, or dangerous, as it does Roy's sister Stanley. The girls' father, Asa Timberlake, the primary point-of-view character and a sensitive introspective man, is described as a poet, but he is a poet trampled by an unsupportive environment and by the bad belle. In many ways a weak and downtrodden man, he represents the last remnant of all that was good in the Old South—its grace, gentility, and soul. Early in the novel, he watches the demolition of his old family home and thinks, as does William Alexander Percy in his autobiography *Lanterns on the Levee* (published in 1941, the same year as Glasgow's novel), of the great men who have gone before him, particularly of his father, who committed suicide rather than witness the downfall of his society. The new way of life is driven by materialism and the shallow pursuit of pleasure, and all that has survived from the southern past are its worst elements—its racism, lust for power, and idolization of women—characterized by William Fitzroy, Lavinia Timberlake, and Stanley, the bad belle.

Though Glasgow uses Stanley as a vehicle for social protest, she does not make this bad belle an artist, as Southworth did with Juliette and Faustina and as Hentz did with Claudia. Instead, this girl, who is "as pretty as new paint" (*ITOL* 322), is more creation than creator, just as the femme fatale was first a creation manifesting the fears of male artists. And this exaggerated creation tramples the dreams and desires of the two artist figures in the novel, Asa, "that sleeping giant, who was also a poet" (*ITOL* 12), and Roy, an interior decorator. Stanley's cruelty to Roy especially, who suffers more than their father because of the bad belle's actions and who struggles to work despite her pain, reflects the danger the femme fatale figure poses for the woman artist. Though the bad belle is an effective vehicle for capturing male attention and making female voices heard, she paradoxically silences other women by perpetuating the stereotype that all powerful women, including women artists, are dangerous. Importantly, however, Glasgow projects herself as *writer* into a male character, the sensitive father, perhaps to portray more completely the artist's seduction and destruction by this enticingly dangerous image of femininity. Because powerful women are seen as sexually dangerous, the woman artist who wishes to avoid such a negative image may be tempted to remain silent, to conceive of her talents (and herself) as masculine, or to reject her sexuality altogether, as Roy will eventually do.

In light of Glasgow's use of the bad belle, the interpretation of this character made in chapter 2 using Lacan's concept of the phallus might be revised. As did the nineteenth-century bad belles, Glasgow's femme fatale "has" the phallus, in the sense that the character carries out masculine acts of power normally denied women in the early twentieth-century South. But unlike her predecessors, Glasgow seems to recognize that the bad belle cannot "be" the phallus for the woman writer, the embodiment and reflection of the writer's own power, because the femme fatale's presence in the novel confirms that women have little power in reality. If actual women were able to exercise power in their own right, then the bad belle as she functions in these novels would be unnecessary. As a result, Glasgow's descriptions of her bad belles—like those of her contemporaries, Scott and Gordon—do not seem inspired by the same passionate desire displayed by Southworth and Hentz. The earlier writers' passionate obsession for their characters confirmed that these femmes fatales "were" the phallus for them, the site and reflection of the writers' greatest power, as the powerful man desires the beautiful woman who affirms his virility and ability to control. But in Glasgow's novel, just as the femme fatale confirms the woman writer's lack of real power in her society, the bad belle Stanley figuratively emasculates the poet Asa and causes the artist Roy to deny her sexuality. Glasgow probably was not thinking about phallic power as she created her characters, but because her descriptions of her bad belle are coldly analytical and mocking, she may have seen the negative implications of this character for women such as herself at the same time she made use of its power for social commentary.

Oddly, Glasgow gives her two main female characters, the sisters Stanley and Roy, male names. Though the novel never reveals how they came by these names, one can imagine their parents hoping for male offspring to carry on the family name and traditions. Glasgow points out that "the calling of girls by family names is a familiar practice in Virginia, especially when there are few boys to consider. Neither of these names strikes me as peculiarly masculine, because the only Roy and Stanley I have ever known were women. In this novel Roy was, of course, merely a convenient abbreviation of Fitzroy." Rather than suggesting their power and masculinity, then, these names suggest instead the appropriation of the women's identities by their patriarchal heritage or a form of patriarchal ancestor worship.[17] Because the men who surround them—uncle, father, husband, and fiancé, the traditional patriarchal figures of the South—are weak or corrupt, however, Glasgow seems to imply that it is time for women to claim authority in their own right. Stanley and Roy embody the positive and negative potentials of feminine strength.

Glasgow repeatedly describes Stanley as innocent, but hers is the innocence of a small child, who out of boredom and a need to define its own ego exerts its will on adults around it. Stanley, however, uses a tool not available to the small child, which makes grown men do her bidding, her sexuality. Tall, fair, with "dusky amber" hair, and "sea-blue" eyes (*ITOL* 22), Stanley has been trained as a coquette by her mother, the invalid Lavinia, who hopes Stanley will break all the hearts Lavinia herself was not beautiful enough to capture. But Lavinia has created a lovely monster she can't control. As the mother observes, "The matter with Stanley is that she is never content unless she is exerting her power. I mean, her power over men. When she complains of her loneliness, she means there aren't any men who amuse her" (*ITOL* 370). This quest for power leads Stanley to destroy the dreams, and in two cases the lives, of those who surround her. During the course of the novel, she jilts her fiancé to elope with her sister's husband, Peter, marries him, and drives him to suicide; then returns to steal back her first fiancé, Craig, who had sought comfort and healing in her sister; and causes a young black boy to be sent to jail for a crime she committed.

A "painted shell of a girl" (*ITOL* 102), a "fantasy clothed in flesh and made living" (*ITOL* 168), a "soulless little pleasure-seeker," Stanley embodies all the shallowness Glasgow perceived in the postwar world. But in the other characters' reactions to her, the weakness of the southern patriarchy is made evident. As Lavinia perceives, Stanley's power is more potent

17. Glasgow, *A Certain Measure,* 258.

with southerners than with others: "It may be the Southern way—I don't know—but they seem to excuse everything because she is young and has beauty. They like beauty, I suppose, more than most people" (*ITOL* 369). Stanley's beauty and the illusion of weakness she projects are her greatest assets, because with them she taps into the male southerner's vanity, possessiveness, and need to protect. Dew celebrates this same "irresistible power" of feminine weakness over masculine strength in his 1835 essay "Dissertation on the Characteristic Differences of the Sexes, and Woman's Position and Influence in Society."[18] Stanley's father observes, "[S]he would always win in the end, not with him alone, but with other men also; and she would win, he told himself, not through strength, but through some inner weakness, whether her own or another's" (*ITOL* 366).

Stanley's weakness is her emptiness and lack of morality, but the weakness of others on whom she preys is the very trait the patriarchal South prided itself on, chivalry. After Peter commits suicide, apparently because of guilt over the elopement, her father somewhat wryly excuses her: "After all, was Stanley, not Roy, the innocent victim? In the effervescent sympathy surrounding them, the solid outlines of facts were partly obliterated. Because of Stanley's youth and her touching plight, the family, and before long the whole community he suspected, would melt into compassion. For this emotional debauch, he told himself, it was not fair to hold Stanley responsible" (*ITOL* 297). And, in the end, she wins back Craig through her need of him (*ITOL* 426). Stanley paradoxically uses weakness as strength to control others and to absolve herself of any responsibility. In the traditional South, this power was supposed to translate into obedience to the man who agreed to be one's lifelong protector, but Stanley ignores this part of the equation.

The man who exerts the greatest control over Stanley is the one who holds the purse strings, her great uncle William Fitzroy. Like Stanley, this elderly patriarch embraces the worst elements of the Old South—again, its lust for power, idolization of women, and racism—along with the shallow materialism of the industrialized New South. But even this usually formidable old man can be controlled by Stanley's petulant demands when they are accompanied by flirtatious smiles and kisses. Like all the men in the novel, his need to protect is mingled with his sexual desire, but this incestuous

18. Glasgow, *A Certain Measure,* 259; Dew, "Dissertation on the Characteristic Differences," 496.

blend is even more deplorable in this man, who is consumed by appetites for which his time has passed. One of Uncle William's many gifts to Stanley is a car, given in honor of her engagement to Craig. After she has jilted Craig and returned home in the wake of Peter's suicide, the car becomes a surrogate outlet for Stanley's destructive sexuality. Recovering from her initial grief and bored because there are no men within reach to torment, Stanley vents her frustration by speeding down Queenborough's streets, a female version of the dissipated, disillusioned new southerner Faulkner depicts in Bayard Sartoris.

It is through the car, a symbol for Stanley's destructive power, that Glasgow links the bad belle with southern conceptions of race. Though the modern femme fatale is no longer marked by African features, many of the Southern Renascence women writers use black characters as shadow figures who have secret knowledge of the white lady's sins. These black characters form visual representations of the bad belle's sexuality and guilt. It is useful to return to Morrison's theory of the role of Africanist characters in American literature written by whites. "[T]he fabrication of an Africanist persona is reflexive; an extraordinary meditation on the self," Morrison states, and "this black population was available for meditations on terror—the terror of European outcasts, their dread of failure, powerlessness, Nature without limits, natal loneliness, internal aggression, evil, sin, greed."[19] Though Southern Renascence women writers do not punish their bad belles, or even allow them to feel guilt, the reader receives a sense of the bad belles' wrongdoing through the black characters who silently follow and observe the belles' evil actions.

The Timberlake family's black laundress in an interior monologue first discloses to the reader that some trouble is brewing between Stanley and Peter. Minerva accidentally witnesses a scene in which the pair stare at each other as if spellbound, completely unaware of her presence: "Not a word, not so much as a speck of a word, passed between 'em. But, never mind, she knew what she knew; and she'd felt the sort of sultriness that whips around in the air when a thunderstorm is all but ready to break" (*ITOL* 89). Later, Uncle William pays Minerva's son, Parry, to accompany Stanley on her drives. The patriarch wants Parry to drive for Stanley, perhaps an attempt to relegate the young white girl's passionate impulses—symbolized by her reckless handling of the car—to a more traditionally appropriate sur-

---

19. Morrison, *Playing in the Dark*, 17, 38.

rogate; but Stanley chooses to revel in her passionate displays, wildly maneuvering her car while Parry watches silently from the back seat.

But Parry is not present when her destructive power veers out of control. Careening the car around a curve at dusk, Stanley strikes a young child returning from her grandmother's with a bouquet of pinks. The child is killed by the car, just as Stanley's own childish innocence is marred by the destructive sexual impulses the car represents. Rather than take the blame for the accident, Stanley blames Parry, as white southerners of the nineteenth century overtly projected their sexuality onto blacks. Everyone accepts her word, and only Parry and his family, with whom he had been home all evening, knew what really happened. It is the sensitive (and, to this point, largely ineffectual) Asa, embodiment of all that was good in the Old South, who finally realizes the truth and forces Stanley to confess. Even so, she escapes punishment: "They had made everything, especially the inquiries, as gentle as possible; and they had both chivalrously regretted the necessity to release Parry and charge a young girl in his place. . . . Watching them, from a corner, Roy had felt vaguely that, by the time the questioning was over, the three men had confused Stanley with the dead little girl. All the horror and pity seemed, through some strange freak of human emotion, to have veered round from the dead to the living" (*ITOL* 421). The bad belle, made terribly powerful by her terrible weakness and beauty, once again manipulates the chivalrous instincts of the southern male. In the film version, starring Bette Davis as Stanley, the young belle flees the house as the police are called and is killed in one last wild drive. The director and screenwriter destroy the femme fatale in the traditional fashion, but Glasgow understands that Stanley, like Annabel, has exactly the right appetite to survive on the southern patriarchy's corrupt remains.

Roy, Stanley's sister and moral opposite, does not fare so well. Though she is not an entirely traditional southern woman (she works to support herself and willingly releases her husband from his marriage vows when he tires of her), Roy embodies all of the traditionally respected traits of the southern lady. According to her father, "[s]he possessed all the qualities . . . that men have missed and wanted in women: courage, truthfulness, a tolerant sense of humor, loyalty to impersonal ends. That men have *thought* they missed in women" (*ITOL* 21). Asa satirically alludes to the fact that what most men really want in a woman is what Stanley has, that they only delude themselves into thinking that they value moral attributes. At the hands of her shallow but alluring sister, this good woman suffers the rejection of two men she loved, who also claimed to love her. The loss does not kill her, but it leaves her spiritually broken, incapable of love. After Craig's departure, she runs out into a rainstorm, meets a stranger about to leave for the war, and spends the night with him. The action is in part a gesture of pity and in part an attempt to flout the values, so faithfully upheld, that had so miserably failed her, not a sexual revitalization. At the novel's close, she returns home to pack her things, preparing to leave the South, which no longer has a place for women like her.[20]

Though she harshly reveals Stanley's faults, Glasgow lets us see that she is a survivor, a woman who has learned to manipulate her environment. And though she praises Roy's virtues, the author shows us that they are outdated in a world where only the worst aspects of the Old South survive. As Wagner observes, Glasgow's own confusion and resentment over southern expectations of women led her to unsex herself as a writer, referring to the author as *he* in *A Certain Measure* and often projecting herself into male characters.[21] Though Glasgow's use of "he" for the generic writer is typical of the time period, so is the notion that the generic writer is typically male. Her use of the masculine pronoun shows that she is affected by such notions, and this and her projection of artists into male characters indicate an unacknowledged confusion about her own role. Through her novels, Glasgow protests against these expectations, using as her vehicle of social protest the sexuality that made women vulnerable or made them dangerous.

EVELYN SCOTT

Like Glasgow, Evelyn Scott (1893–1963) embodies the conflicted feelings about the past that characterize, according to Tate, the Southern Renascence writer. Born Elsie Dunn in Clarksville, Tennessee, Scott summed up her relationship to the past by saying that she was impelled, as a writer, "to protest the lingering antebellum tradition under which I grew up . . . 'both literally and metaphorically,' I have traveled far from the South of my childhood." But later, in the autobiography *Background in Tennessee*, she concluded she could never escape her southern heritage and that her identity was formed by her early experiences in Tennessee.[22] This ambivalence about

20. In *Beyond Defeat,* the posthumously published sequel to *In This Our Life,* Roy returns to the South with the child of this union.

21. Wagner, *Ellen Glasgow,* 117.

22. D. A. Callard, *"Pretty Good for a Woman": The Enigmas of Evelyn Scott* (London: J. Cape, 1985), 4; Evelyn Scott, *Background in Tennessee* (New York: R. M. McBride, 1937), 2–3.

the South finds expression in her writing through her female characters'
sometimes desperate attempts to thwart sexual conventions.

In her own life, her confused attempts to escape the past without quite
letting go also led to dangerous sexual behavior. At age twenty, Scott ran
away with a man more than twice her age and changed her name to elude
her parents and her lover's family. Scott had much in common with the bad
belle. Regarding Scott's many romantic liaisons, D. A. Callard speculates
on a possible link between Scott's sexuality and her southern past: "What
percentage of her ideas on sexual freedom derived from Freud, feminism
and the 'new woman,' and how much was merely an extension of feminine
coquetry, the actions of a southern belle who did, rather than simply flirted?"
Callard's comments draw attention to a paradox associated with the bad
belle in southern women's writing. Appearing on the surface to be the opposite of the conventional "nice" girl, the sexually manipulative woman
has, upon closer inspection, much in common with the traditional southern
coquette. In Scott's frustration over public response to her first elopement
she makes a conscious objection to society's common classification of
women as one of the paired opposites: "If I had been older I would have
been called a 'vampire.' As it is, I was 'seduced.' In any case I am not to be
allowed any decent self-responsibility for my acts." Unlike Glasgow and her
nineteenth-century predecessors, Scott admits to a promiscuity of which
other vocal women were accused, and she claims agency by refusing to be
labeled an innocent victim or wicked villain.[23]

Scott admittedly tried to seduce every man she met, at least mentally,
and she had difficulty being friends with other women because of sexual
competition. Again, Scott's behavior underscores a problem inherent in the
bad belle character. This strong woman not only victimizes men but she
also victimizes women and resists any opportunity for positive female relationships, sending messages of female divisiveness along with the author's
social protest. Though Scott neglected to combat this problem in her own
life, her work shows that she was aware of the dangers. She uses her bad
belle to point out the weakness in the social structure, but at the same time
she condemns the woman's cruelty to both men and women. Though Scott
saw in herself traits of the bad belle, like Glasgow she did not extend her
own artistic traits to this character. Instead, the artist becomes the bad
belle's victim, emphasizing this figure's silencing potential.

23. Callard, *"Pretty Good for a Woman,"* 154, 10.

Scott's first published book, *Precipitations* (1920), a collection of poems, illustrates her concern with women's sexuality and is characterized by what Callard describes as "a violent female eroticism." The violence is more against convention and romantic illusions than against people. Sometimes the female is the passive, but not unwilling, recipient of this imaginative violence, as in "Summer Night": "The thick-witted drunkard on the park bench / Touches a young girl's breast / That throbs with its own ruthless and stupid delight." But sometimes the female is the source of figurative violence. As Mary Wheeling White points out, in the poem "Lullaby," "Scott draws on the archetype of female sorceress and destroyer": "She is Death enjoying Life, / Innocently, / Lasciviously." Here we see a very early and brief representation of the femme fatale, who will figure more prominently in her second book, *Narcissus* (1922). The title of this poem, "Lullaby," indicates a pattern in Scott's representation of the bad belle similar to a pattern later twentieth-century writers will employ. In both Scott's poem and *Narcissus,* the bad belle is a threatening sexualized mother, perhaps a version of the devouring mother Scott borrowed from her readings of Freud in the early twenties. This depiction could also be, consciously or unconsciously, somewhat autobiographical. Her son, Creighton, described the constant sexual activity in the home among Scott's bohemian friends and said that he was occasionally the object of adult advances and Freudian experimentation. His mother would scold and spank him if he protested or got in the way when unwanted.[24]

Though set in New York rather than in the South, *Narcissus* employs the same dual classification other southern women writers use, the dangerous, manipulative woman versus the passive, submissive woman. Julia, the bad belle, is stepmother to her counterpart May, reversing the traditional pattern in which the young coquette relinquishes her willfulness and flirtation to assume the role of compliant and pure lady. Much younger than her husband, Julia is close enough in age to May to view her as a potential rival. Like Southworth's Juliette, Julia collects men. Her conquests during the novel include—in addition to her husband—an artist of approximately her own age, the husband of an older friend, and (in spirit at least) her stepdaughter's eighteen-year-old boyfriend. A creature of consuming vanity, as

24. Callard, *"Pretty Good for a Woman,"* 49; Mary Wheeling White, *Fighting the Current: The Life and Work of Evelyn Scott* (Baton Rouge: Louisiana State University Press, 1998), 62; Callard, *"Pretty Good for a Woman,"* 62–63.

the title indicates, Julia cannot love another. After beginning an affair with Dudley, the artist, she arranges a dinner at which he and her husband are present. But she remains emotionally distant from their encounter: "Suddenly she realized that both these men were strangers to her, that she loved and wanted only herself" (*N* 58). It is this lack of emotion that gives her destructive power.

Julia first unnerves Dudley, her artist lover. As she leaves him for the last time, "Dudley felt a swift pang of despair. Not because she was gone, but because her going left him again with the problem of reviving the hallucinations of greatness. It was not easy for him to deceive himself" (*N* 145–46). Dudley longs for her to "be" the phallus, to reflect for him his delusions of his own greatness. But Julia is more concerned with her own power and ego. Like Glasgow, Scott chooses a man as the artist figure and makes him the bad belle's victim. In both these writers' works, as in that of Mitchell and Gordon, the male artists grow weaker as the destructive women grow stronger. Dudley is a disguised version of actual male artists Scott knew, but he is also similar to Scott herself. By projecting her artistic traits into a male character but making Julia's character so closely resemble Scott's conduct in her personal life, thereby figuratively dividing herself, Scott reveals an awareness of the social values that limit powerful women—values which hold that artists should be men, that creativity and self-expression in women translate into promiscuity, and that sexuality makes women bad.

Scott not only criticizes the bad belle, however, she also condemns Dudley, and perhaps her censure is also directed outward toward society and inward toward herself. Her criticism of Dudley the artist may be directed at all who, like him, fall for such a shallow trap as Julia's. As a parody of the femme fatale, Julia's machinations are so blatant and her lack of emotion is so obvious, the reader finds ridiculous those who believe in her. Perhaps Scott also criticizes herself through Julia. Scott has self-consciously divided and misrepresented herself, projecting her socially unacceptable sexuality onto a bad female character and her artistic ability onto the traditional male artist. Though she was not completely silenced, perhaps she admonishes herself and other women artists who mute their voices because of society's intimidatingly negative conception of female power.

Scott's condemnation of Julia, Dudley, and all her characters reflects her interest in Freudian interpretations of power and sexual development. The author depicts Julia's lovers' unsuccessful attempts to work through their oedipal fantasies using Julia. Watching her prepare to leave after he has made love to her for the first time, Dudley feels desperately isolated: "He could not bear the sense of her separateness from him. He was obsessed by curiosity about her and a lustful desire to outrage her mental integrity. He could not bear the feeling that the body which possessed him so completely yet belonged to itself" (*N* 9). His thoughts are reminiscent of Beauvoir's description of the male's obsessive attraction to and fear of female sexuality: "His mistress, in the vertigoes of pleasure, encloses him again in the opaque clay of that dark matrix which the mother fabricated for her son and from which he desires to escape. He wishes to possess her: behold him the possessed himself."[25]

Similarly, the greatest desire of Julia's second lover, Charles, is to rest his head in her lap and tell her about himself, but at the same time he half-fearfully longs to have sex with her to subdue her. Julia and her lovers' responses to her read like a textbook case of Freudian narcissism. In "On Narcissism: An Introduction," Freud writes that "the human being has originally two sexual objects: himself and the woman who tends him, and thereby we postulate a primary narcissism in everyone." The infant sees the mother as an extension of himself because she satisfies his earliest autoerotic desires for food and comfort. The love of the mother, therefore, becomes an extension of the infant's narcissism. Freud goes on to explain the development of narcissism in adult women and the male response to it:

> With the development of puberty the maturing of the female sexual organs . . . seems to bring about an intensification of the original narcissism, and this is unfavorable to the development of a true object-love with its accompanying sexual over-estimation; there arises in the woman a certain self-sufficiency (especially when there is a ripening into beauty). . . . Strictly speaking, such women love only themselves with an intensity comparable to that of man's love for them. Nor does their need lie in the direction of loving, but of being loved; and that man finds favor with them who fulfills this condition. The importance of this type of woman for the erotic life of mankind must be recognized as very great. Such women have the greatest fascination for men, not only for aesthetic reasons, since as a rule they are the most beautiful, but also because of certain interesting psychological constellations. It seems very evident that one person's narcissism has a great attraction for those others who have renounced part of their own narcissism and are seeking after object-love.

Scott was a Freudian in the twenties when she wrote this novel, and she no doubt modeled her characters on his theories. Julia's narcissism feeds that

---

25. Beauvoir, *Second Sex,* 164.

of her male admirers, and their attempt to associate her with mothering indicates an attempt to return to the blissful narcissism of infancy.[26]

The oedipal yearnings of these twentieth-century hollow men also reveal a need to take the place of the father, a place they would occupy by completely possessing the mother, to reclaim symbolically their position as authoritarian patriarchs. The lady is the vehicle they use to approach their past importance, just as the South at the beginning of the twentieth century clung to the lady's image as the last vestige of its past glory. Seidel comments on the confusion the dual role of southern womanhood created for actual women: "What happens if a girl—having had a successful season as a belle and married as she ought—refuses to relinquish the personality of a belle in order to become a sober matron? The transition from belle to matron requires an entire shift of personality traits, from coquette to helpmate, from flirt to nurse, from child to mother, from indulged and self-concerned to selfless and self-sacrificing."[27] Apparently this dual role creates a similar confusion for men; when the flirtatious coquette becomes a man's wife, she suddenly seems just like his mother.

Julia refuses to indulge her lovers' fantasies by playing the nurturing lady. She gives herself to them sexually, but her emotional indifference destroys them. Statuesquely tall and dignified, Julia looks the part of the lady, but, as Seidel points out, she is happy in her role as coquette. When Julia ends the affair with Charles, her second lover, he first stalks her, then drinks to erase her from his mind. But her image continues to haunt him: "(In the depths of me, this awful despair. Horror, horror, horror. Something clutched and dragged him into himself.). . . . (Some woman's throat white like that. Bent back. Lilies on a windy day. I shall die.)" (*N* 249). He longs for lilies, the image of purity and ladyhood Julia would not offer him. This need arrests him in a perpetual emotional infancy, preventing him from becoming the powerful, mature man he wants to be.

Julia's husband, Laurence, is also her victim. Needing an audience for her conquests, Julia confesses her indiscretions, ostensibly to relieve her conscience. Rather than make a scene, Laurence is aloofly dignified, removing himself to the guest bedroom but keeping up a front of domestic harmony. His self-possession challenges Julia's sense of her own power, and she does not rest until she wins his declaration of love and his humiliation:

26. Sigmund Freud, "On Narcissism: An Introduction," in *Collected Papers*, authorized translation supervised by Joan Riviere (London: Hogarth Press, 1934), 4: 45, 46.

27. Seidel, *Southern Belle*, 34.

"She was pressing his head against her. His lost head. It lolled. It was hers. Everything was hers. She had taken him, and was exposing his love for her. This would be the hardest thing to forget. Could he ever forget? He gave himself limply to her exultance. 'You've killed me, Julia. What is there to forgive? Yes, I love you. I love you'" (*N* 262). This figurative decapitation—his head lolling as she takes possession of it—represents Julia's emasculation of her husband. Enchanted by the beautiful coquette, Julia's husband and lovers long for her to become the lady who will restore their sense of power and self-worth. Instead they find a manipulative narcissist who uses their need to strengthen herself.

To Paul, May's boyfriend, the inapproachable Julia appears threatening from the start, but in his mind the danger is also associated with motherhood. After leaving May's house frustrated one afternoon, he falls asleep dreaming of naked bodies, including Julia's: "There were breasts in the darkness. He was afraid. He could not wake up. He was fear and he was afraid of himself. He was against naked breasts that held him, that he could not see" (*N* 49). Still young and unsure of himself, Paul longs for the beautiful older woman at the same time he despises her for making him feel like a child. Julia encourages his awkward infatuation because, ironically, for her he "is" the phallus: in his eyes she sees an image of her power and her own greatest love, herself. Julia's manipulation leaves the boy longing for death in the shape of "white breasts like sculptured things" (*N* 244), but her actions have more tragic results for her stepdaughter.

Unable to touch the object of his passion and resentment, Paul lashes out at an easier target, May. Always eager to please, fifteen-year-old May lies passive and uncomprehending as Paul forces sex upon her. Afterward she feels she has done something wrong, and rather than tell anyone and risk disapproval, she moons around the house crying, waiting for Paul to come back and wishing she were dead. She dutifully erases any small traces of her personality and will: "In the enormous evening only a little shiver of self-awareness was left to her. She tried to imagine that, because she was ugly and impure, Paul had already killed her. The strangeness and exaltation she felt came to her because she was dead. She loved him for destroying her" (*N* 133). Rather than eliciting approval or even pity, her quiet, timid behavior reaps only scorn and irritation from Julia and revulsion from Paul. Even more than the men in the novel, May, the passive traditional girl, is victim of the bad belle.

Julia engages in her liaisons matter-of-factly and with very little subterfuge, not shrinking or feigning modesty as did even the bad belles of the nineteenth century. As did Glasgow, however, Scott uses the one black character in the book to reflect the guilt associated with Julia's affairs. Nellie, the family cook Julia thinks of as "a lean old savage of many lovers" (*N* 62), silently appears at strategic moments, making Julia feel inexplicably uncomfortable. Nellie appears right after Julia's first tryst with Dudley, and Dudley delivers his farewell letter via Nellie. Without understanding why, Julia does not know how to act around her servant, and she feels as if the black woman watches her, holding some secret knowledge. Just as Julia needs the admiring gaze of men to recognize her worth and fully experience her narcissistic desire, she also seems to require the accusatory gaze of her servant to experience a sense of conscience, the knowing eyes of the other serving as a mirror for her guilt.

Nellie serves as a shadow figure for May as well. After being raped by Paul, May goes to the backyard to think of him, but she is disconcerted by the knowledge that Nellie stands in the doorway watching her: "She wanted to avoid the eyes of the old woman" (*N* 132). Julia, like most other femmes fatale in twentieth-century literature, has "very white" skin (*N* 59), and she is associated with "the annihilating quality of whiteness" (*N* 13) and with white "sculptured things" (*N* 244). May, her counterpart, has similarly fair features, but she seems literally to pale in comparison, dimmed by the brilliance of her more attractive stepmother. The black shadow figure seen and imagined in connection with violent sexuality may represent the characters' guilt, providing at once eyes that accuse and a dark symbol for sin itself. In the nineteenth-century works discussed that employ the bad belle, the reader sees the character through the desiring eyes of the author, thereby sharing her desire. In this novel, however, because the point of view shifts to that of the observed, the reader shares in Julia and May's uncomfortable experience of the seemingly judgmental gaze. We, therefore, share in both characters' experience of guilt, implicated for either our own destructive desire or passive self-effacement, or for participating in a society that makes these appear as the only options for women.

We may return here to Sander Gilman's observation that visual art from the Middle Ages onward used black figures to indicate illicit sexual activity. The artists often paired a white woman with a black female servant, who served as a visual marker for the white woman's promiscuity. According to Gilman, "The primitive is the black, and the qualities of blackness, or at least of the black female, are those of the prostitute."[28] Scott seems to use Nellie in a similar way, except that she places the reader in the scene beside the white characters through point of view. Though this modern writer imagines a world of sexual freedom, through the incriminating gaze she also seems to advocate sexual responsibility. The fact that the marker of irresponsible sexuality is the black woman recalls sexual attitudes of the southern past. Though Scott does not explicitly critique racist acts in this novel, she does reveal her feelings on the issue in *Calendar of Sin* (1931). Memory Burgess, the main female character, moves to the South to work in a school run by the Freedman's Bureau. In response to her attempts to educate African Americans, she faces attacks from Klan members and the threat of sexual violence. Her name, Memory, suggests her past sexual indiscretions that plague her, and perhaps also the burden of past southern transgressions that haunt the author. Because Nellie in *Narcissus* has the power to inflict the accusatory gaze, perhaps she also represents the black female victims of white sexual irresponsibility, victims of the same social structure that creates the dichotomous roles of passive-good woman and powerful-evil woman.

Though *Narcissus,* the southern-born author's first novel, is not set in the South and though it was not written while Scott lived in the South, it can still be read as a parody of southern types. By taking the symbol of the Old South, the lady, and placing her in the modern world, in a city that epitomizes twentieth-century America, Scott critiques the false ideals of both present and past. The male characters attempt to reclaim their self-respect by controlling women, offering them heavy symbolic import while attempting to deny them agency and personal freedom. Likewise, the Old South placed its women on a symbolic pedestal while denying them basic rights. In the dichotomy of womanhood represented by Julia and May, we see the tension created by the dual roles expected of women under the old ideal. That the beautiful and manipulative woman survives in the modern novel while her more modest and pure counterpart is all but erased shows an indictment of the twentieth century, whose superficiality breeds hollow materialism and feeds on simple souls, but these two characters' fates are also a censure of the culture that clings to the past by trying to shape its women into helpless ladies such as May. As Scott reveals, however, the dan-

28. Gilman, "Black Bodies, White Bodies," 227–28, 248.

gerous woman, though she survives, is a threat to creativity. Though Scott tried to resist this stereotype in her own life, rejecting sexual restrictions as well as the label of "vampire"—while still writing novels—the stress eventually took its toll. Late in her life she suffered from mental illness, transforming herself from the femme fatale to the madwoman.

MARGARET MITCHELL

Gone with the Wind (1936), Margaret Mitchell's only published book, is the most popular southern novel of all time. The work in many ways closely parallels Mitchell's life, and in it she works out her ambivalence toward the southern ideal of ladyhood, a mold into which she was cast. Though born at the turn of the century, Mitchell (1900–49) learned at an early age the mythology of the Old South. Rewriting history, her elders told her that Atlanta had been made the capital of Georgia the same year she was born, instilling an identification with her native city that was later transferred to her heroine, Scarlett. As was her heroine's, Mitchell's fit with her society was uneasy from the start. According to Elizabeth I. Hanson, Mitchell was "controlled and admonished . . . for not being a conventional 'belle,' for not marrying early and well, for not producing heirs." Also like Scarlett, the young Mitchell, though quite successful with men, was disapproved of by the women of her community for her unconventional behavior.[29]

In many details, the plot of *Gone with the Wind* parallels incidents of Mitchell's life. Just as the sainted Ellen O'Hara dies of typhoid while Scarlett struggles to return to Tara and her mother's protection, leaving her husband a grieving empty shell, Mitchell's mother, whom she admired for her strength and goodness, died of influenza during World War I while her daughter was away at Smith College. Mitchell returned home after her freshman year to care for a father who never recovered from the emotional blow of his wife's death. In *Gone with the Wind,* Scarlett's first husband, Charles Hamilton, whom Scarlett barely knew, dies at the beginning of the Civil War. Similarly, after only a brief romance, Mitchell became engaged to a young man with the same initials, Clifford Henry, who was killed when he went off to fight in the First World War. And Mitchell's first husband, Red K. Upshaw, whom she divorced because of his abusiveness, had much in common with the swashbuckling Rhett Butler. Upshaw's reputation in po-

29. Elizabeth I. Hanson, *Margaret Mitchell* (Boston: Twayne Publishers, 1991), 10.

lite society was unsavory, and in his youth he had been dismissed from the Naval Academy, just as Rhett was dismissed from West Point. As Hanson puts it, "He had a capacity, similar to Rhett's, for extraordinary charm coupled with violent and cynical passions. No man would torment or appeal to Margaret Mitchell more."[30]

Unlike Scarlett, however, Mitchell rejects the violent passions of Upshaw, first for a career as a newspaper reporter, then for a more stable husband, John Marsh, and finally, with the support of Marsh, for a career as novelist. Marsh, however, censored Mitchell's first efforts at novel writing because he disapproved of her manuscript— predating Faulkner's *Absalom, Absalom!*—which dealt with miscegenation and incest. After this initial disappointment, Mitchell set out to create a portrait of the "decorous deviousness" required of the southern belle. The parallels between Mitchell's life and that of her heroine indicate that she saw similarities between her role as a southern lady during World War I and the Great Depression and that of a southern lady during the Civil War and Reconstruction. The South had not changed much in sixty-plus years.[31] By placing an exaggerated version of herself in the novel, Mitchell expresses her ambivalence about the past, the present, and her place as a woman writer in this transitional South. But as Scarlett's interactions with an artist figure reveal, the bad belle's actions, though necessary for survival, are detrimental to creativity.

If we read *Gone with the Wind* autobiographically, the character that most nearly resembles Mitchell is the quintessential belle gone bad, Scarlett O'Hara. But the author seemed unsure of who was the actual protagonist. In an interview, she said that "she began to wonder . . . what the ladies of the Daughters of the Confederacy organizations, and the Civil War veterans would say about her making a woman like Scarlett the heroine of her novel. . . . she had meant for Melanie, the ideal Southern woman, to be the leading character, but . . . somehow Scarlett had simply taken over." O'Brien notes that Mitchell referred to Scarlett in a letter as a "far-from-admirable" woman, but "at the Atlanta premier of the film, she acknowledged her heroine to wildly cheering friends as 'my Scarlett, my poor Scarlett.'" In fact, even readers of the book have had differing opinions as to whom they like best. Helen Taylor writes that in a 1957 survey of American high school girls, most said they "identified" with Melanie Wilkes, but

30. Ibid., 31.
31. Ibid., 52.

106 The Belle Gone Bad

in 1970, the majority of a similar group chose Scarlett.[32] Just as South-worth's wicked Juliette and Milton's defiant Lucifer claim the admiration of both author and reader, Mitchell's Scarlett in her rebellion seems to steal the spotlight. Scarlett inspires desire not only in her male victims but in her creator and in readers as well. Like other southern women writers, Mitchell sees both good and bad in the bad belle, and like other Southern Renascence women writers, she sees that the bad belle's worst qualities—her deceitful-ness, shrewdness, manipulativeness, and superficiality—are the very traits that enable her to survive in the fallen South. Also like her contemporaries and her predecessors, Mitchell sees both good and bad in the ideal southern lady. Paradoxically, the good lady's best qualities—trust, self-sacrifice, and loyalty—are the ones that make her unfit for the modern world.

Though these female characters are nearly opposite physically and sym-bolically, both Scarlett and Melanie are threatening to the artist. Ashley Wilkes, the man least fit to survive the hard materialism of the new world, the man suited for nothing but the life of a country gentleman, the man who longs to "read, hear music, and dream" (*GWW* 212), is the closest the novel comes to portraying an artist figure. Significantly, as did Scott and Glasgow in their feminist novels, Mitchell projects her artist self into a male character. Her main character, Scarlett, displays no artistic talents. She lives in the new world, where making money is her primary interest. Her beauty, strength, and air of mystery and danger make her an excellent subject for the artist, but her materialism and pragmatism are far removed from the traditional artist's creativity and vision. In an important scene, Scarlett steals into Melanie's room to read Ashley's love letters, hoping to deter-mine from the missives whether he truly loves Scarlett or his wife. Instead of trite lover's phrases, she finds heartfelt and sober meditations on the na-ture of life and war, communication that indicates a deeper bond between husband and wife than she can understand. Scarlett dismisses these letters, along with Ashley's feelings for Melanie. Much as the New South portrayed by Mitchell has no place for the quiet beauty cherished by the Old South, Scarlett does not value the artist's words because they do not fit the formula she expects. Paradoxically, Melanie, Scarlett's opposite and representative of the Old South, also says she does not understand her husband's ideas,

---

32. Jones, *Tomorrow Is Another Day,* 333; O'Brien, "Race, Romance, and the Southern Literary Tradition," 165; Helen Taylor, *Scarlett's Women: "Gone with the Wind" and Its Female Fans* (New Brunswick, N.J.: Rutgers University Press, 1989), 78.

though she cherishes his words. Mitchell reveals that both stereotypes of womanhood, the passive-good lady and the powerful-bad belle, inhibit, in the long run, genuine artistic expression.

But these two ladies are types Mitchell's readers immediately recognize, and they serve as excellent vehicles for social criticism. Set in the Old South but written in the New South, *Gone with the Wind* employs many existing stereotypes about the South and, through its great popularity, creates many new ones. As Taylor points out, though Scarlett is to many a symbol for the antebellum South, modern women see themselves in her: "Identified with a brand new city (Atlanta), new people (the carpetbaggers and scalawags), and new money (industrial rather than agricultural economy), Scarlett O'Hara becomes the very symbol of the new woman, recognized as such by 1940s wartime women workers and mothers, 1960s liberationists and careerists, and 1980s 'Me'-generation postfeminists." To modern readers then, Scarlett embodies the past, present, and future, but Melanie represents only the strengths and weaknesses of the Old South.[33]

Even in her appearance, Scarlett as bad belle blends the traits traditionally employed by antebellum women writers with those employed by Southern Renascence women writers. Though she has pale skin and green eyes, Scarlett has raven black hair and the fiery temper associated with the exotic temptresses of antebellum novels. Like her antebellum analogue's, Scarlett's eyes, though green instead of black, are used as hypnotic focal points of her feminine powers. In the opening scene, she flutters "her bristly black lashes as swiftly as butterflies' wings" (*GWW* 3) to convince the Tarleton twins to shift the conversation away from the dull topic of war. She also sweeps these lashes strategically at Charlie Hamilton at Twelve Oaks, stimulating his tongue-tied ardor. And it is her beautiful, tearful eyes that first pluck Frank Kennedy's heartstrings in Atlanta. Melanie, on the other hand, does not resemble the golden beauty whose fairness contrasts with the dusky sexuality of the bad belle in most antebellum novels. Mitchell first describes her as a plain, sweet, and timid girl, with brown eyes, brown hair, and a childish figure. Beneath this mousey exterior, though, is "a sedate dignity about her movements that was oddly touching and far older than her seventeen years" (*GWW* 68). Physically, Melanie resembles the washed-out modern good girl May in Evelyn Scott's *Narcissus*, but spiritually she more closely favors the queenly Eulalia of Hentz's *The Planter's Northern Bride*.

33. Taylor, *Scarlett's Women*, 105.

In Mitchell's novel, set in the South during a war fought to end slavery, the racial marking that had all but disappeared from Glasgow's and Scott's representations of the bad belle is once again more obvious. Like Stanley and Julia, Scarlett has a dark shadow figure who seems to possess a secret knowledge of her sexual power, but this figure for Scarlett is much closer and more active than for the other modern bad belles. It is Mammy who teaches Scarlett the feminine wiles she so skillfully uses to keep men at her mercy, Mammy who sews the dress from velvet curtains in which Scarlett goes to Atlanta for the tax money, and Mammy who discovers and aids Scarlett's plan to steal Frank Kennedy away from her sister. Rhett Butler, the man who knows Scarlett best, seems to sense the symbolic connection between Scarlett and Mammy. Attempting to win the old lady's approval, he buys her a red taffeta petticoat while on honeymoon with Scarlett. Mammy finally puts on the petticoat after the birth of Rhett and Scarlett's child and shows her new affection for Rhett by coyly lifting her skirt to reveal the petticoat's shiny red hem. This scene may seem disturbingly inappropriate, until we see Mammy as guardian of Scarlett's sexuality, to whom Rhett, the skillful lover, makes offering, as would a supplicant to a fertility goddess. In her role as liaison, Mammy also distances Scarlett from the passion that would make her vulnerable.

Like antebellum bad belles, Scarlett is also dark-visaged. Perhaps Scarlett's bad qualities are so titillating and dangerous because through them she steps over the boundaries of race and class. Though she plays her role as belle to perfection, the role is based on deceit. Underneath, Scarlett is fiery, dark, and sexualized, the traits reserved by her culture for slave women or white trash, such as Emmie Slattery. As Darden Asbury Pyron and Roberts point out, Scarlett is associated with the color red rather than white: "So how white is Scarlett? Not very; she is, as her name implies, as red as her land and in her redness . . . lies her femaleness, her physicality, her sexuality: all that is denied by whiteness."[34] Mitchell does not actually tint Scarlett black, but through Mammy's petticoats she calls up, then blurs the nineteenth-century symbolism that labeled sexuality black and purity white. As her earlier repressed novel indicates, Mitchell wished to reveal and comment on southern miscegenation. Perhaps through Scarlett and Mammy, she hints at what she was unable to directly assert through her first book.

34. Roberts, *Myth of Aunt Jemima*, 178–79.

Another link between Mitchell's book and the nineteenth-century representations of race and sexuality is Rhett Butler. As Joel Williamson has
shown, Rhett, the most passionate and virile character in the novel, is
described over and over again as "swarthy," "dark," "black," or animal-like.
Furthermore, Rhett is not a southern gentleman; he refuses to do the hon-
orable thing by marrying a young lady with whom he had been accidentally
stranded overnight, and he approves of Scarlett's unladylike outbursts. Not
only does Mitchell associate Rhett with dark sexuality, but Jones believes
she also links him with evil incarnate, the devil:

> his eyes glint, he watches Scarlett like a cat watching a mouse hole, he prowls
> with a contained ferocity, and he has an uncanny ability to read other people's
> minds. Most striking of all is Rhett's astonishing ability to appear on, and to
> leave, the scene at exactly the right moment. To choose only a few examples:
> he manages to appear just as Scarlett is sobbing over Ashley during the war;
> just as the family appear at the train station to find out the casualties; just as
> they prepare to evacuate the city; and just as the last of Aunt Pittypat's chick-
> ens is cooked.[35]

As black devil, Rhett forms a visual representation of a figure implied in the
works of nineteenth-century southern women writers and present in the
nineteenth-century imagination in general. For example, Southworth's bad
belle figures Juliette Summers and Sinai Hinton are both said to be in
league with Satan, from whom they get their inspiration and their dark seductive powers. Witches were also popularly believed to sleep with the
devil. Like her nineteenth-century counterparts, Scarlett does frequently receive help from the Satan-figure Rhett, and he often tempts her by request-
ing sexual favors as payment for his services. But Rhett, too, is a complex
character, and Mitchell shows us that despite his hard and sinister facade, he
is—especially in his concern for Scarlett, Melanie, and Bonnie Blue—also
kind and sometimes vulnerable. The famous scene in which Rhett carries
Scarlett up the stairs finally to possess her mentally and physically has often
been read as a rape scene meant to suggest the Reconstruction fear of black
on white rape in the South. Earlier, however, Scarlett is actually attacked,
her bodice ripped, by a black man as she drives alone on the streets of
Atlanta, but it is another black man who saves her from the assault. Though
the movie version masks these scenes and characterizations, the intent of

35. Joel Williamson, "How Black Was Rhett Butler?" in *Evolution of Southern Culture*, 97–
98; Jones, *Tomorrow is Another Day*, 346–47.

the novel seems to be more to expose and question sexual-racial stereotypes than to reinforce or create them.

Despite all these similarities between *Gone with the Wind* and the actual antebellum novels, one major difference that separates this work from its predecessors and links it to its Southern Renascence contemporaries is that the bad belle survives. And though she sometimes receives aid from Rhett, her major victories take place in his absence. Scarlett survives, like her contemporaries, by manipulating the men who would control her. From the novel's beginning, Mitchell shows that Scarlett is aware of the limiting nature of her role but that she is nonetheless willing to push those limits. While dressing for the barbecue she complains: "I'm tired of everlastingly being unnatural and never doing anything I want to do. I'm tired of acting like I don't eat more than a bird, and walking when I want to run and saying I feel faint after a waltz, when I could dance for two days and never get tired. I'm tired of saying, 'How wonderful you are!' to fool men who haven't got one-half the sense I've got, and I'm tired of pretending I don't know anything, so men can tell me things and feel important while they're doing it" (*GWW* 53). Though Scarlett revels in her power to attract beaux, she resents the lies necessary to capture their attention. Mitchell adds her authoritative censure of the system to Scarlett's childish one: "There was no one to tell Scarlett that her own personality, frighteningly vital though it was, was more attractive than any masquerade she might adopt. . . . [F]or at no time, before or since, had so low a premium been placed on feminine naturalness" (*GWW* 54). Clearly, Mitchell indicates that Scarlett's behavior in this scene and in subsequent ones is the result of an intelligent and spirited woman's attempt to adapt and prosper in a society that does not value her intelligence or spirit. Throughout the rest of the novel, Scarlett struggles to negotiate this system in a way that will allow her to satisfy her desires while remaining in the society's good graces.

As with the bad belle in both the antebellum novel and the Southern Renascence novel, it is Scarlett's skill at playing coquette—the sexually enticing yet seemingly innocent and helpless woman—that allows her to manipulate the men around her by using their supposed strengths as southern gentlemen against them. But Scarlett is successful with these men only when she follows the rules of conduct against which she protests. Her forthright and unladylike declaration of love to Ashley reaps only humiliation, because it is evidence of a fiery spirit Ashley admires but fears. Scarlett's first and easiest conquest is the callow Charles Hamilton, from whom, by blushing and batting her eyes, she entices a marriage proposal as revenge against Ashley. Scarlett takes advantage of Charles's romantic notions of his own gallantry and her maidenly modesty to encourage a speedy wedding.

Scarlett's next attempt to win a husband, again for money, fails, because she forgets the rules she learned as a child. Wearing a green dress made from her mother's curtains, she attempts to stoke the fire of Rhett's ardor to procure the money she needs for taxes. She succeeds as long as she flatters, "flutter[s] her thick lashes up at him," and "manage[s] a pretty confusion and a blush" (*GWW* 382). But as soon as he notices her rough and blistered hands, indicating the unladylike employment in which she has been recently engaged, and Scarlett drops the illusion of helplessness to bluntly state her purpose, Rhett gains the upper hand. Unable to offer cash, he offers advice instead: "When you are trying to get something out of a man, don't blurt it out as you did to me. Do try to be more subtle, more seductive. It gets better results. You used to know how, to perfection. . . . You are forgetting your early training" (*GWW* 388). As Rhett indicates, skillful deceit is a necessary accomplishment for a lady who hopes to win favors from a gentleman.

Though Scarlett angrily rebuffs his refresher course in feminine stratagems, she puts them to use with the next man she meets, obtaining better results. By pretending to be a helpless, ignorant, admiring woman and by concocting the lie that Suellen had jilted him for another man, Scarlett wins the love and the money of her sister's fiancé, Frank Kennedy. She plays on her victim's masculine pride and his obligation to protect the weak, manipulating him to form an alliance that proves profitable to Scarlett but fatal to him. Lured in because of his obligation to protect, one of the defining traits of the southern gentleman, Kennedy participates in a Klan raid to avenge Scarlett's insulted honor and is killed. Though Scarlett does not intentionally kill him, he is made vulnerable to her by their roles in the southern social system.

Judith Butler, commenting on Joan Riviere's 1929 essay, which identifies exaggerated womanliness as overcompensation for a desire to be masculine, says the "mask" of womanliness of "women who wish for masculinity" can be interpreted as an attempt to disguise their power (to deny "having the phallus") to avoid "retribution by those from whom it [power-the phallus] must have been procured through castration." Scarlett figuratively castrates her men, but her exaggerated femininity ensures they feel no pain. Butler goes on to say that "What is hidden [behind the mask of womanliness] is not sexuality, but rage."[36] Scarlett in fact uses her sexuality, or at least the appearance of it, both to mask the rage she feels at her society's demand for feminine passivity and to circumvent that demand. She wears the mask to usurp masculine power and to avoid retribution by those from whom she has stolen that power. But in stealing her sister's intended, Scarlett follows a pattern established by earlier Southern Renascence bad belles: Stanley steals Roy's husband and Julia steals May's boyfriend. Scarlett views her sisters as "natural enemies in pursuit of the same prey—man" (*GWW* 60). The bad belle's manipulations, though an effective means of gaining power in a world that ordinarily reserved power for men, threaten other women and even disrupt the ties of loyalty to family. Later southern women writers will react against this problem.

Scarlett's complaints about the deceit inherent in the belle's position in society and her success when she employs this deceit against men made vulnerable by their chivalrous ideals form an indictment of the Old South's social order. But like other Southern Renascence writers, Mitchell casts a critical eye toward her own time as well. After the Civil War, when the southern way of life had fallen, money became the sole aim of a new breed of people. For Scarlett, "everything except money lost its value once it was hers" (*GWW* 676). Once she is rich, she associates with a crass set of Yankees and builds the gaudiest house she can imagine, forsaking without regret all the values her once-worshiped mother had taught her. Scarlett is the harbinger of a new era, Mitchell seems to say, in which a person's worth is measured, not by character, but by capital. The emptiness and tawdriness of Scarlett's obsession eventually drives away the one man who had always accepted her true nature. At the end of the novel, Rhett, now a mockery of his former strength and magnetism, flees her presence to rediscover the comforts of the past. But Mitchell also lets us know that only Scarlett's fierce desire for money and her ability to obtain it keep her and those she cares for alive.

Scarlett's assumption of the role of provider is another indication of the new era's moral failure. As did Glasgow and Scott, Mitchell contrasts the unexpected strengths of the new woman with the weakness of the new man. With one third of southern manhood dead, one third maimed, and one third demoralized after the war, these women writers seem to say that it is time for the matriarchal South to emerge. Even in Mitchell's generation, women struggled for the right to earn their own livings without suf-

36. Butler, *Gender Trouble*, 51, 52.

fering the type of ridicule Scarlett faced. For example, when Sue White struggled to obtain a law degree in the twenties, says Wheeler, "They called her 'impractical' and 'visionary.' They told her 'It was about time I was getting married, anyhow.' "[37] Mitchell suggests that the manipulations of the bad belle are necessary because the men who once ruled were now incapable and the good women never had the necessary skills. All of the men in Scarlett's life—her father, Charles, Frank, Ashley, and Rhett—want to protect her, as true southern gentlemen should, but they each fail her at some crucial point or prove less competent providers than Scarlett herself. Charles dies of pneumonia, leaving her pregnant at the beginning of the war; her father succumbs to grief at the loss of his wife; Frank is not the shrewd manager Scarlett is; Ashley is unsuited for anything but lofty ideas; and Rhett always pulls away when Scarlett needs him most: on the road to Tara when fleeing Atlanta, when the tax money is due, when catty women discover her in an embrace with Ashley, and finally, when she realizes that she's loved him all along. To survive, Scarlett must take the place of these men who have lost their former stature. Relinquishing the role of nurturer, which was her mother's role and one expected of a true lady, Scarlett becomes the father figure. She thinks and conducts business like a man while continuing to practice her coquettish charms, a threatening combination to those who stand in her way but the sole means of survival for her family.

Melanie, on the other hand, baffles Scarlett by continuing to be a lady after all of her finery and elegance are gone. As Scarlett's counterpart, Melanie fulfills the role Scarlett abandons, nurturing Scarlett's children, the men in the family, and Scarlett herself. Melanie refuses to abandon the ideals of her past, even though the culture that established those ideals has died. Though Melanie has the courage to help Scarlett riffle through the belongings of a dead Yankee, she will not condescend to meet the new Yankee governor who might make her social position in Atlanta more comfortable. Mitchell seems to admire Melanie's moral character, but by having her die while Scarlett prospers, Mitchell makes it clear that Melanie's time has passed and that Melanie, though good, lacks the physical stamina to survive in the fallen South. Symbolically, it is Melanie's desire for motherhood—the crowning glory of the southern lady, during which her potential for womanly devotion and self-sacrifice reaches its height—that destroys her.

37. Wheeler, *New Women of the New South,* 85.

Mitchell's novel, perhaps more than any other of the Southern Renascence, shows the presentness of the past, the poverty and turmoil of Reconstruction mirroring the poverty and turmoil of the thirties. By allowing Scarlett, the corrupt heroine, to prosper through social and economic upheaval, Mitchell seems to say that desperate times require desperate measures. The old way of life has ended, and those who cling to it become the victims of those smart enough and unscrupulous enough to manipulate the codes of the past. These codes, however, continue to victimize Scarlett as well. Despite her intelligence and strength, she cannot reach her goals by a direct route, but must use deceit and coquetry in a society that prefers weak women. Metaphorically at least, Scarlett and, by implication, all strong women of Mitchell's time draw shallow breaths beneath their corset stays.

CAROLINE GORDON

Reared in the same milieu as Glasgow, Scott, and Mitchell, Caroline Gordon (1895–1981) also struggled early with her socially defined role as woman, but she seemed to accept her place more easily after converting to Roman Catholicism in young adulthood. Gordon outwardly accepted the teachings of her faith that the wife should be subservient to her husband, and one of her last novels, *The Malefactors* (1956), contains an epigraph by Jacques Maritain: "It is for Adam to interpret the voices that Eve hears." Though Gordon strongly believed in these conventional gender roles, they were not so easy to practice. Her husband, writer and Southern Agrarian Allen Tate, was far from the masculine ideal. Often drunk, unfaithful, and emotionally insecure, he was not an effective moral guide. Gordon's own problems with alcohol abuse and a violent temper also contributed to an unstable marriage, but the couple continued to work at their relationship, reconciling and remarrying after their divorce in 1946. They finally divorced permanently, to Gordon's great disappointment, in 1959.

Gordon's acceptance of traditional gender roles created difficulties for her as an artist. According to Nancylee Novell Jonza, Gordon viewed writing as a masculine prerogative: "The act of writing forced women into awkward postures, she believed: they would have to deny or mask their sex—write like men—in order to gain approval." And Veronica A. Makowsky writes that the late work *The Malefactors* "indicates Caroline's increasing ambivalence toward her role as an artist who is also a woman. If Adam has the interpretive role, why is Eve writing all these novels?" Gordon also suffered feelings of artistic inferiority to Tate, who, though his reputation as a Fugitive poet predated and surpassed Gordon's artistic renown, actually wrote and published less than (and most readers would say not as well as) his wife.[38] She nevertheless continued to write autobiographical novels, creating characters which are composites of herself, Tate, and their literary friends. Gordon often used the bad belle in her novels, but in *The Strange Children* (1951) and *The Malefactors*, her use of this character forms an outlet for her uncertainty regarding her dual role as a woman and an artist in the South.

Though her notion of gender roles was conventional, her use of the bad belle is not. If Margaret Mitchell's historical novel forms a link between the Southern Renaissance writers' attitudes toward gender and sexuality and those of the antebellum writers, then Caroline Gordon bridges the gap between the Southern Renaissance and contemporary literature. With a long career beginning in the 1920s, Gordon usually is considered a Renaissance writer, but *Strange Children* and *Malefactors* were written relatively late in her career. In these novels, a slightly more mature belle gone bad survives, as she does in the works of other writers of Gordon's generation. But in Gordon's work, no clearly opposite good lady is destroyed while the bad belle prospers. Instead, as will happen more clearly in the work of contemporary writers, the artist figure, a composite of Gordon, Tate, and other writers they knew, is the primary victim of this femme fatale.

Set at Benfolly, an old southern estate modeled and named after one on which Tate and Gordon lived in the thirties, *Strange Children* recounts, from the point of view of Lucy Lewis, her parents' and their writer-friends' odd behavior. The Civil War, chief source of creative inspiration for Lucy's father, Stephen, and for Uncle Tubby, lurks in the background. But the focal points of the story are the religious conversion of Mr. Reardon and the affair and elopement of Mrs. Reardon with Uncle Tubby, who does not realize that this bad belle is mad. James E. Rocks believes this novel enacts a southerner's quest for meaning in a new era:

> From the beginning of her career, when she was sympathetic to the Agrarian movement, to her conversion to Roman Catholicism, Miss Gordon examined and rejected her Southern heritage in an effort to secure a set of beliefs that would replace the traditions of her defunct ante-bellum morality. . . .

38. Nancylee Novell Jonza, *The Underground Stream: The Life and Works of Caroline Gordon* (Athens: University of Georgia Press, 1995), 38; Veronica Makowsky, *Caroline Gordon: A Biography* (New York: Oxford University Press, 1989), 208.

> In all of her fiction . . . Miss Gordon admits that the agrarian ethic of the
> South before the Civil War will no longer serve the regrettably altered world
> of the modern commercial South.

Rocks believes Gordon dramatizes this quest through Lucy, the central intelligence of the novel, who in the end chooses the authentically spiritual Kevin Reardon over the beautiful and hypnotically alluring Isabel Reardon.[39] Isabel may symbolize the false quest of the Southern Agrarians, whose major goal was a return to the agricultural economy of the Old South but who also longed for a more romantic era with ladies and gentlemen presiding over serene plantations, doing little—like Ashley Wilkes and, indeed, like the Agrarians themselves—besides reading, thinking, and writing. Isabel is a parody of the lady, who serves as focal point for all southern dreams of a glorified past.

Gordon indicates that this ideal threatens the artistic and spiritual integrity of those who follow it. Although in the novel Isabel is originally from the Midwest, Gordon modeled the mad woman poet on several writers of her acquaintance, including Katherine Anne Porter and Zelda Fitzgerald, two former southern belles famous for their coquetry, the latter infamous for her mental instability. Gordon prepares the reader for the entrance of this femme fatale by references to the undine tale, which Lucy reads, and to Keats's "La Belle Dame sans Merci," which Uncle Tubby obsessively quotes. In both these works, seemingly inhuman women (the undine is a water sprite) use their bewitching powers to lure mortal men to their destruction. Rocks believes the medievalism of these allusions ties into the Catholic theme and the quest motif he has pointed out in the novel.[40] But they could just as easily refer to the false quest of the Agrarians. The romantic notion of chivalry, in which courageous gentlemen protect and idolize pure ladies, gilds the southerner's reverential backward-glancing. But in the undine story and in "La Belle Dame sans Merci," the knight aids a lady whose helplessness and beauty form a facade for treachery. Like the knight, Tubby seems to seek Isabel as a muse, and like the lady, Isabel turns out to be an antimuse, leading Tubby into a life of certain misery. Significantly, the bad lady is herself a failed poet, revealing Gordon's religious and social qualms about her role as a woman writer; Isabel also deadens the creative

39. James E. Rocks, "The Christian Myth as Salvation: Caroline Gordon's *The Strange Children*," *Tulane Studies in English* 16 (1998): 150–51, 156.

40. Jonza, *Underground Stream,* 279; Rocks, "The Christian Myth as Salvation," 154.

endeavors of her artist follower, showing, as did Glasgow, Scott, and Mitchell, that the image of the femme fatale silences artistic expression.

When Isabel first appears in the novel, she and Tubby recite lines from "La Belle Dame sans Merci." Tubby returns from a walk with Lucy to find that Isabel and Kevin have just arrived:

> Her [Lucy's] mother stared at her. "Where have you been?" she asked. "We've looked everywhere for you."
>
> Uncle Tubby laid his hand on Lucy's shoulder. "She took me to her elfin grot," he said.
>
> The lady looked at Lucy before she looked at him. She was tall, and thinner, even, than Mama. She shook her head and her hair fell farther back on her shoulders. It was the same color as Lucy's and the same length. Her eyes were the color of the periwinkle blossoms that grew in the old graveyard at Merry Point.
>
> She said, "Tubby, *don't* shut your wild, wild eyes!" But you couldn't hear the rest of what she was saying, for Uncle Tubby had put his arms about her and was kissing her. As Lucy gazed at them she would have wept but all eyes were upon her. (*SC* 94–95)

Not only does Isabel enthrall Tubby with her beauty, but she also mesmerizes young Lucy. Seen through Lucy's awestruck eyes, Isabel appears to be the feminine ideal— tall, thin, elegant. Beyond this, she has something in common with Lucy. Her hair is the same color and length as Lucy's, she is thin like Lucy's mother, only more so, and she is the woman Lucy could someday become. But her unusual colored eyes, a source of power for many literary femmes fatales, remind Lucy of flowers that grow in the graveyard. This image evokes a feeling of hypnotic stillness as Lucy, Tubby, and the reader gaze into Isabel's eyes, but it also sounds a note of warning. Despite the beauty of this Edenic setting and the lady, who serves as chief symbol for the idealized past, decay and stagnation are in the air at Benfolly. The graveyard not only recalls the fact that the southerners who inhabited that glorified past are all dead but it also comments on those now living at Benfolly. Just as "no birds sing" in La Belle Dame's elfin grot, at Benfolly, where literary figures congregate, no writers write.[41]

In the past, Tubby, the bad belle's chief victim, wrote the long poem about the Civil War "If It Takes All Summer," and he plans to write a new one, "Conspiracy of Pontiac." No longer able to write poetry, Stephen

41. Keats, "La Belle Dame sans Merci."

works on a Civil War history. Reading the novel biographically, most readers assume Stephen is modeled after Allen Tate and that Uncle Tubby is a composite of male writer-friends Robert Penn Warren and Ford Maddox Ford. But as artist figures experiencing the same inability to write with which Gordon often struggled, they no doubt also represent many of her anxieties about her creative abilities. Instead of creating anything new, they drink, gossip, and rehash old stories, trying to find a battle "[n]obody's ever done anything on" (*SC* 26). That is, they do that until Isabel appears, at which time Tubby puts into practice all the ideals about which he has read and written to save the "damsel in distress" (*SC* 27).

Isabel plays the damsel in distress so that Tubby will help her out of an unsatisfactory marriage. As an aspiring poet and Midwestern girl of modest means, she married Kevin primarily for his money. Kevin, however, since his religious conversion, plans to give all his money to a group of monks and live in monk-like simplicity himself. Tubby, having received fifty thousand dollars from Hollywood for the rights to "If It Takes All Summer" and having recently divorced, presents an excellent means of escape. Isabel arranges for Tubby and the Reardons to meet together at Benfolly, where she plans to make the exchange of husbands. On a few occasions, the lovers use Lucy as a cover for their talks, believing that she is too young to understand. But she sees more than they think she does: "The gentlemen all seemed to be afraid of these strange ladies, but they were always going around where they were" (*SC* 172). Though she does not fully comprehend the nature of the relationship, it holds a strange attraction-repulsion for her, as do the knights and ladies she reads about in books.

Only one person knows all that goes on between Isabel and Tubby. Much the way Mitchell, Scott, and Glasgow do, Gordon links a black character to the forbidden sexuality of the bad belle. Relieving boredom one hot afternoon by walking in the woods with the family cook Jenny, Lucy spies upon Tubby and Isabel making love behind some vines. Actually, she sees only Tubby and doesn't know what he is doing, but she senses by the look in his eyes that another body lies beneath his: "They had stared straight into hers. But his gaze had merely happened to fall upon her face. He had seen her and he had not seen her. And if she and the others had not stood there he would have stared straight before him in the same way, as if he were looking beyond whatever was before him, at something that was not there and never could be there, no matter if you looked all your life" (*SC* 220). The look indicates that "La belle dame sans merci / Hath [him] in thrall," but Lucy does not understand.[42] Relying on old sexual codes, however, Gordon links the sexual act to the only black character in the novel, Jenny, who acts as a barrier between it and Lucy. Ironically, the family servant is the only one with a sufficient spiritual basis to clearly see and judge Tubby's and Isabel's sins. Jenny serves as a sexual interpreter for the reader, making clear the importance of what Lucy sees, and she serves as a protector for Lucy, shielding her from the dark sexuality in the woods. With a face "kind and wise, but a little sad," Jenny also serves as the missing or ignored morality of the group. Similar to Nellie in Scott's *Narcissus,* Jenny seems to hold secret knowledge about the family's sins and the possibility of redemption, but she does not know how to share it (*SC* 219). For the modern writers, the black characters are no longer the object of illicit sexuality, as they were in the nineteenth century. The writers continue to associate sexual indiscretions with black characters, but instead of participating in the indiscretions, the black characters silently judge them. This reversal may exhibit the modern notion of the noble savage, the simple-minded other who is morally superior because he/she has not been tainted by the dissoluteness of the modern world. But it may also be an expression of the writers' racial guilt, a way of atoning for white society's once labeling African Americans animalistic and immoral and a way of pointing out the hypocritical corruption behind the labels.

The sexuality Jenny judges fascinates young Lucy, but it must compete against the equally enticing profound spirituality of Kevin. Soon after Kevin's arrival, Lucy steals from his room an ornate crucifix, charmed by its beauty and sensing its symbolic import for him. She keeps "the little man" in a cloisonné box, which Isabel had given her after their first evening at the house. The box, like Isabel, is beautiful but empty. Lucy instinctively fills it with the Christian symbol, hiding both until the night Tubby and Isabel elope. Isabel leaves in the night, untouched by the consequences of her actions, free to manipulate Tubby until his money is gone and then to find another rescuer-victim. At this time, though there were hints before, the reader learns of Isabel's incurable madness and realizes that Tubby, the southern artist, is doomed. Like Southworth and Evans, Gordon links her bad belle to madness, connecting these two symbolic means of protesting the limited spheres afforded to women in society. As if to compensate Kevin for his loss, Lucy returns his crucifix, casting the box which held it aside.

---

42. Ibid.

Crying, she confesses her crime, and receives Kevin's absolution. Lucy, the child of the South, represents its future. Torn between the empty worship of the old agrarian ideal—symbolized by the beautiful belle gone bad—and the true spirituality of Catholicism, Lucy makes what Gordon sees as the right choice.

Gordon uses the bad belle similarly in her next novel, *The Malefactors*. Here, Cynthia, the femme fatale, is an aspiring poet, and like a poetic succubus, she attaches herself to failing southern writer Tom Claiborne, hoping to absorb some of his talent or to at least be seen with him by the right people. Here we see the same dynamic between the bad belle and the artist Gordon employed in *Strange Children*. She not only reveals her ambivalence about her role as a woman writer by projecting herself as artist into the mediocre poet femme fatale, but she also shows how threatening this figure can be to artistic expression generally by having her serve as antimuse to the male poet, Tom. As in *Strange Children*, Gordon appears to censure herself through this exaggerated character as much as she censures society's attitudes. Though Cynthia does not actually silence Tom (for years, he has been hiding the fact that he can no longer write), she lures him into accepting her by making him believe that her youth and beauty will inspire him with new creative energies, as the beautiful lady of poetry was wont to do. When this illusion shatters, he is left, like the knight in "La Belle Dame sans Merci," "alone and palely loitering."[43]

Having long felt an emptiness in his marriage to Vera, Cynthia's older cousin, Tom leaves his wife, hoping the new relationship will revitalize his waning poetic abilities. Though her physical charms fascinate him and though he respects her work, Tom soon learns that there is something missing in Cynthia: "She doesn't know how other people feel. She has to make it up . . . she is a woman with moveable ways!" (*M* 268). Like the moon (a feminine symbol) for which she is named, the face Cynthia reveals changes constantly. She pretends a love for Tom she does not feel, and when he does not bring her the recognition or the connections she had hoped for, she chooses a new man before the old one is out the door. Tom knows Cynthia will always get what she wants: "You will be a fool to worry about her. . . . There are eight million people in New York. And no dearth of sick intellectuals. I believe that Willy Stokes is the next prospect" (*M* 302). But the encounter leaves Tom a broken man. One reviewer described *The Malefactors*

43. Ibid.

as "the spiritual hangover of the Lost Generation," and that label accurately describes the alcoholic ennui of the central artist figure.[44] But Gordon provides healing redemption. Searching for his wife and having changed little, Tom finally has a spiritual epiphany in a Catholic chapel. With his new faith, he plans, at the novel's close, to return to Vera and reclaim his rightful place as moral head of the household.

Though Caroline Gordon was tormented throughout her marriage by Tate's affairs, sometimes with Gordon's friends and relatives, the bad belles in these two novels are more than just "other women" and their allure is more than simply physical.[45] As do Glasgow, Scott, and Mitchell, Gordon uses the bad belle as a symbolic vehicle for her commentary on southern society past and present. For Gordon, the belle gone bad is an icon for the empty, romantic, and poetically seductive past still worshiped by the Agrarians. Through the femme fatale's destruction of the artist figure, she shows that this obsession with chivalrous southern history is not sustaining in literature or in life. For Tubby and for Tom, this false quest drains their poetic abilities and their spirit.

The bad belle in Gordon's work survives, as she did in the works of the other Southern Renascence women writers discussed in this chapter. But Gordon changes the pattern used by her contemporaries. Glasgow, Scott, and Mitchell destroy the bad belle's counterpart, the ideal lady, as if to say the seductress's tactics are the only way for a woman to survive and prosper in a world created by and for men. Their message reflects their anger and resentment of male domination in the traditional southern setting and their attempt to assert their feminist voices. Unlike her contemporaries, though, Gordon offers an alternate survival strategy for both women and men, spiritual renewal through Christianity, perhaps as compensation for the loss of the Old South's creeds. This religious faith endorsed in her novels reflects, of course, Gordon's individual world view. But some of the themes she introduced reappear in the works of more recent southern women writers. The bad belle's threat to the southern artist recurs in more recent uses of this figure; and a child figure, a central intelligence who must escape the dark lady's corrupting influence, like Lucy in *Strange Children,* will also be important to southern writers in the final half of the twentieth century.

44. Brainard Cheney, "Caroline Gordon's *The Malefactors,*" *Sewanee Review* 79 (1971): 361.
45. Makowsky, *Caroline Gordon,* 180.

3 TO CALL MYSELF AN ARTIST
Destroying the Bad Belle

The Southern Renascence bad belles were powerful and somewhat frightening representations of women, embodying at once the author's rage against and criticism of society. But the modern woman sees herself in a different light. During the last half of the twentieth century, the roles of women changed in many ways, even—though perhaps more slowly—in the South. World War II helped change the region by bringing in people from the outside and by boosting the economy after the depression. Although society still expects sexual modesty and restraint more from its women than from its men, the "sexual revolution" of the 1960s created a more open atmosphere, in which women experienced greater sexual freedom than in any other period. Furthermore, the woman's rights movement of the 1970s and 1980s, on top of changes gradually brought about by women voting for more than fifty years, helped introduce new laws to protect women in the home and out. Despite women's continued primary responsibility for child care in most families, in the last decades of the century more women worked outside the home than not, creating in the 1980s the images of "Super Mom," the woman who could succeed in both the man's world and the woman's world, and "Mr. Mom," the man who took primary responsibility for child rearing.[1]

Contemporary southern women writers experienced the benefits of

1. Bartley, *New South*, 8, 423–24.

greater freedom and equality for women. But their lives were not entirely free from tensions caused by lingering attachments to the old southern social structure. Their mothers were of a generation influenced by the stereotypes of southern belle and southern lady, and their literary role models immortalized these figures in their works. Elizabeth Spencer, one of the earlier contemporary writers included in this chapter, writes of facing parents who believed that placing oneself in the public eye by writing novels was an improper activity for a well-brought-up young lady. Though this concept of ladyhood may seem distant from the reality of the late twentieth century, it still held sway in the South and influenced the works of a new generation of writers. Consequently, the bad belle has not disappeared from the novels of the modern southern woman. Like their predecessors, contemporary southern women writers Eudora Welty, Elizabeth Spencer, Lee Smith, and Kaye Gibbons use the bad belle figure to critique the southern social system, particularly as it relates to the roles of women. Unlike their Southern Renascence predecessors, however, these contemporary writers do not allow the dangerous woman to survive to influence yet one more generation of southern women.

They refuse to allow her to survive because, though antebellum and (more blatantly) Southern Renascence women writers used the bad belle as a vehicle for social protest and critique of the patriarchal system, their parody of this image, created by the system to symbolize feminine power, perpetuates that system. As Judith Butler puts it, "The 'I' who would oppose its construction is always in some sense drawing from that construction to articulate its opposition; further, the 'I' draws what is called its 'agency' in part through being *implicated* in the very relations of power that it seeks to oppose." Parodying societal attitudes, therefore, though it may be a means of voicing dissatisfaction, is not enough to uproot those attitudes. Again, according to Butler, "The citing of the dominant norm does not . . . displace that norm; rather, it becomes the means by which the dominant norm is most painfully reiterated as the very desire and the performance of those it subjects."[2] The bad belle as used by southern women writers parodies society's concept of powerful women as evil, immoral, and unwomanly, or womanly only on the outside. But this figure also calls attention to most women's lack of real power in society, and it forces the women writers to make their points through indirection and manipulation, the flimsy tools consigned to women in patriarchal society.

2. Butler, *Bodies that Matter*, 122–23, 133.

Although Scarlett survived and prospered in the fallen South, she was able to do so only by outwardly playing to perfection the role of the weak, helpless woman while inwardly scheming to usurp masculine power. And though Mitchell and the other women writers of the Southern Renascence who employ this figure indict southern males for creating the society in which the belle gone bad flourished, they create a figure who, except in the fact that she survives and makes the men look as bad as or worse than herself, resembles the evil females of Haggard and countless other misogynist male writers. Showalter describes Haggard's most famous novel, *She,* as follows: "Haggard's *She* was one of the great best sellers of the 1880s. The story of a mysterious African Kingdom ruled by an immortal white queen may seem paradoxical because it is about the search for a matriarchal goddess. Yet Haggard's heroes seek this goddess only to destroy her. *She* is about the flight from women and male dread of women's sexual, creative, and reproductive power." Gilbert and Gubar address the problems caused when women writers adhere to male literary models that portray women as weak and helpless or make strong women appear unnatural, denying—even as the writers themselves illustrate—that a woman can be both intelligent and "womanly": "[S]elf-denial may become even more than self-destructive when the female author finds herself creating works of fiction that subordinate other women by perpetuating a morality that sanctifies or vilifies all women into submission."[3] Granted there is nothing submissive about Scarlett, but her early readers, even Mitchell herself, saw her as a "bad woman," and they could be led to believe that all powerful and successful women are somehow "bad." Even if we do not see Scarlett as a villain, she shows us that the only way to succeed in a man's world is to play the man's game while slyly subverting his rules for selfish ends.

As Hélène Cixous writes in "The Laugh of the Medusa," women have the power to end the cycle: "We must kill the false woman who is preventing the live one from breathing." Contemporary southern women writers allow their female characters to reject this negative concept of female power and instead become powerful by drawing on positive examples of feminine strength. By destroying the bad belle without restoring patriarchal authority, as did her nineteenth-century predecessors, the contemporary southern woman writer destroys negative stereotypes associated with the expression of independent feminine creativity. In the works of Welty,

3. Showalter, *Sexual Anarchy,* 83; Gilbert and Gubar, *Madwoman,* 69.

Spencer, Smith, and Gibbons, the bad belle is most often a beautiful and intelligent mother figure (reflecting her potential influence on a younger generation and the longevity of the stereotype that the writers are finally laying to rest), who has learned to succeed in the male world by using her manners, charm, and looks to manipulate men. In contemporary literature, the stereotype that links sexuality and blackness is no longer as important as it was to antebellum and Renascence writers, and this change reflects changing southern race relations. But other stereotypes have taken its place. Instead of associating the bad belle's dangerous sexuality with African blood, these writers associate it with class. The femmes fatales in these novels are often women of lower classes seeking to improve their economic and social standing and using their sexuality as the means to climb. Over and over again, they are described with vampire imagery to insinuate both the vital physical energy their sexual appetites drain from their mates and the moral, financial, and social benefits they usurp. Even in modern times, open sexuality in women is looked down upon, as is free expression of voice (particularly outspoken women are considered trashy and unladylike). Recent controversies of daytime TV talk shows such as *Jerry Springer* show that these class stereotypes still persist. On these shows, working-class people, usually women, loudly share their unconventional sexual exploits with millions of viewers. Ellen Willis, who writes commentary for the *Nation,* argues that these working-class people are being exploited by the media and by the dominant middle classes so the rest of us can feel "superior." The middle class views working-class Americans as sexually deviant, indiscreet, and unintelligent, and the talk shows spotlight such traits.[4] Because of their class and social climbing, the femmes fatales of contemporary southern women writers are not southern belles in the traditional sense. Perhaps "would-be" belles is a better name for them, because in their efforts to climb, they use the same techniques as the belles gone bad already discussed.

One can debate whether this class bias reflects personal shortcomings and lingering stereotypical assumptions held by the women authors. Perhaps, instead, Welty, Spencer, Smith, and Gibbons self-consciously use their would-be belles as types or symbols of the silencing denigration soci-

---

4. Hélène Cixous, "The Laugh of the Medusa" in *Feminisms,* 338; Ellen Willis, "Bring in the Noise," in *Reading Culture: Contexts for Critical Reading and Writing,* Diana George and John Trimbur, eds. (New York: Longman, 1999), 37.

ety has traditionally heaped on women's self-expression. Numan V. Bartley argues that by the 1980s, "the most self-consciously southern of southerners had come to be not defenders of the old regime but promoters of the new order."[5] These writers do not embrace this disparaging label—that an assertive, outspoken, and sexual woman is of lower moral and social standing—on the literal level, but they use the character as a parody of this stereotype to call attention to it and to exorcize through its destruction what it represents to the writers' creative psyches. For the bad belle is not only dangerous to men, she is dangerous to other women as well. By killing off these characters, the women writers destroy the stereotypes through which patriarchal society limits feminine self-expression.

Rather than contrast the bad belle with a weaker woman who follows the rules, as the Southern Renascence writers did, contemporary southern women pair her with a daughter figure, usually an intelligent and talented young artist. Through the young girl's struggle to escape her threatening mother, the contemporary women writers portray their own efforts to escape the limiting roles imposed on them by traditional southern society. But in addition to their personal escape, by literally or figuratively destroying the bad belle, these writers free themselves and the next generation of women writers, symbolically represented by the girls in the texts, from the weight of centuries of negative literary representations of women. By destroying the bad belles in their works, these four contemporary southern women writers kill the mother both within the text and without. Not only does the daughter's rejection of the mother within the text enact the normal (according to Freud) oedipal rebellion by which the child establishes its autonomy, but it also enacts the author's mutiny against her literary precursors' representations of women.[6]

The contemporary woman writers' destruction of the bad belle differs from that of the nineteenth-century writer in that the proper patriarchal power structure is not reasserted at the end. According to the Freudian model of gender-identity development, which examines dynamics in traditional families, "Only he [the father] can connect the daughter to the public world. . . . Yet he can withdraw his permission at any time, especially if she attempts to bring the mother (female identity) into that world." In

5. Bartley, *New South*, 449.

6. The dynamic described here resembles Harold Bloom's theory of the anxiety of influence, whereby the writer overthrows his literary forefather through his writing, resisting the elder's influence in a type of oedipal rebellion.

these traditional mother-father pairings, the mother represents physical and emotional comfort but also "all that is not civilized and not rational."[7] We can see this model represented in the plots of nineteenth-century southern women writers and in the lives and works of Southern Renascence women writers. Though Glasgow, Scott, and Mitchell all expressed a deeper sympathy for their nurturing and passive mothers, in their temperaments and in their public roles they more closely resembled their strong, authoritarian fathers. And in these Renascence writers' works, their femmes fatales make the same choice or, in some cases, they model themselves after equally unattractive and assertive mothers, as do Glasgow's Annabel and Stanley. The younger daughters (May, Bonnie Blue) in these works face the unattractive options of following in their mother's footsteps, thereby learning to manipulate the male system, or being swallowed by the strong lady's desire to control. Only in Gordon's late Renascence work do we see that there may be an alternate path.

In their works, contemporary southern women writers revise these patterns of influence whereby strong women must reject their mothers and identify, at least in their actions, with their fathers or whereby they must follow their manipulative mother's example. In the works by Welty, Spencer, Smith, and Gibbons that are examined, the father figure, though loving, is weak and ineffectual and therefore not a useful role model for the would-be artist. After rejecting the bad mother, and lacking a strong father, the daughter-artist heroines seem to create themselves. They become, in a sense, their own artistic creations, a symbolic embodiment of the work the writer herself creates.

EUDORA WELTY

The career of Eudora Welty (1909–2001), the earliest of the contemporary writers examined, began in the Southern Renascence, and in some ways she can be seen, like Caroline Gordon, as a transitional writer. Her late work, however, more closely fits the paradigm working in Spencer's, Smith's, and Gibbons's use of the bad belle. Welty does not describe facing the same derision from editors and publishers at her career's beginning as do other women writers of her generation, perhaps because she met her friend and

---

7. Jane Flax, "Postmodernism and Gender Relations in Feminist Theory," *Signs* 12 (1987): 634, 631.

literary agent Diarmuid Russell early on. In her autobiography *One Writer's Beginnings* (1984), Welty mentions her father's objections to her planned career as writer, but his disapproval seems to have been based primarily on concern for her financial well-being and distrust of fiction itself: "Though he was a reader, he was not a lover of fiction, because fiction is not true, and for that flaw it was forever inferior to fact. If reading fiction was a waste of time, so was the writing of it" (*OWB* 89). Her father objected to fiction writing, not necessarily to a woman writing fiction. Though he did give financial support for her education and very early career, only her mother gave emotional support (*OWB* 88). Her father's death, when she was in her early twenties, deprived Welty of the opportunity to prove to him that she could be a successful writer and to hear his words of praise (*OWB* 89).

Perhaps because her father died just before her career began, fathers in Welty's works are not portrayed as limiting patriarchal figures. As Louise Westling notes, "There is no hostility to males, but they are always seen from outside; fathers are beloved but peripheral or dead or dying."[8] Women, on the other hand, are much stronger and more central in both her life and work. In her autobiography, Welty writes of visiting her mother's family home in West Virginia as a child, where her grandmother and mother preside over a cluster of adoring and unruly uncles, "the boys" (*OWB* 57–58). She also reminisces about influential female teachers, particularly Miss Duling, the principal of her elementary school. Exercising authority over adults and children of Jackson, Mississippi, alike, Miss Duling had come alone from Kentucky because of her love of teaching, the challenge provided by Mississippi schools, and presumably the chance for independence. As Welty tells us, "She's not the only teacher who has influenced me, but Miss Duling, in some fictional shape or form, has stridden into a larger part of my work than I'd realized until now. She emerges in my perhaps inordinate number of school teacher characters. I loved those characters in the writing" (*OWB* 26). Most of the female authority figures in Welty's works show the same firmness and caring that her real-life role models, her mother, grandmother, and teachers, provided in her life. And perhaps her strong daughter-artist characters, who seem to create themselves without role models, are at least in part inspired by Miss Duling, the ultimate authority in the young girl's education, who appears detached from all per-

8. Louise Westling, "Fathers and Daughters in Welty and O'Connor," in *The Female Tradition in Southern Literature*, 116.

sonal connections of family or romance. Welty says that she identifies with these strong, independent, and devoted women who often appear in her works as mother-teacher characters and sometimes as daughter–budding artist characters (*OWB* 110).

But strong women are not always positive role models in Welty's work. And these negative examples demonstrate Welty's awareness of the obstacles that strong women often face in southern society. Like many other southern women writers, Welty uses the bad belle as a hyperbolic version of society's traditional view of powerful women, an image that the woman artist must escape to pursue her craft. In *The Robber Bridegroom* (1942) and *The Optimist's Daughter* (1972), a daughter-artist character struggles against a highly sexual, threatening mother figure, threatening because she embodies all the negative stereotypes of strong, independent women in a traditional society—coldness, manipulativeness, deceit, moral depravity—the very characteristics that allowed the bad belles of the Southern Renascence to survive. But her negative aspects are threatening not only because she exerts control over the daughter-artist, acting as a barrier to her attempts at self-expression and creative growth, but also because in her capacity as mother she (actively or passively) threatens to mold the daughter in her own image. In both of these works, Welty undermines the power of the traditional femme fatale by making her a comic figure or a grotesque and by literally or figuratively destroying her at novel's close.

In *Robber Bridegroom,* a very early work, Welty employs and destroys her version of the bad belle, but the author does not, as she will in her late work, grant complete autonomy to the daughter-artist, placing her instead under the seemingly more benevolent influence of a masculine hero. This novella, set in the frontier days of Mississippi's Natchez Trace and filled with mythic, historical, and literary allusions, has a fairy-tale quality, enhanced by the character Salome, who is in part the classic wicked stepmother and in part the evil seductress whose name she bears. The fact that Welty first engages the femme fatale character in a work that draws on fantasy and fairy tale rather than on the tradition of domestic realism that characterizes most of her works suggests that she is consciously exploring exaggerated feminine types here. The biblical Salome, one of the earliest examples of the femme fatale made even more infamous by Oscar Wilde's 1893 drama, dances for the delight of the lustful King Herod and so enchants him that he grants her any favor she might request. Prompted by her mother, she requests and is given John the Baptist's head on a platter.

Interestingly, Salome's mother prompts her evil deeds, just as the femme fatale mother in contemporary southern women's writing threatens to indoctrinate her daughter in her stereotypical methods. Here, Welty is at once revising the Bible and a traditional fairy tale, two sources that have been used for generations to indoctrinate children into the society's values and gender roles.

Unlike her namesake and unlike her southern literary predecessors, however, Welty's Salome is not physically alluring. In fact, she is so ugly that the Indians who capture and kill her first husband are frightened of her and set her free (*RB* 23). But Margaret Mitchell tells us that even Scarlett was not beautiful, only enchanting, and Welty exaggerates the typical incongruities of the femme fatale character to point out its absurdity. Despite her grotesque appearance, Salome exhibits the behavior of the traditional femme fatale. After the Indian attack, Welty tells us, she has nothing "left but ambition in her destroyed heart" (*RB* 24). And so Salome convinces Clement Musgrove, who along with his young daughter also survived the attack, to marry her. Salome is obviously the more powerful of the pair, growing stronger as her husband grows weaker, seeming to sap his strength in the night, like a female vampire, and transferring that energy into her own acquisitiveness. Under cover of darkness, this would-be belle uses her body to extort material comforts from her husband: "Salome, my new wife, entreated me in the night to build a better house, like the nearest settler's, and so I did" (*RB* 25), and "he remembered how in her times of love Salome was immeasurably calculating and just so, almost clocklike" (*RB* 27). Salome uses the same tools as Scarlett, less subtly, for her survival. Nineteenth-century doctors regularly attributed this vampire-like quality to the nymphomaniac, who could, they said, "suck the life and exhaust the vitality of her male partner." And Peter Schmidt points out that "the obverse of an infantile fantasy of women as eternal breast is women as a sexual vampire, smothering the male and draining him of vital fluids rather than providing him with them."[9] Welty—as will Spencer, Smith, and Gibbons— links the woman's sexuality to a more material need that enervates her husband. The woman's insatiable desire is for wealth and social prestige as much as, or sometimes instead of, sex. The writers invoke the stereotypes that link sexuality with lower classes and manipulation with femininity. By eventually destroying the bad belle, they challenge these connections.

9. Showalter, *Sexual Anarchy*, 180; Peter Schmidt, *The Heart of the Story: Eudora Welty's Short Fiction* (Jackson: University Press of Mississippi, 1991), 65.

Through the other side of Salome's persona, the wicked stepmother, Welty plays on another ancient stereotype that labeled bright, outspoken women as witches. Based on no clear evidence, Salome is able to instruct her husband to buy and sell at exactly the right times, so they soon become wealthy landowners. And she also uses her powers against her stepdaughter, Rosamond. Like the wicked stepmother in the "Snow White" fairy tale, Salome envies the girl who is her opposite in almost every way: "Rosamond was as beautiful as the day, Salome was as ugly as the night" (*RB* 33). She sends her stepdaughter into the dangerous woods, as did the queen in "Snow White," hoping she will be killed. Like fairy tales and like the nineteenth-century novels already examined, Welty's *Robber Bridegroom* invokes the opposites of light and dark to designate good and evil. But as the antebellum southern women writers hinted, dark and light, good and evil, are just parts of one whole. This suspicion prompts Musgrove's musings on the contrast between his beautiful first wife and Salome: "All things are divided in half—night and day, the soul and body, and sorrow and joy and youth and age, and sometimes I wonder if even my own wife has not been the one person all the time, and I loved her beauty so well at the beginning that it is only now that the ugliness has struck through to beset me like a madness" (*RB* 126).

Musgrove's analysis of his situation resembles Gilbert and Gubar's reading of the "Snow White" tale, in which the wicked stepmother queen is just an older, disillusioned version of the good, dead queen who was Snow White's mother. Having internalized the king's voice in the mirror, the queen becomes jealous of Snow White, who represents all the stepmother once was and is no longer. Men, the seven dwarves and the prince, help Snow White survive the older woman's onslaught, but male society created the rage that inspires the evil deeds and that threatens Snow White in the first place. Unfortunately, Snow White, once she marries the prince, is destined to become the queen, whose disillusionment will eventually turn to evil rage: "There is, after all, no female model for her in this tale except the 'good' (dead) mother and her living avatar the 'bad' mother."[10] Likewise, in Welty's tale, Rosamond is not only in danger of the harm that may befall her in the woods because of her stepmother's evil designs, but, should she survive, she is also in danger of following in her stepmother's footsteps, of being forced into the niche society has carved for the powerful woman who does not fit her designated role.

10. Gilbert and Gubar, *Madwoman*, 38–42.

Like Salome, Rosamond is a powerful, creative woman. But whereas Salome directs her creative energies to the acquisition of wealth, Rosamond is an artist figure. The girl sings beautiful songs and creates fantastic stories, for which, in her traditional life, she finds no audience. After being sent by her stepmother on a dangerous errand in the woods, Rosamond returns safely with a tale of a giant mother panther who carried her home in its mouth:

> [S]he did not mean to tell anything but the truth, but when she opened her mouth in answer to a question, the lies would simply fall out like diamonds and pearls. Her father had tried scolding her, and threatening to send her away to the Female Academy, and then marching her off without her supper, but none of it had done any good, and so he let her alone. Now and then he remarked that if a man could be found anywhere in the world who could make her tell the truth, he would turn her over to him. Salome, on the other hand, said she should be given a dose of Dr. Peachtree. (*RB* 38–39)

Welty presents here the alternatives for a young talented woman. As we have seen in chapter 1, a young lady at a female academy learned, among other things, to avoid the temptation of reading novels—books of lies—and to be properly reserved in her own written correspondence. A traditional education at a female academy would, therefore, teach Rosamond to be suitably retiring and submissive, and if that failed, a strong husband would surely silence her. As a last resort, physical violence administered through a peach-tree switch would curb her tongue. Welty's ironic voice lies behind these remedies. The author's and the reader's sympathies are clearly with the young artist, but both the father, the representative of male authority, and the stepmother, the stereotypical negative image of female strength, would silence Rosamond's artistic expression, her lies "like diamonds and pearls." In Welty's novel, however, the father, already under the power of a strong female and doting on his beautiful daughter, is not the major obstacle. Salome's wicked influence is the greater threat.

Welty shows that even now, in their strong, independent natures, Salome and Rosamond have much in common. To Musgrove's threat of a tutor, Rosamond responds, "Never! I will learn it all for myself" (*RB* 39). Similarly, Salome, who has directed her husband's life throughout their married years, defies the first person to try to control her, her Indian captor: "'No one is to have power over me!' Salome cried, shaking both her fists in the smoky air. 'No man, and none of the elements! I am by myself in the world'" (*RB* 160–61). She is a woman without male control: dangerous, erratic, and evil. Rosamond, though sweeter, is also defiant and uncontrolled and represents a similar latent threat. But Welty shows the pair growing close as mother and daughter only when, desperate to see her mysterious lover's face, Rosamond takes the advice of her evil stepmother: "There has to be a first time for everything, and at that moment the stepmother gave Rosamond a look of true friendship, as if Rosamond too had got her man by unholy means" (*RB* 122). In a variation of the Psyche and Eros myth, Salome gives Rosamond a potion to remove the berry stains from her bandit lover's face, and, as in the myth, he deserts his lover for her betrayal, jumping out the window.

As her beloved disappears, Rosamond realizes the mistake of following her evil stepmother's advice. But here, rather than allowing the artist figure to thrive on her own, as will happen in a later novel, Welty abandons her feminist message, relinquishing Rosamond to male control. Finding herself on her own after everyone she knows has been captured by Indians, instead of taking advantage of her independence to sing her songs and tell her stories, Rosamond seeks Jamie, her bandit-lover, to whom she speaks only the truth. Already visibly pregnant, Rosamond abandons her creative voice to create babies, as a good wife should. Upon seeing her father after many years, she happily describes her new middle-class life that is almost comically commonplace in this tale of magic and fantasy: "Jamie Lockhart was now no longer a bandit but a gentleman of the world in New Orleans, respected by all that knew him, a rich merchant in fact. . . . They were the parents of beautiful twins . . . and they lived in a beautiful house of marble and cypress wood on the shores of Lake Pontchartrain, with a hundred slaves, and often went boating with other merchants and their wives, the ladies reclining under a blue silk canopy; and they sailed sometimes out on the ocean to look at the pirates' galleons" (*RB* 183–84). No longer the daring bandit and his stolen bride, Jamie and Rosamond are a settled married couple who now, like the rest of society, imagine the bold exploits of real pirates from the comfort and safety of conventional lives. Though Welty restores Rosamond to patriarchal control, she does not silence her voice entirely. When Rosamond's father questions the truth of her tale, she takes him "to see for himself, and it was all true but the blue canopy" (*RB* 184). Her creative voice adds the one dash of color to her ordinary life.

This early tale of Welty's ends conventionally, with a happy marriage. And as male authority is restored, the evil female is destroyed. The biblical

Salome's power lay in her seductive dance, and in her final act of defiance, Welty's Salome also dances. But Salome's more closely resembles the self-destructive, mad dance of the queen in "Snow White." Salome's rebellion reaches Luciferian proportions as she boasts to her Indian captors that even the sun obeys her command to stand still, and she proceeds to dance until it will do so. But the sun is a male god, and he continues to rise despite her frenzied movements. Salome's dance, this strong but evil woman's independent artistic expression, is a futile defiance of ultimate male authority that finally ends in her own undoing. She dances herself to death.

Welty's early attempt to revise a fairy tale and to revise her Southern Renascence predecessors is, from a feminist standpoint, disappointing. Although she seems to recognize the limiting stereotypes implied in each of these earlier forms and to recognize, as will her literary heirs, the threat the stereotypes pose for the young woman writer, she finally resorts to an orthodox ending, marriage and death for the unconventional female characters, that more closely resembles the novels of nineteenth-century women writers.

In her last novel, *The Optimist's Daughter*, Welty again destroys the bad belle, this time figuratively, but here the artist-daughter figure remains independent. In this most autobiographical of her fiction, perhaps, Welty finally liberates herself from the cultural conceptions the bad belle parodies. As the heroine, Laurel McKelva Hand, comes to terms with her own past, the reader can see that it is the author's past as well. Published first as a story in the *New Yorker* just after the illness and death of Welty's mother, this book depicts the West Virginia homeland of Laurel's mother, which is in many details identical to that of Welty's mother's as described in *One Writer's Beginnings*. Though the main character differs from the author in many ways, this fictional artist figure is, perhaps, an exaggerated projection of Welty's anxieties about her profession as writer.

Laurel, a widowed designer, lives in Chicago, where she had gone to college and married another artist. She seldom sees her family, even after the death of her mother leaves her elderly father on his own, and she is therefore surprised when he marries a much younger woman. As the novel opens, Laurel visits her father after a year-and-a-half absence to accompany him and his wife to an eye specialist for vision problems he has recently experienced. His increased frailty, coupled with Laurel's sense that the young wife, Fay, is not worthy of him, awaken Laurel's feelings of guilt. Fay herself puts accusatory words to Laurel's suppressed feelings. As they both take a break from tending the Judge following his eye surgery, Laurel goes to her stepmother's room to find out more about her. All her relatives have died back in Texas, Fay says. "Oh, I wouldn't have run off and left anybody that needed me. Just to call myself an artist and make a lot of money" (*OD* 37). Fay would never dream of calling herself an artist, so these words are a direct attack on Laurel.

Fay is not the only one to accuse Laurel. The day after her father's funeral, the neighbor ladies sit on the porch of his home, keeping Laurel company and disparaging the Judge's young widow. Finally, her father's elderly friend, Mrs. Pease, says what all appear to be thinking: "Laurel is who should have saved him from that nonsense. Laurel shouldn't have married a naval officer in wartime. Laurel should have stayed home after Becky died. He needed him somebody *in* that house, girl" (*OD* 136–37). Though Welty never married and never moved away from her Mississippi home, perhaps she felt the same tensions between family and career that Laurel did. Lucinda H. MacKethan links Laurel's guilt to the guilt Welty describes in *One Writer's Beginnings*, when she first begins traveling to New York to publish her stories: "The torment and guilt—the torment of having the loved one go, the guilt of being the loved one gone—comes into my fiction as it did and does into my life. And most of all the guilt then was because it was true: I had left to arrive at some future and secret joy, at what was unknown, and what was now in New York, waiting to be discovered. My joy was connected with writing; that was as much as I knew" (*OWB* 103).[11] Welty, however, appears to have handled these emotions differently than did her character. From 1955 to 1970, during the long illnesses of her brothers and her mother, Welty published nothing but a children's book. In *Optimist's Daughter*, she perhaps works out her feelings toward the obligations that interrupted her own work for fifteen years by imagining a woman who neglected them.

But Welty does not condemn Laurel. She allows her the freedom to do what she herself was unable to do. And Welty grants her this freedom by destroying the symbolic representation of the negative traits society attributes to women who place their own desires above those of others. Fay is a comic belle gone bad, almost a grotesque, like Salome of *Robber Bride*. Younger than her new stepdaughter, she—like many of her nineteenth- and

11. Lucinda H. MacKethan, *Daughters of Time: Creating Woman's Voice in Southern Story* (Athens: University of Georgia Press, 1990), 55.

twentieth-century precursors—is a classic gold digger who marries up in the world, having met the Judge while working in the secretarial pool. But as with Salome, Fay's social leap seems to be greater than that of any of the early bad belles we have seen, and her overt sexuality is portrayed as a direct indication of her lack of breeding. In women, unconstrained passion of any type, whether expressed physically or verbally, signifies the lower classes. We see an early representation of this idea in Faulkner's *The Sound and the Fury* (1929), where Caddy's and her daughter Quentin's promiscuity and their unwillingness to hide it accompanies, and perhaps speeds, their family's social and economic decline. As racial differences and stereotypes lost some of their meaning in the second half of the twentieth century, other biases seem to have taken their place in southern conceptions of sexuality.

All surface and selfishness, Fay is a parody of society's image of independent-minded women. As Welty herself said of Fay in an interview with Gayle Graham Yates, "You could scratch the skin and there wouldn't be anything under it, the way she would see things. And to me, that is horrifying and evil, almost sinful."[12] Welty self-consciously uses this character as a symbol of "evil," not of feminine evil, but of the evil society enacts against women through such silencing clichés as Fay herself. Her selfishness and superficiality are at first so extreme that the reader cannot take her seriously, indicating her parodic function. To the doctor's explanation of her husband's condition and the necessary eye surgery, Fay's only response is "I don't see why this had to happen to me" (*OD* 15). And during his slow recovery, Fay becomes petulant and abusive because the Judge does not rise from his hospital bed to take her dancing. Her selfishness reaches a destructive height when, on her birthday, she screams at him that "enough is enough!" and attempts to pull him from the bed. The shock proves too much for the old man, and he silently passes away.

Despite her selfishness and superficiality, Fay has managed to capture Judge McKelva's heart. Though Laurel cannot understand what her father saw in Fay, the reader cannot miss it. The green stiletto-heel shoes and matching dangling earrings with which Fay tries to tempt the Judge from what turns out to be his deathbed are talismans of her dangerous sexuality, fit for the original Salome. Later, when Laurel and Fay return to the family home and Laurel wakes Fay, the stepdaughter is shocked to see the sensu-

12. Gail Graham Yates, "My Visit with Eudora Welty" in *More Conversations with Eudora Welty*, Prenshaw, ed. (Jackson: University Press of Mississippi, 1996), 97.

ous peach satin covering the windows and bed in what was formerly Laurel's parents' dignified bedroom. And here she also notes the same green shoes "placed like ornaments on top of the mantel shelf" above the bed (*OD* 75). Fay uses her femininity and sexuality—the classic tools of the femme fatale—as a lure. Underneath her feminine exterior, however, she is not compliant and self-sacrificing, as a true lady would be.

Laurel later hears from the town ladies of her father and Fay "billing and cooing" scandalously over Sunday dinners at the Iona Hotel. These same catty women who rip Fay to shreds wonder why "all the men think they need to *protect* her" (*OD* 136). Like the dangerously seductive women characters of earlier southern women writers, Fay exploits gender stereotypes to use the patriarchy's power against itself. Ruth M. Vande Kieft sees this same social criticism implicit in the Judge's relationship with Fay: "Judge McKelva's protective love leads to a need to indulge women (a possible indictment on Welty's part of superficial southern male gallantry). This turns into a form of self-indulgence as he marries his second wife, the cheap, self-centered Fay Chisom."[13] Because Fay appears small and vulnerable, like Glasgow's Annabel and Stanley, men want to help her, and she takes advantage of this desire.

In connection with sexuality, Welty uses the one African American character in the novel in a way that marks a transition between Southern Renascence women writers' treatment of race in relation to the bad belle and that of later contemporary women writers. In the Southern Renascence works discussed in chapter 3, black women characters were often used as silent shadow figures who knowingly observed the actions of the bad belles and registered for the reader the guilt the seductresses themselves did not feel. Through this association, the early twentieth-century writers called attention to southern stereotypes that proclaimed the promiscuity (while hiding the sexual violation) of African American women. Welty uses Missouri, the judge's black housekeeper, in a similar way. It is Missouri who disapprovingly tells Laurel that Fay habitually sleeps late and has breakfast in bed, an indication of her sensuality, her laziness, and her attempts to climb the social ladder (Missouri does not want to wait on the unworthy woman because of Fay's background, but she does it for the Judge); and it is Missouri who sends Laurel upstairs to find the seductive transformations

13. Ruth M. Vande Kieft, "The Love Ethos of Porter, Welty, and McCullers" in *The Female Tradition in Southern Literature,* 250.

wrought by Fay on the bedroom (*OD* 73–74). Later, however, Missouri's support helps Laurel overcome the negative influence of the bad belle. Missouri helps shoo from the house a chimney swift that haunted Laurel through the night, a symbolic action for the artist's overcoming her guilt at having left her family (*OD* 194–95). This nurturing role of a black domestic servant will appear more clearly in Smith's and Gibbons's work.

Missouri's nurturing role is minimal in this novel, and Laurel must do the real work of freeing herself. In her symbolic capacity, Fay attracts all the condemnation that Laurel, and perhaps Welty, fear. Fay is not only a seductress, she, like Welty, is also a master at fabricating tales. When Fay's large and boisterous family arrives for the Judge's funeral, the reader learns that Fay lied when she told Laurel all her family was dead. In *Robber Bridegroom*, Welty links Rosamond's lies to creative self-expression. Fay's lies, however, highlight her selfishness and hypocrisy. Welty's point may be that any woman who expresses herself creatively runs the risk of society's censure, just as Rosamond reaped her parents' disapproval. Fay merely attempts to recreate herself, as Rosamond did and as Laurel will have to in the end to escape her guilt. As MacKethan points out, Fay, unlike Laurel, feels no guilt for her departure from home nor, apparently, any compunction for the lie in which she named her family dead, but "Fay . . . can make Laurel feel like a betrayer, for Laurel has never reconciled her daughter self with her artist self."[14] Seeming to feel almost nothing, yet able to inspire anxiety in Laurel, Fay personifies Laurel's struggle with her own needs, the needs of her family and friends, and the community's negative stereotype of the independent woman. In short, Fay is the woman Laurel fears she will become, or fears the community will see her as, if she pursues her goals rather than theirs.

As with the wicked stepmother in *Robber Bridegroom*, Fay's greatest threat is her influence on the daughter-artist. But in *Optimist's Daughter*, the threat is not so much that Laurel will become Fay but that she will begin to see herself in the negative stereotype Fay embodies and guiltily relinquish her creativity. John Edward Hardy points out similarities between the two characters he believes Welty intends for her readers to notice. Both are widows in their forties, both are alone in the world, and both jettison the past. And Fay, like Laurel, goes to her family home after the funeral to settle her relationship with the past. In a moment of personal despair and

14. MacKethan, *Daughters of Time*, 93.

self-doubt, Laurel begins to identify similarities between herself and the woman she despises. Longing to tell her mother about Fay's role in her father's death, she realizes that this deed would equal any of Fay's in its selfishness: "Father, beginning to lose his sight, followed Mother, but who am I at the point of following but Fay? Laurel thought. The scene she had just imagined, herself confiding the abuse to her mother, and confiding it in all tenderness, was a more devastating one than all Fay had acted out in the hospital" (*OD* 157).[15] The daughter-artist secretly fears she is no better than the would-be belle.

Schmidt argues that "Welty's early stories explor[e] the different fates available to eccentric or 'mad' women . . . [as] an attempt to confront her own anxieties about how to validate her imaginative activity as a writer." He goes on to say that "Welty's best comedies, early or late, capture how women either resist or are petrified by stereotypes of the feminine." Throughout this late novel, Laurel's mother, Becky, stands as the counterpoint—the alternative—to Fay. The proper lady—who, significantly, is dead before the novel begins—Becky knew how to act and what to say in social situations, but perhaps more important, Becky knew when to say nothing at all. On the last night Laurel spends at home, trapped in her mother's sewing room while hiding from the chimney swift, she confronts the memory of her mother's suppressed rage that spilled forth near the end of her life. Having left her family in West Virginia to be with her husband in Mississippi, as Welty's mother had done, Becky longs to return to them on her deathbed. To the Judge's empty promise that he will take her there, Becky vents her pent-up rage at a lifetime of sacrifice: "'Lucifer!' she cried. '*Liar!*'" (*OD* 150). What Becky seems to be experiencing is guilt for having abandoned her family (she tearfully remembers her mother's sacrifices for her, hands bleeding from ice on the well in winter [*OD* 151]) and anger at having been required to do so. Welty's mother apparently suffered similar feelings near her death, peevishly demanding that an old piano be returned to the house so she could hear and sing a song of the West Virginia hills she had left long before (*OWB* 67). Becky and Welty's mother also share a love of literature, both having rescued volumes of Dickens's works from burning houses, but neither is able to indulge her own creative voice. According to Jan Nordby Gretland, "the main character of *One Writer's Beginnings* is

15. John Edward Hardy, "Marrying Down in Eudora Welty's Novels" in *Eudora Welty: Critical Essays,* Prenshaw, ed. (Jackson: University Press of Mississippi, 1979), 114.

named Chestina Andrews Welty [Eudora Welty's mother]; and the book's thematic drama is a coming to terms with the memory of the woman."[16] Perhaps in *Optimist's Daughter,* the novel written just after her mother's death, Welty also comes to terms with the memory of her mother, whose life was so much like that of her character Becky. Here Welty also comes to terms with the possibility of her mother's opposite, Fay, the woman she might fear becoming if she does not follow in her mother's footsteps. What Laurel, and perhaps Welty, seem to learn from the night alone in Becky's sewing room is that everyone has had to leave someone behind and that a life of self-denial rewards no one in the end. She owes it to her mother's memory and to herself to live her own life.

While both the image of the lady and the bad belle threaten the woman artist's liberation, Laurel's final confrontation with expectations takes place over a symbolic token of patriarchal heritage and masculine creativity. A breadboard, made by Laurel's husband's skilled and loving hands, has been defiled by Fay's careless use. Laurel, as she raises the symbolically and physically weighty breadboard above her head to strike Fay, suddenly realizes the power that lies within herself and makes her stronger than her stepmother. Hitting Fay with this heavy piece of handcraft would not only bring Laurel down to Fay's level, but it would also mean a retreat to the fortress of patriarchal family, symbolized by the breadboard her husband made. She has her own art, she does not have to guard the family's creative past. It is her own creativity, Laurel realizes, that gives her the passion both to fight against her annexation by society's expectations and to love those who were part of that society. Her recognition of her strength in contrast to Fay's emptiness allows her figuratively to destroy the bad belle, the image that threatens to silence all independent women. Leaving the breadboard behind, she flies back to her Chicago art world, her memories safe but unencumbered by self-sacrificing devotion. In rejecting Fay, however, she also appears to reject sexuality altogether. Unlike her stepmother's milieu, which she disdains, Laurel's world (and Welty's?) is apparently asexual, and love lies buried with her husband. As a transitional writer between the Southern Renascence and more recent writers, Welty liberates the woman's voice, allowing her to express her ideas without the moral censure that pre-

---

16. Schmidt, *Heart of the Story,* xvi, 131; Jan Nordby Gretland, "An Interview with Eudora Welty," in *Conversations with Eudora Welty,* Prenshaw, ed. (Jackson: University Press of Mississippi, 1984), 171.

viously accompanied such freedom, but she cannot liberate her body. For Welty, artistic liberation seems to demand a sacrifice of sexuality.

Schmidt, writing of Welty's short stories, believes Welty encourages the reader to "evolve from identifying with a Medusa to identifying with a Sibyl, from self-destructive rage and guilt to empowering acts of disguise and revision."[17] This message is repeated in her last novel. In many ways, Welty is a transitional figure in southern women writers' efforts to critique their society and liberate themselves from its negative representations of women like them. Although Laurel escapes being silenced by male domination or being silenced by fear of the label "bad woman" more successfully than does Welty's Rosamond, her destruction of the bad belle image is only figurative and only in Laurel's mind. The image of Fay—the stereotypes associated with assertive female voice and sexuality—still lives on in Welty's Mississippi. Later contemporary writers Spencer, Smith, and Gibbons depict the struggle to create more overtly and portray the struggle's outcome more optimistically through a more literal destruction of the bad belle. These later writers also free their daughter-artist characters at an earlier stage in life and show their readers the artistic products of the woman artist's liberation.

ELIZABETH SPENCER

Elizabeth Spencer (1921–) writes and speaks of the tension she experienced when her talent led her in directions other than those her family and her Mississippi community had envisioned for her. Spencer's decision to become a writer caused great distress for her parents, who were actually disappointed when she telephoned home from Italy with news of the contract for her first book, *Fire in the Morning* (1948), because, as Spencer says in her memoir, "They had thought I might be engaged" (*LH* 189). Her parents imagined a traditional life for their daughter, one that involved an early marriage, several children, and perpetuation of the female values and roles with which she had been reared. Consequently, when they read her first book, they were ashamed of their young, unmarried daughter's use of profanity and her knowledge of sex (*LH* 191). Rather than surrender to the pressures of home, Spencer left after being home from Italy for only two days. The young southern woman writer experienced similar disapproval

---

17. Schmidt, *Heart of the Story*, 263.

from southerners outside her family. Southern Agrarian Donald Davidson, Spencer's professor at Vanderbilt, told her, upon learning of her desire to write, that she would do better to get married (*LH* 188). Although Spencer was not compelled to put her writing career on hold, as was Welty, and though she distanced herself from the expectations of her community by moving with her British husband to Canada, the fact that this early discouragement surfaces in interviews, in her recently published memoir, and in her latest novel shows that its effects have lingered.

Like Welty, Spencer uses the bad belle to parody and finally exorcize these confining expectations. Also like Welty, Spencer's most successful use of this figure comes in her latest novel, but she explores the threatening aspects of the bad belle less successfully in an earlier work, the short story, "Judith Kane" (1968). In this story the title character is an aesthetic "creation" who destructively manipulates men. In her narcissism, Judith rivals Scott's Julia; she loves most her own image reflected back to her in another's eyes. The ending of the story, however, leaves both the narrator and the reader unsatisfied because the wraith-like Judith is left roaming the dusk toward the man who both fears and desires her. But her power also touches the female narrator, who seems to be the voice of the young Elizabeth Spencer: "Where would she lead him to, where would she drop him when she moved furiously on to some other high perch, to astonish and confound whoever found her there? My heart filled up with dread. For him, I guess; that was where the dread started, but it had a way of spreading: it was more than just for him" (JK 258). The young woman's dread is also for herself, who had earlier looked to Judith as a role model of independence and an object of envy because of her great beauty. The bad belle's menace is not exorcized from this tale, and she continues to haunt the narrator at its close, Judith having literally stolen the last bit of the narrator's story when she forces her to confess that she cared for Judith's latest conquest. Because the bad belle escapes unscathed and we see her detrimental effect on the artist figure, this story resembles that of the Southern Renascence writers discussed earlier.

Spencer finally exorcizes the negative stereotypes embodied by the bad belle in a late work, *The Night Travellers* (1991). One of the most intriguing characters in this Vietnam War novel, a work populated by intriguing characters, is Kate, an aging belle gone bad. Kate is a trained scientist, doing animal research with chemical weapons, and it is her combination of beauty, coldness, and intelligence that men find so frighteningly fascinating. In *Night*

Travellers, through Kate and her daughter, Mary, Spencer revisits the traditional figure of the femme fatale, dismantling it to open new space for the woman artist and to reverse some of the damage done by earlier misogynistic representations of women.

Elizabeth Spencer knows one incarnation of the femme fatale particularly well, the mermaid. Prenshaw has explored Spencer's use of this myth in the story "Ship Island" (1964), subtitled "The Story of a Mermaid," and Spencer has commented on her interest in the mermaid figure.[18] But the mermaid has a dark side that is relevant to the discussion of the femme fatale in southern women's writing. Like the siren and the undine, the mermaid lures sailors from their ships with her beauty and enchanting voice, leading them to their deaths in her watery home. Hans Christian Andersen's fairy tale "The Little Mermaid" presents a much tamer version of this seductress, who, after her alluring power is removed, transforms into another stereotype, the self-sacrificing angel. In exchange for a leg-growing potion, a witch cuts out the little mermaid's tongue, silencing the beautiful voice with which the mermaid planned to win the prince's heart. In Andersen's story, the little mermaid has no soul, and to gain one she must please the prince and become his bride. The story graphically displays the denial of female subjectivity by male representations of women, showing that a mind and a voice are things a good woman may have only through a man's patronage. In mermaid lore in general, it is the maid's beautiful voice, her creativity, that gives her the power to seduce men and lure them to their deaths; in a male-dominated culture, any woman with an independent voice is a dangerous woman.

But in *Night Travellers*, Spencer splits the two sides of the mermaid, the dangerous seductress from the artistic woman, giving them separate bodies in Kate, the belle gone bad, and in Kate's daughter, Mary, the dancer. Read this way, the two women become symbolic characters, the mother representing the women who silence other women, the daughter embodying the independent woman artist emerging from the shadow of male control. In other words, Kate is at once the bad belle within the novel, seducing and controlling men, and a symbolic embodiment of the bad belle in society, silencing the creative woman. By destroying the bad belle as character and

---

18. Prenshaw, *Elizabeth Spencer* (Boston: Twayne Publishers, 1985); Elizabeth Pell Broadwell and Ronald Wesley Hoag, "A Conversation with Elizabeth Spencer," in *Conversations with Elizabeth Spencer*, Prenshaw, ed. (Jackson: University Press of Mississippi, 1991), 71.

symbol, Spencer allows Mary, the artist, to stand alone. Free of the stifling representation that previously had defined and limited her, Mary gains subjectivity, a soul, and keeps her artistic voice. After Mary's desertion, Spencer registers the dangerous woman's decline, figuratively destroying the image by which women were labeled threatening objects of hate. In doing so, she frees the woman artist, herself and Mary, from the negative stereotypes associated with feminine creative power, allowing her to speak her own voice for her own purposes.

Mary Kerr Harbison dances from earliest childhood. Her dance teachers covet her presence in their classes, one even begging to teach her "free of charge" when her mother claims they can no longer afford lessons (*NT* 13). For this slight girl, "an essence with nothing solid about her" (*NT* 5), dancing is more than a hobby, it is her primary mode of expression. An only child with a distant mother and a sickly father, Mary has learned to keep quiet. When she has something to say, she says it with her feet. Likewise, in Andersen's "Little Mermaid," after the maid has lost her tongue, she expresses herself through dance "as none had ever yet danced." But, in her case, though the prince is "enraptured by it," she still fails to touch his heart.[19] In her early life, Mary feels a strong devotion for her father, who is more approachable and tender than her mother. But when she attempts to express her feelings for him through the exuberance of dance, combining her two greatest loves, the results are catastrophic. Meeting her father walking home one hot summer day, she begins to dance, gaining his praise and admiration. Not strong enough to withstand the hot sun, however, her father suffers a heart attack, and after lingering only a short time, not long enough to tell Mary's mother it wasn't Mary's fault, he dies.

And Kate does blame Mary for his death. "Didn't you know better," she asks (*NT* 12), believing that Mary's dancing lured her father into the strong sun where he withered. Like the mermaid's, Mary's voice seems dangerous, and her mother's accusing coldness (she even brings it up again years later) almost silences her: "She was sinking down then, no higher than her mother's strong firm ankle, insect-sized on the gigantic stage of the world's business. Even back in the room, grasping his hand, she could not find her voice again" (*NT* 13). For the first time, the reader can see that Mary is out of her element in the everyday world. Next to her, Kate seems like a giant,

19. Hans Christian Andersen, "The Little Mermaid," in *Favorite Tales of Hans Andersen*, M. R. James, trans. (Boston: Faber and Faber, 1978), 94.

capable woman, who takes it upon herself to silence her daughter. Shortly after the funeral, she cancels Mary's dancing lessons, believing her instructor, Madame Delida, is a bad influence. And when Madame Delida comes to the house begging for the privilege of teaching Mary, Kate locks Mary in her room. Finally breaking free, Mary finds her teacher packing a trunk, and the older woman leaves her with these words: "This town will never be good to you, my treasure. You, too, will learn someday" (*NT* 14). This woman artist has learned the fear and scandal that the ordinary world attaches to her art, and she emphasizes that Mary, too, is an outsider. Just as the classic femme fatale image silenced generations of women artists, Kate, as symbolic character, stifles the creative voice of her daughter.

But Spencer hints that Kate herself may have played a role in weakening her husband. Don first notices Kate because she "had golden hair and was always like a princess" (*NT* 15), and she marries him because he is a law student from a prominent family. Soon after the marriage, however, his health begins to fade: "He was never robust and his sensitive face aged sooner than it should have. Most of his hair went early on" (*NT* 16). He seems to waste away as Kate grows more beautiful and vital. After an argument between Kate and Mary, he explains to Mary her mother's disappointments: "'Your mother,' he was going on, half to himself, 'deserved better than me'" (*NT* 6). When Mary does not understand his meaning, he laughs, telling her she will understand someday. Mary assumes that he means his health, but the reader senses that he also refers to his inability to satisfy such a strong, ravishing wife. Like Welty, Spencer uses vampire imagery to allude to the insatiable desire attributed to the femme fatale, and she ties this enervating quality to class. Not only does Kate exhaust her husband physically, but she depletes him financially as well. Born to a poor family of farmers, she married Don for his family's money and his earning potential, and she complained throughout their marriage of his inability to fulfill that potential. Once again, the strong, ambitious, and sexual woman is equated with lower classes and with gold digging. This association, Spencer implies, threatens to silence young women who would express themselves freely. Perhaps Don also hints darkly that Kate will one day destroy Mary as she destroyed him and then Mary will understand.

Spencer, however, does not treat Kate only as a stereotype or as a symbolic figure. The characters' concrete interactions within the text illustrate the destructive role this figure has on women's relationships with other women. From the independent woman's perspective, the most dangerous aspect of the bad belle is not that she seduces and destroys men in myth but that she seduces and destroys other women in reality. Women who see their beauty as their greatest strength must abandon potentially supportive relationships with other women for fear of diminishing their own enchanting power.

Learning more about Kate, the reader realizes that she has a cold and manipulative quality and seems to lack true motherly affection. Before Don's death, the father and daughter share a bond, which leaves Kate on the outside, and she is jealous of their love. Late in the novel, Mary, watching her mother from a distance, summarizes Kate's feelings: "[T]he lovely, impeccable, talented, efficient, desirable woman—waiting for the one true touch of the adoring, unchanging, passionate lover. For her there had never been a child. . . . Lover into father: what right did they have to change like that? Children take what lovers have, they take it right away" (*NT* 186–87). Kate's resentment of her daughter takes the form of physical and emotional abuse; she spanks Mary with a silver hairbrush and locks her in her bedroom or a closet as punishment. At times, though she is Mary's biological mother, Kate, like Welty's Salome, seems the wicked stepmother: "[E]very room she entered, there was never any doubt that Kate Harbison was the most attractive woman who could be there. *Mirror, mirror on the wall . . .*" (*NT* 286). As did Welty in *Robber Bridegroom,* Spencer revises this fairy tale, but instead of capitulating to a conventional marriage at the end, she eventually frees the daughter-artist. Like the aging queen of the fairy tale, jealous of Snow White's growing beauty, Kate resents Mary's influence over the men in her life. Again and again, she belittles her daughter and tries to get her out of the way. Kate not only wants the king to herself, she tries to seduce the prince as well.

A few years after Don's death, Kate begins to drink too much ("It was getting known about" [*NT* 34]) and to see other men. Her endeavors to find a new husband contain at once a pathetic and sinister quality, both of which stem from her awareness of playing a role: "On free afternoons, Kate Harbison would dress in her soft-colored silks with the sandals so neat and the stocking sheer, and in the corner on the chaise longue she would wait for somebody who just thought he might drop in . . . happy to find her with the lamplight spinning its web, an aureole soft around her bright hair, put up so skillfully. She might have been on a stage, playing out this part written for her, or somebody in a book" (*NT* 41). Like a beautiful black widow, she calmly awaits her prey; but the reader also senses that on many occasions there is no gentleman caller to witness her display. None of the men Kate meets is of suitable quality, and as soon as she becomes aware that her drinking and socializing interfere with her work, she ends the evening ritual.

Her daughter's boyfriend, however, though she does not approve of his politics, holds a special fascination she cannot shake. At the first family dinner to which Jefferson Blaise is invited, Kate subtly flirts with him, trying to unsettle and distract him from her daughter, for whom she believes he is a bad match (*NT* 49). But when Mary and Jeff's relationship develops despite Kate's objections, she invites him for a private meeting. Whether because she is attracted to him or because she is attempting to break up her daughter's liaison, Kate makes a pass at Jeff. Her beauty is not without its effect—Jeff later says she is the sexiest woman he ever saw (*NT* 76)—but he senses danger and breaks away to safety.

To Kate, then, Jeff becomes the one who got away, and she does not easily shake the image of this young, attractive man. She wonders, "However would Mary Kerr know what to do with him? What could the child understand about the nature I know he has?" (*NT* 83), and her nights are disturbed by erotic dreams of him. But soon Kate finds more suitable companionship and her attention turns, for a time, away from Mary and Jeff. On a business trip, she meets Fred Davis, a man she needs more than she loves: "What he had, of course, was obviously money" (*NT* 101). She needs Fred to take care of her in the manner she feels she deserves, and she plays her body like an ace in the early stages of their relationship, laying it down for him at exactly the right moment. As her interest in the new man increases, Kate begins to see Mary's dancing, which she had previously viewed as a childish hobby, as a means to get her daughter out of the way. She borrows money to send Mary away from Kingsbury to a dance school in Winston, and it is there, exiled by the dangerous woman's amorous manipulations, that Mary first comes to her own as an artist.

At the auditions, her moves so impress a famous dancer from New York that he joins her on stage during the audition. Away from her mother, Mary grows as an artist, and Kate begins to feel threatened by her daughter's independence. When she goes to see the school's program, Kate brings Fred along, thinking of it as a quaint family outing. The violence embodied by the recital, however, shocks and disturbs her. In a scene reminiscent of Sylvia Plath's "Daddy," the dancers play children rebelling against their mothers until, at the end, children and mothers join in an angry mob circling the one remaining holdout, chanting: "Mother, we're through.

Mother, you bitch, we're through" (*NT* 96). Instead of rebelling against the father, as Plath did, these young female dancers rebel against the bad mother, as Mary will eventually rebel against Kate and as contemporary women writers rebel against negative representations of women portrayed by their literary foremothers. Kate takes the piece personally, but even her distress works to her advantage in the new relationship. Finding her unusual vulnerability charming, Fred tells her she may "go all to pieces" if she wants to, adding, "Women crying . . . they're nice to hold" (*NT* 101). On the way home from Winston, they spend the night together for the first time, and not long after, he invites her to his New Jersey home, where they soon marry.

But the two halves of the mermaid, the seductress and the artist, once separated, are at odds. Again, just as the image of woman-as-evil often silences the voices of creative women, the symbolic bad belle mother tries to regain control of her independent daughter. As the traditional mermaid would think, what good is a beautiful voice unless you use it to lure sailors into the deep? Kate sees Mary's dancing as a way to catch the eye of a man of quality or to win a fellowship to a good school (where she may catch the eye of a man of quality). As Sally Greene points out, Kate attempts to impose on Mary the attributes of the southern belle, which make potent weapons in the hands of the bad belle.[20] In Kate's eyes, Mary wastes her time and her talent, throwing herself away on bohemian dance troupes and men without prospects, such as Jeff. Kate has an image in her mind of what Mary should be and later, when Mary comes to take her own daughter away from Kate, we see the physical proof of that image: "It was a full page torn from a magazine, a cigarette ad or some such. It showed a girl in a fluffy pure white dress standing with a boy in duck trousers and a yachting coat. They were leaning together, woodwork and graceful posts and peaked roof—so beautiful, both of them. So charming, social, entirely right. *It is what she'd dreamed I would be,* I thought" (*NT* 199). But Mary rejects the role of coquette, rebelling against all her mother represents, and pursues her art for its own sake.

Driven to a frenzy by her inability to control her daughter, Kate arrives at Mary's dorm drunk one afternoon, ranting about a political article written by Jeff's friends. When Mary refuses to be silenced by her diatribe, Kate

20. Sally Greene, "Re-Placing the Hero: *The Night Travellers* as Novel of Female Self-Discovery," *Southern Quarterly* 33 (1994).

becomes violent: "She hit so hard I had blood on my tongue. It was time to leave her, her mad, long, blond hair tearing out of the pins and coiling up into the wind" (*NT* 148). The mermaid's two parts, the seductress and the artist, clash; in this scene, the mother becomes a monstrously beautiful Medusa (another version of the femme fatale), hair coiling about her head, while the daughter is described as a slight urchin-like creature who cares only for Jeff and for the dance. As Virgie Rainey, a creation of Spencer's friend Eudora Welty, learns from a painting of Perseus and Medusa, for there to be heroes, there must also be victims.[21] For Mary to save herself, to become the powerful, creative woman she longs to be, she must break free of her mother, even if she must destroy her in doing so. Alone, Mary becomes the little mermaid on land, shorn of seductive powers, but, in Spencer's version, she is still able to speak her voice.

But the mermaid on land, especially without its manipulative powers, is vulnerable to man. Free of Kate, Mary's struggle still is not over. Though her lover, Jeff, never tries to stop her dancing (one attraction for Mary is that when she tells him she's a dancer, he takes her seriously [*NT* 25]), his own work is always more important. He tries to save the country from the war machine, while she is "into" dancing. Tellingly, the first time she dances for him, she cuts her foot in the sand, and the first time they embrace, he bruises her side. Rather than warning her, this pain seems to bind her to him: "It was the bruised spot that kept crying for him. I would hold my hand on it at night, but still it kept insisting" (*NT* 137). Like Andersen's Little Mermaid, who willingly accepts the tearing agony of growing legs to meet the prince, Mary cherishes her pain as a reminder of Jeff's presence. Andersen's mermaid, stripped of her power, becomes a self-sacrificing angel, whose only desire is to please the prince. Seidel explores the connection between this kind of masochism and the upbringing of the southern belle: "The narcissist, who is trained to seek the attention of men and who thereby develops only traits with which to do so and ignores and suppresses any others (such as assertiveness, intelligence, logic, confidence), is a person whose sense of worth is achieved only through the attention of others. If that attention is removed, the person is left feeling worthless, a failure, perhaps deserving of punishment for her inadequacies. Since punishment brings attention, negative though it is, such attention is preferable to no at-

21. Eudora Welty, "The Wanderers," in *The Golden Apples* (New York: Harcourt, Brace, 1949; reprint, New York: Harcourt Brace Jovanovich, 1977), 275.

tention at all."[22] The stereotype of the self-renouncing good woman is another means of seduction of which the woman artist must be wary.

Like the Little Mermaid, Mary sacrifices everything for Jeff. When they discover she is pregnant, Jeff wants to keep the baby, but Mary is unsure. She goes into the night alone to think: *"My body is all I have . . . using it, that's what's happening . . . making use of it"* (*NT* 152). Even if Jeff does not realize the sacrifice involved in their predicament, Mary does, and she contemplates escaping to a watery refuge, suicide. But the couple moves to Canada, where they marry, and Mary leaves behind her home and family. Pregnant, she also loses her ability to dance, her creative voice, like Welty's Rosamond.

In Canada, without a support system, Mary is first emotionally, then physically abandoned by Jeff. When, sick and tired, she loses interest in sex after the baby arrives, Jeff has an affair with their landlady and friend, Madeline. Then, feeling stifled by exile in Canada, Jeff returns to the United States to write for an underground newspaper. He leaves Mary behind to care for the baby, with only an unreliable network of war activists for support. As Dorothy Dinnerstein points out, Western culture, until very recently, sanctioned a division of labor through which men were identified with the lofty pursuits of the mind and women were identified with the mundane processes of the body.[23] Idealist that he is, Jeff pursues the life of the mind, the important work of shaping culture, leaving Mary at home to do the messy job of rearing his offspring. To add insult to injury, shortly after Jeff leaves, Mary finds a love note to him from Madeline, learning of the affair when she is unable to confront him. Isolated, surrounded by fair-weather friends and drugged hippies, Mary is again out of her element.

When Andersen's Little Mermaid fails to please the prince, when he pursues and then marries another, she dies, dissolving into sea foam. Likewise, Mary, abandoned by her husband and without the money to pay for the dancing that "balances" her, attempts to vanish from the cruel world in which she finds herself. Leaving her baby with a neighbor, she tries to hang herself from a heating pipe in her apartment, only to be cut down at the last moment by rescuers the vigilant neighbor summons. Given back her life, Mary must rediscover herself on her own terms. Without the interference

22. Seidel, *Southern Belle*, 36.
23. Dorothy Dinnerstein, *The Mermaid and the Minotaur: Sexual Arrangements and Human Malaise* (New York: Harper and Row, 1976), 133.

of her mother, the bad belle who represents society's fears and limitations of women, and without the man who sentences her to a life of domestic drudgery, the creative woman begins to emerge on her own. Mary establishes a circle of friends and begins to dance again. Rediscovering her artistic voice is a major part of Mary's healing, and the first thing she does when released by the authorities is borrow money for dance lessons. As if to mark her rebirth, Mary Kerr adopts a new stage name, Marie Caree, by which she becomes known as a talented professional. Mary never relinquishes her love for Jeff, and as they renew their relationship on more equal footing, Spencer allows the young woman artist positive sexual expression as well. But Mary finds her center in herself, establishing her independence and self-worth while focusing on her art.

Mary's escape from home marks the beginning of her journey to independence, but it also marks the beginning of her mother's decline. Spencer, however, allows the reader to see enough of Kate to view her as a victim. In allowing the reader to feel sympathy for the bad belle and making her a well-developed character rather than a one-dimensional grotesque, Spencer differs from Welty. In Spencer's version, we can see the would-be belle both as a type representing all such images of women in literature and in life and as a real woman seduced into adopting the strategies of the femme fatale. Though Kate is a capable scientist, at home she never talks of her work, cherishing instead a vision of her own allure: "Early in her marriage, Kate Harbison heard some mention of Scott Fitzgerald, whom she then read. What happened between her and the pages set in Long Island, New York City, Paris, and the south of France cannot be known, and she did not often mention the books, but something shone for her out of them with no sign of going out, became a guiding star, an idea of how she, when she wasn't doing her job, was going to be" (*NT* 17). The dangerous woman, as glamorously portrayed in Fitzgerald's novels, seduced Kate. According to Fiedler, Daisy Buchanan is the epitome of the American femme fatale, "the girl who lures her lovers on, like America itself, with a 'voice . . . full of money.'" Daisy is rich and beautiful, attributes America idolizes, but these very characteristics give her destructive power.[24] These works would naturally reinforce the southern belle ideal that permeated Kate's childhood South, for Zelda Fitzgerald, on whom many of Scott Fitzgerald's female characters are modeled, was an Alabama belle herself. Kate carries this

24. Fiedler, *Love and Death,* 300.

image with her like a mask, and though it provides her with manipulative power, it also traps her in a limited role.

She thinks of Fitzgerald when she first meets Fred. On a business trip to Atlanta, she descends the long, elegant escalator to the lobby of her expensive hotel, knowing how good she looks:

> Her golden hair was up and the light made varying designs upon it, while plants, gliding past, obliged her with nimbly changing frames. *Someone should see me,* was what she almost thought.
>
> Someone did. . . .
>
> Neither of them could help but notice that blond and dark made them an attractive pair. How much did it matter? It mattered to Kate. It mattered to Scott Fitzgerald. (*NT* 90)

Her beauty catches Fred's eye. But to Fred, a rich and respectable man, Kate is the perfect showpiece, a trophy wife, someone to take on exotic vacations who will look stunning on the deck of a cruise ship or wearing graceful evening clothes. Kate is like an expensive bauble or a thoroughbred horse (which he actually compares her to), and Fred treats her as such. He does not respect her work, the one thing that focuses Kate on something beyond herself. He procures an unchallenging position for her in the science department of his pharmaceutical company and insists that she take summers off; eventually he discourages her from working at all. With nothing to do all day but look beautiful, Kate broods on her daughter's absence and on Jeff, now her daughter's husband. She begins to come unwound.

Deprived of her work, with only her beauty left to give her life meaning, Kate tortures herself with the memory that Jeff refused her, preferring instead her daughter. Before Jeff disappeared from Kingsbury, Kate had visited his apartment, telling herself she went to discuss Mary's welfare. When he insolently accuses her of having other motives, she leaves confused and angry, but the encounter lingers and becomes magnified in her dreams: "And then her dreams took on where that left off, and they roiled in gigantic beds together . . . . A distant glimmer of the sea, the French coast. Zelda and Scott about to arrive" (*NT* 100). Jeff and Mary's relationship reminds her of the romantic love she will never have (both her marriages were for prestige and money), and his refusal reminds her that her youth and beauty are fading. When he dismisses her final advance, at a political rally in New York, Kate is stung to the core (*NT* 287). She returns home a drunken wreck, no longer an asset, but an embarrassment to Fred on their expensive vacations.

It is in this state that the deadly power of the femme fatale reaches its destructive height. To preserve the value of "this beautiful creature," Fred decides to act on Kate's earlier suggestion to have Jeff permanently removed from the scene (*NT* 316). He uses his political connections to have Jeff found, at which time he is given the option of going to Vietnam or to prison. Jeff chooses the war. But when Kate learns of this trap, she suffers a total collapse: "Her voice when it came, was strained and altered. 'You as good as killed him.' She buried her face entirely, sideways into her arm. She kept speaking, leaning her cheek into the banister, lips moving against the wood, so that he could barely make out words: 'I never meant this . . . never meant it. I swear I—' She was not speaking to him: he knew that" (*NT* 361). She speaks not to Fred but to herself. Though Fred cannot be absolved, Kate believes her manipulations have sentenced her son-in-law to almost certain death, and the self-reproach is paralyzing. Faced with her guilt at destroying her daughter's marriage, as well as the object of her infatuation, Kate transforms from a bad belle to a pathetic, wrecked creature, leaving Fred considering psychiatrists and lithium.

But Mary, without Jeff, survives. Surrounded by her dance company in a country house in Montreal, she is finally in her element. As Spencer said in a recent interview, one important message in *Night Travellers* is "the persistence of art and how art can be sustaining . . . . The thing that art forms is a community for itself wherever it goes. If a person were attached to poetry or writing or sculpture, you could always find others within the art world and make a community for yourself, and I think that was a very sustaining force with her [Mary] in the book."[25] Surrounded by friends who respect and admire her voice, Mary seems at peace. She realizes she has grown beyond the limitations set for her by her mother's image: "*Voices call, dwindling but never quite extinguished, outside from beyond the snows. Jeff will appear like that again; the voice must be Mother's, she the lost wanderer, calling; I the fixed point at home*" (*NT* 364). Basking in the afterglow of a successful performance and giving advice to a younger dancer, the once fragile and timid Mary is now centered and confident. In her symbolic characterizations, Spencer destroys the misogynistic attributes of the mermaid without silencing her creative voice. The ending of Spencer's novel offers hope to future generations of women artists. Sure of herself after having found her community, Mary turns to look at her daughter, Kathy: "In the firelight

25. Entzminger, "Interview with Elizabeth Spencer," 614.

they were happy around her. Mary cautioned Kathy, who behind them was swinging on the banister of the stairway, too high up, but sure she would never fall" (*NT* 365). Free of the inhibiting image of the evil female, Kathy will benefit from the guidance of a strong woman speaking her own voice.

In the end, the woman artist more clearly triumphs over negative stereotypes of powerful women in Spencer's novel than in Welty's. In *Optimist's Daughter,* Laurel's triumph over Fay and all she represents is subtle and subject to debate. Instead of triumphing, Laurel could be running away. Spencer, however, shows the actual decline of the bad belle, a decline precipitated by the belle's manipulations. Also, though Laurel returns to her career as an artist at the end of *Optimist's Daughter,* the reader does not see how she fares in Chicago and does not see the product of her artistic endeavors. In Mary, Spencer portrays a strong woman artist creating her art, inspiring her daughter and readers alike.

LEE SMITH

Lee Smith (1944–), born more than twenty years after Spencer and in a different part of the South, still experienced similar conflicts about becoming a writer. Smith describes her feelings of separation from the community that surrounded her in the mountains of Grundy, Virginia, where she grew up: "I felt very isolated. I felt kind of like a little princess in a sense. . . . I felt sort of embarrassed to live in town, and I had friends whose lunch would be buttermilk and cornbread in a mason jar. But I lived in town, and my mother was from the Eastern shore and had pretensions." Smith's feelings of isolation seem to be prompted by differences in class and education rather than gender, but they still produced anxiety when she began to write: "I still feel a lot of guilt because I didn't grow up in the 'hollers.' I didn't have a father who went down in the mine every day. So you say, you haven't any right to write about people who never ventured more than nine miles from the place they were born in." Though Smith's parents encouraged her to write, releasing her from traditional gender expectations by saying she didn't "have to marry a doctor," her anxiety about being "a little princess" in the eyes of community reveals concern about class and gender distinctions, alike.[26] The equivalent masculine label, "little prince," would not

26. Irv Broughton, "Interview with Lee Smith," in *The Writer's Mind: Interviews with American Authors,* Broughton, ed. (Fayetteville: University of Arkansas Press, 1989), 280, 281, 282.

carry the same negative connotations. Not only is a little princess wealthy, but she is also a pampered and *selfish* girl who values herself and her needs above everyone else's, as does the princess of traditional southern society, the demanding and manipulative belle. In addition, Smith links her anxiety about being considered a little princess to her mother's eastern pretensions, though it was her father's store that placed her family at a higher economic status than the Grundy miners.

Smith further connects her uneasiness about writing to gender and class expectations when she discusses her submerged passion for literature while at Saint Catherine's School: "We were just all on fire with reading and writing. I'd been that way for a long while, but I'd sort of hidden it because I was at St. Catherine's. My father had sent me off to St. Catherine's to turn me into a lady, and it wasn't okay to be that way."[27] Saint Catherine's seems to resemble the nineteenth-century female academies, which Rosamond was threatened with in *Robber Bridegroom*. In the eyes of the school officials and apparently in Smith's father's eyes as well, an intense interest in reading and writing were incompatible with ladyhood. Here Smith expresses an early awareness of the class bias to which Welty and Spencer allude in their novels. Passionate women—women "on fire" with anything, even reading and writing—are not ladies. This negative association is bound to unsettle the young woman writer, who sees that the traditional icon "southern lady" is the greatest threat to her creativity but who also learns from the traditional southern mythology that her only other options are "white trash" and "jezebel."

In other interviews, Smith broadens her dissatisfaction with limiting institutions that prescribed women's roles to include marriage and the church and indicates that her discontent with traditional gender roles informs her fiction writing. Speaking of a particularly passive character, Crystal of *Family Linen,* Smith said, "I think a lot of women have—a tendency to be passive, because our expectations have been set out for us by other people—our mothers, our men. . . . I had come to a point—and a lot of my friends had come to a point—where that was failing us."[28] Through her novels, Smith overcomes the obstacles she faces as a woman writer breaking conventions in the South and offers alternatives for herself and other women left incomplete by the passivity and self-sacrifice traditional society

27. Ibid., 283.
28. Rebecca Smith, "A Conversation with Lee Smith," *Southern Quarterly* 32 (1994): 22; Dorothy Combs Hill, "An Interview with Lee Smith," *Southern Quarterly* 28 (1990): 11.

demands. Like Welty and Spencer, she opens this new space by destroying the negative representations of powerful women embodied in the belle gone bad.

Smith's sense of the impediments she faced as a woman writer manifests itself in her first book, *The Last Day the Dogbushes Bloomed* (1968), written when she had just escaped the influences of parental authority and community expectations to become a student at Hollins College in Virginia. Smith portrays the daughter-artist's triumph over negative conceptions of strong women more directly than Welty and Spencer because she, unlike her predecessors, allows the daughter to narrate her own story. The author dramatizes her early concerns about gender expectations through a mother-daughter pair, whom the narrator, a younger daughter named Susan, calls the Queen and the Princess. Smith has said that the Queen is a made-up character, not someone from her own life, but that she was inspired in part by literary characters such as Scarlett O'Hara.[29] The narrator's description of the Queen, like the Old South's notion of chivalry, seems to spring from fairy tales and romantic legends. Like Welty and Spencer, Smith chooses to revise a fairy tale, a vehicle through which moral values and gender roles traditionally have been passed from generation to generation. As the nine-year-old Susan, up past her bedtime, watches an adult cocktail party from the stairs, she transforms her parents and their friends into characters from a children's book: "The Queen was there, and Daddy, and the whole royal Court. They were having a grand ball almost, except nobody was dancing. But it was like the grand ball in the red book except for that. The Queen was . . . a night sun, glittering and bright, and all the people were like night flowers around her. The lady night flowers were pink and blue and black and white. They were all shimmery, and their teeth were very white. . . . The men were black and white and straight up and down. They were handsome" (*LDDB* 43). These adults play their roles to such perfection they become two-dimensional in the young girl's description. They are motionless, colorful clichés. The Queen, Susan's mother, the evening's focal point and the epitome of charm and grace, influences all.

But though Susan does not realize it, her descriptions reveal that the Queen's influence is not always benevolent. Through the Queen's interactions with the men in the novel, we see that she is a charming and beautiful femme fatale. Significantly, her husband is not the King, but Daddy, the

29. Lee Smith, telephone interview with the author, 6 January 1998.

only partygoer who is not a member of the royal Court. To Susan, Daddy's warmth and sensitivity make him more human and approachable, but less suitable for royal service than the other, more urbane, adults. But, as a failed painter, Susan's father reveals in his dual role as husband and artist the bad belle's threatening power. Bored one afternoon, Susan discovers hidden away in the basement her father's telling portrait of his wife: "The picture was a face, the face of the Queen. It didn't look like the Queen too much, only it was. The whole back of the picture was black and the face grew out of that blackness until you knew the white part of the face wasn't really white but only lighter black. The mouth was too big. It opened and opened until it almost had everything inside it, all the other pictures and me too" (*LDDB* 119). This portrait reveals that in the eyes of her husband, the Queen is a devouring woman, a female vampire, beautiful and horrifying. Here again, as in Welty and Spencer, the acquisitive bad belle is associated with the female vampire's deadly power of seduction and depletion. Daddy has sacrificed his artistic career for an office job to support his wife in queenly fashion, but still she is dissatisfied with their middle-class life. Even Susan sees that the Baron, a silver-haired sophisticated man, makes a more suitable match for the Queen. After an affair with the Baron, which Daddy is unable or unwilling to stop, the Queen eventually abandons her family for the new man, leaving shame and despair in her wake. When Susan sees her father's portrait of her mother, she says that it almost swallowed "all the other pictures and me too" (*LDDB* 119). This painting's awful beauty disturbs this sensitive child, and her reactions remind the reader that to contemporary southern women writers, the bad belle presents the greatest threat to her daughters, the young creative women who in the past had found the Queen's way of getting ahead to be the only one available or whose creativity was limited by artistic representations that made all powerful women appear evil and devouring like the Queen.

It is easy to see the Queen's immediate influence on her older daughter, Betty, whom Susan calls the Princess. Betty, now eighteen, has just returned from Paris, where she has grown to look even more like a princess, with "long yellow hair to hang out of towers" (*LDDB* 3). The older daughter imitates her mother's appearance and manners in everything from drinking coffee, to laughing, to ridiculing her father and her predictable boyfriend, Tom Cleveland. The Princess, a younger, more innocent version of the Queen, will, as in Gilbert and Gubar's reading of "Snow White," someday become the Queen herself. But when her mother abandons the family for the Baron, Betty responds with shame and disgust, rejecting all her mother stands for. In her retreat from her mother's course, she seeks comfort in a more conventional relationship and becomes engaged to Tom. Ironically, by abandoning her attempts at self-definition and seeking safety in a convenient marriage, Betty chooses the same path her mother chose eighteen years earlier, when she married Daddy upon discovering she was pregnant with Betty. Although the Princess tries to find a new direction, she follows in her mother's footsteps.

Susan, the young narrator and the story's central artist figure, reveals this soap-opera drama from her naive and undiscerning perspective. Though she chronicles the lives of her friends and family, Susan's own struggle to find an independent voice directs her tale. She must claim this independence not only from the negative influence of the bad belle, the stereotype of the strong-willed woman, but also from silencing male authority. The summer she is nine, remembered "summers and summers since," she begins to exercise her creative control over the world around her. Susan, a budding writer, names the bushes at the edge of her yard "dogbushes," because she found a dog there once, and she creates imaginary lives for all the tiny creatures at the "wading house." Even at such a young age, she recognizes the limitations of the traditional female role in society—"to have big blobby things flopping around all the time in front of your chest and to kiss boys"—but she sees no way to escape it (*LDDB* 41). She associates make-up, diaphanous clothing, tinkling laughter, and cumbersome body parts with the Princess's and the Queen's allure. But Susan's power lies in "all the muscles in [her] legs" (*LDDB* 41) and in her active mind. Much to Susan's dismay, however, the Princess tells her that she too must someday roll her hair and paint her lashes with mascara, so she can "look beautiful all day long and make all the men fall in love" with her (*LDDB* 39). Her struggle will be to maintain her own strengths against the Queen's condescending laughter and the Princess's attempts to improve her.

Susan must also withstand another silencing element, traditional male authority, which takes the form of an imaginary man, Little Arthur, invented by the demonic boy Eugene to control the other children's games. Little Arthur, an old man with a black coat and large black boots, carries a loaded gun, a symbol of his masculine power, which the children immediately respect. They vote Little Arthur president of their new club, and because Eugene is the only one who can see or talk to the imaginary leader, this physically weak but wicked boy dictates the club's activities. Susan dislikes Eugene from the start, but she feels a special reverence for and fear of the mysterious Little Arthur, and she willingly does what he asks. The individual boy does not control her, but the tradition of masculine authority represented by Little Arthur does. Under his guidance, the children poke at pictures of naked women in books, and Susan sorrowfully thinks of their action's implications for herself: "I thought about how it would be to be punched there, not now but later when I got fat. When I got beauty. I didn't even want to get beauty if I would get punched" (*LDDB* 95). Susan intuits that their actions indicate male and, by extension, societal contempt for the feminine. In the best-case scenario she imagines, feminine beauty consigns one to silent pages as the object of another's gaze. In the worst case, however, this beauty and its requisite silence invite abuse. Eugene's aggression toward Susan takes a final extreme form when, under the guise of a game he invented called Iron Lung, he sexually assaults her while her friends hold her down: "I tried to yell and say no but I couldn't talk and I couldn't breathe either because I was so sick, and they held my hands and my legs down hard" (*LDDB* 162). Eugene's humiliation and domination of Susan take away her voice.

But Susan does receive help and comfort from one character in the novel. Elsie Mae, the family's black cook and nanny, occupies the role normally filled by a mother, seeing to all of Susan's emotional and physical needs while the other members of the family act out their adult drama. Subservient, kind, loving, nurturing, and asexual, Elsie Mae is the traditional southern mammy, and as Fox-Genovese points out, the mammy is the opposite of the jezebel in every way except in race.[30] As we have seen, nineteenth-century southern women writers often allude to the jezebel figure in their tales of the bad belle. In doing so, they critique the South's absurd conventions that assigned sexual roles to women based on their race and call attention to the moral hypocrisy of white men who indulged in miscegenation. The Southern Renascence writers also draw on the stereotype that links African American women to promiscuity, using a black character to direct the reader's gaze toward the sins of her white mistress. The judgmental position of this character perhaps indicates a sense of guilt regarding past sexual sins committed against African American women. But in this early novel, Smith has her heroine identify with the jezebel's asexual opposite. In rejecting the bad belle's influence, Susan seems to reject sexu-

---

30. Fox-Genovese, *Within the Plantation Household,* 292.

ality altogether. In her later novel, however, Smith will have her heroine overcome the physical limitations of the woman's conventional role, showing that a woman can be sexual and still be good.

Neither Smith nor her contemporaries attempt to destroy her real mother, but only her inheritance from her literary foremothers. Consequently, these writers sometimes project motherly qualities onto characters who are the visual opposite of their bad belles, their literary foremothers, and the white society that created the belles. The fact that Smith and, as will be shown later, Gibbons exchange one black stereotype for another may indicate the authors' limited perception, but in *The Last Day the Dogbushes Bloomed* every character except Susan is one-dimensional and stereotypical, which may simply indicate the young narrator's limited perception. Though Elsie Mae fills a stereotypical role, her nurturing positively influences Susan's creativity. Elsie Mae's quiet stories about her own life comfort the child and make her think of her father's paintings hidden in the basement. The black character remains a shadow figure in the works of these recent southern women writers, but instead of personifying and critiquing the negative image of passionate women, including women artists, the figure mothers the young writers' repressed creativity struggling to emerge.

Susan's creativity finally does emerge when she symbolically defies male authority and rejects her mother's influence. Finding out about Eugene's malicious deeds, a friend's father tells the children that he has killed Little Arthur, reclaiming the power usurped prematurely by the male child. Susan resists the man's authority, knowing that the patriarchal power for which Little Arthur stood is still alive but that she need fear it no longer. Later, she has a phallic dream in which she imagines her thumbnail grows so long and strong that it splits Betty's nail file in two and forces the Queen and Little Arthur to stand so far away from her they cannot touch her. With the grotesquely growing nail that turns Susan into a freak but protects her from silencing influences, she appropriates male authority and power. Though Susan remembers her mother's and Little Arthur's power, she has now gained control over them: "I had fixed my mind up so it was cut into boxes, sort of like the boxes eggs come in. In one box I put the Queen; and in one box I put Little Arthur . . . . That way, if I ever wanted to think about anything I could just pull it out of its box and roll it around in the part of my head that was not boxed in. When I got tired of it I could close it back up in its box" (*LDDB* 173). As an artist, Susan begins to order her own experiences, shaping them into a controlled story, organizing them for later use.

Finally, she rejects the ultimate male authority, God, whom she had earlier equated with Little Arthur. Unable to pray to God, she calls out instead to the flowers, stars, and the tops of the trees: "Everything talked to me, it was all the same, they wrapped me up in their green talking like a Christmas present. I could pray to anything" (*LDDB* 180). Free from silencing control, Susan finds her source of inspiration and her voice.

At the novel's close, Susan puts on a "new yellow dress and . . . new red shoes without straps" (*LDDB* 180) to go out to dinner with her father. Though her actions may seem an attempt to take the place of the Queen or the Princess by dressing up for Daddy, her sign of love is far different from the condescension and frustration the two older women expressed to him earlier and shows that she is moving toward her own voice. As the story itself, told by Susan "summers and summers since," bears witness, Susan does not abandon her newly discovered voice at the last minute. Instead, dressed in her painter's colors, she embraces her artist father as her true role model.

Smith's *Oral History* (1983), a more complex novel, focuses on an entire community rather than on a single mother-daughter relationship, but this novel is also, to a large extent, about women telling stories. One character, Red Emmy, the femme fatale, influences the lives and the stories of all the women narrators. Red Emmy, the clan's rejected matriarch, dooms the patriarch's daughters to lives of discontent and despair. Though far from the belle gone bad in appearance and manner, this mountain woman is strong, independent, and sexually free, traits that threaten the patriarchal social structure and result in her ostracism. The community labels Red Emmy a witch, vilifying and silencing her and condemning future generations of its strong, creative women to a similar fate.

Granny Younger, the community healer and midwife, who narrates the section in which Red Emmy first appears, describes her as a witch with supernatural powers to change shape, control animals and people, and inhabit the body of another. Born under mysterious circumstances and living alone in the mountains after her father's death, Red Emmy, like E.D.E.N. Southworth's evil bad belles, reputedly consorts with the devil, who inspires and strengthens her. Like all femmes fatales, her power manifests itself through her sexuality. Awestruck, Granny Younger describes Red Emmy's first appearance to Almarine, the clan's patriarch:

> The skin of her back showed the whitest white that Almarine ever seed, and her hair fell all down her back to her waist. And that hair! Lord it was the

reddest red, a red so dark it was nigh to purple, red like the leaves on the dog-
wood tree in the fall. . . .

Her eyes was as black as night . . . . Her hair hung all down her back like
one of them waterfall freshets along the path and her breasts were big and
white with her nipples springing out on them red as blood.

"My name is Almarine Cantrell," he said, "and I aim to take you home."
(*OH* 34–35)

Red Emmy has the traditional attributes of the femme fatale, the long,
beautiful hair and the dark, magnetic eyes. As Sonya Smith Burchell observes,
Smith's frequent use of the color red to describe this woman is "symbolic of
passion or evil."[31] Red Emmy's beauty has an intoxicating effect on Almarine, but he desires to take her home, where he will figuratively mute her
bright colors by placing her under his authority and beyond the eyes of others.

Red Emmy's beauty also seems to have an intoxicating effect on Granny
Younger and on the writer and the reader. Smith shows us here, as did
Southworth and Hentz in the nineteenth century, that few are able to escape the femme fatale's power of seduction. Granny's fascination may stem
from envy; the healer has power in the community, but mainly because she
uses it to aid the patriarchal domestic structure and because she is too old
to be considered a sexual being. Red Emmy breaks down gender divisions,
because she is sexual and powerful at the same time; she is, in this sense, the
phallic woman, and Granny may envy her freedom. On the other hand,
through her eventual destruction, Red Emmy "is" in the Lacanian sense the
phallus for Granny (and for Smith?), because it is Granny's influence that
leads to her destruction. Granny uses her power to drive out this dangerous
woman, so Red Emmy becomes the site and reflection of Granny's great
strength.

But first, Red Emmy, who desires Almarine as much as he desires her,
comes to him in her own time. And once in his household, she refuses to
moderate her appearance or her behavior. Red Emmy's aggressive sexuality,
through which she appears to grow stronger as Almarine grows weaker,
arouses Granny Younger's suspicions about her evil intentions and invites
her condemnation. Once again, Smith uses vampire imagery in a way that
links sexuality and class. Not only does the community believe that Red
Emmy saps Almarine's physical strength by making love to him and by "rid-

31. Sonya Smith Burchell, "Female Characterization in Lee Smith's *Oral History:* Superstition, Sexuality, and Traditional Roles," *North Carolina Folklore Journal* 42 (1995), 106.

ing" his body in the night as a witch, but she is also a social climber who usurps his position as head of the household. Although everyone in this community is poor, Almarine owns his own house and land, whereas Emmy reportedly had been living in a cave on top of the mountain. Believing Almarine's life to be in danger, Granny advises him to drive the pregnant Emmy from his house. He follows the old woman's advice and soon meets a younger, appropriately passive woman, Pricey Jane, to take as his new bride.

Red Emmy, then, becomes like Lilith, the rejected matriarch of the clan. According to *Funk and Wagnalls Standard Dictionary of Folklore, Mythology, and Legend,* "Taking cue from *Gen.* I, 27, which tells a different story of creation from that of the earlier-written version in *Gen.* II, rabbinical tradition developed the text, 'male and female created he them,' to indicate that God made Adam and Lilith from the dust at the same time . . . . But Lilith would not acknowledge Adam, the man, as her superior in creation; she would not be his servant, for she was created at the same time. Therefore she left Adam and was turned out of Paradise. God then made Eve from Adam's rib." The original powerful woman Lilith leaves paradise to consort with the devil and beget demon children. Because of her rebelliousness, however, God punishes her by destroying her offspring, and she retaliates by stealing human children: "girls especially were in danger."[32] Like her mythical counterpart, Red Emmy also wreaks her vengeance on the descendants of the patriarch. The mountain community believes she curses Almarine's next wife, causing the wife to die from drinking "dew poisoned" milk, and that this curse passes to each female descendant. The curse, however, does not come from Emmy's witchcraft but from a community that sentences its women to lives of constrained passivity and rejects those who resist conformity. Not only does Smith use Red Emmy as a parody of patriarchal society's concept of strong women, as Welty used Fay, but, as did Spencer in *Night Travellers,* Smith also allows us to sympathize with the femme fatale as a victim of her society's expectations and constraints. The cursed offspring, Pricey Jane's daughter, Dory, and Dory's daughter, Pearl, in their discomfort with traditional roles, resemble more closely the rejected matriarch Red Emmy than their meek biological mother, and their resistance seals their fate. Society condemns to tragic lives and empty deaths those assertive women who follow Lilith's lead.

32. Leach, *Funk and Wagnalls Standard Dictionary of Folklore,* 622.

Though Smith shows the community's and Almarine's physical silencing of Emmy's sexual self-expression, it is puzzling that the author silenced Emmy verbally before the book was published. In manuscript form, the novel contained a section written from the point of view of Red Emmy, which revealed she was not a witch but a troubled woman who had been sexually abused as a child. Smith's editor advised her to take this section out, leaving the book with "an unexplained mystery at its core."[33] Though the deletion may have been a wise editorial decision, Smith's authorial act mirrors centuries of repression of women's voices. Because she does not conform to societal conventions, Red Emmy is vilified, ostracized, and finally her voice is cut from the novel as she is cut from the community. Perhaps Smith's decision was in part a conscious attempt to use this character as more of a symbol than a fully rounded character, just as Welty seems to use her femmes fatale to stand for stereotypes of powerful women. Whether because of conscious strategy or unconscious influence from traditional models, until near the end of the novel Smith allows only those women who reinforce the community's values (significantly these women are also described as asexual), such as Granny Younger, Rhoda Hibbits, and Ora Mae Cantrell, to speak. Even Jennifer, the pseudointellectual college student and last female descendant of the patriarch Almarine, who narrates the beginning and ending frames of the novel, speaks in the language of *her* community, middle-class suburbia, at the expense of authentic self-expression.

The fates of Dory and Pearl show that the negative representations of powerful women form a self-perpetuating cycle, a curse handed down from mother to daughter. Pricey Jane's only surviving child, Dory, is the first victim of Red Emmy's curse, a curse enforced by the patriarchy and its class structure embodied, in this case, by Richard Burlage. Having fallen in love with the outsider Richard Burlage, Dory defies her community and her family to be with him. Like Red Emmy, Dory expresses herself with her body. As Richard writes in his journal, "We went straight to my corner bed and made love as no mortals have ever made love before! She answered my passion with her own, taking me beyond all boundaries of physical sensation I had ever experienced or even imagined. And then, stretched body to body on my bed-tick, our legs intertwined so that I could feel the sticky semen (mine!) all over her thighs, and only then she told me" (*OH* 154). Richard figures sex as a dialogue, in which Dory speaks freely to him. The

33. Hill, "An Interview with Lee Smith," 15.

act also loosens Dory's real voice, and she tells this outsider of the inexplicable violence within her community, her father having just been shot by another man in a dispute about a still.

Richard prides himself in having marked Dory with his semen, but her sexuality is beyond his control. Eventually, their passion overpowers Richard, leading to his wasting illness, similar to that Almarine experienced with Red Emmy. Like a female vampire, Dory drains Richard's strength, and once again her debilitating powers are linked to class. Dory also has pretensions to rise above her background, hoping to join Richard in the modernized world he has told her about, a world where, he secretly fears, she will injure his social standing, as she has imperiled his health. Dory's free speech and free sexuality identify her class too obviously; she will never fit in where proper women remain properly subdued. Finally, ill and threatened by the community, Richard returns to his upper-class home without Dory. Though he makes a halfhearted attempt to send for his lover, his note never reaches her, and his abandonment resembles Almarine's rejection of Red Emmy, for Dory, too, is pregnant. Dory's attempts at self-expression have proved costly, for now she no longer fits into her own community, but, expecting twins like Welty's Rosamond, she has no way to escape. She settles into a marriage of convenience and into a patient, dreamy silence, listening for the train that might carry Richard back. Finally realizing he never will come, she lays her head on the tracks and commits suicide.

Dory's daughter Pearl suffers a similar fate, inheriting the curse as she inherits the gold earrings that were Pricey Jane's, then Dory's. Troubled always by an inexpressible longing for better things, Pearl settles into a respectable, passionless marriage that leaves her discontent and still searching. Pearl teaches high school, until her attempt to reach a student becomes tangled with her sexual impulses, causing catastrophe. Though her actions are inappropriate, Pearl, like Red Emmy and Dory, expresses herself through her body. In part, her decision to run away with her student is inspired by her desire to help him understand his artistic potential, and at the end of their affair, when she decides they must return home and face the consequences, he tells her that she was the best teacher he ever had (*OH* 279). After the affair, Pearl, again like Red Emmy and Dory, is outcast, pregnant, and stifled. In her sister Sally's telling of the tale, we hear nothing more about Pearl, except that the baby came prematurely and Pearl died of complications. The curse of Red Emmy is passed on, not through any witchcraft, but through the community's limiting expectations. Women who step beyond the boundaries find themselves rejected and silenced. Like Red Emmy, Dory and Pearl step outside societal boundaries through their threatening sexual openness, which is linked to their attempts at self-expression. Also like Red Emmy, and like the nineteenth-century mad-women in attics, Dory and Pearl are driven insane by the constraints of a society that refuses to grant them a voice.

Two women escape the curse to express themselves freely, verbally and sexually. To obtain this freedom, they, unlike the dreamily waiting Dory and the hungrily searching Pearl, reject the illusions, good and bad, society offers them about love, men, and women. They also, out of necessity, become comfortable living on society's fringes. Justine Poole, owner of the Smith Hotel, loves to gossip with her male boarders and to sleep with many of them, as well as with Aldous Rife, the community's disillusioned minister. Although she has fond memories of her husband who died young, "an absolutely still point in the middle of Justine's mind, a boy-man, not ever going to age or get fat or get sick" (*OH* 188), she has no such romantic illusions about her living partners: "Fucking is fine as far as it goes. But it's nothing more than a prick in your belly and that quivery flash and a man's hot breath in your ear. . . . It don't matter who the man is, nor what it means to him, nor what he *thinks* it means. . . . [I]t don't mean a thing in this world but a man and a woman clamped together in a bed behind the closed door having nothing to do with all the rest of it, with death or fate or sudden sorrow" (*OH* 188–89). A woman who has "a way with a dollar bill," Justine has a man's head for business and a stereotypical male attitude toward sex, which differs widely from the attitude men stereotypically believe *women* should have about sex. But this attitude frees her. The thought of marriage never enters her mind, nor does the thought of guilt. Though she lives alone, except for periodic boarders, this aloneness becomes, instead of isolation, independence. And Smith links Justine's sexual freedom to her verbal freedom. As Justine lies in bed with Aldous Rife, with whom she has had a casual affair for twenty years, she outspokenly gives her opinion on Hoot Owl Holler's residents while engaging in foreplay. Smith inserts the news that "Aldous is erect now" (*OH* 186) between two sentences of the couple's conversation, as if the sex and the talk were interconnected. For Justine, they are. To express herself freely, she must defy gender conventions that constrain women.

Sally, Dory's daughter and Pearl's half sister, escapes the curse in the same way Justine does. Although Sallie's first husband married her to "save" her, Sally has no romantic illusions. As she says of herself and her second husband, "Another way we are, Roy and me, is *down to earth*" (*OH* 238). Roy is a lineman for Appalachian Power, and as his job title suggests, the couple lives on the social fringe of their community, refusing to get ahead or even to plant grass in their yard "so [they] won't have to mow it" (*OH* 239). Sally and Roy are comfortable with their class standing, just as Sally is comfortable with her sexuality and with the sound of her own voice. They act as equals in the bed and outside of it, and their common attitudes as well as their relationship's insular nature distance them from their community. Corinne Dale contrasts Sally's situation to Red Emmy's and points out the link between Sally's ability to express herself physically and verbally:

> Sally has suffered from passion; like Red Emmy, she was abandoned by her lover when she was pregnant. Sally has also suffered from repression: she married a man who "didn't believe in talking to women and he never said one word, just roll over and go to sleep" ([*OH*] 234). But Sally escaped this sexual and linguistic silencing. Her second husband Roy is a tireless lover who likes to hear her talk, even while they are making love. And Sally's two favorite things, talk and sex, show that she has reconciled the language of the body with the language of the mind.

Like Justine, Sally achieves the freedom for assertive verbal and physical self-expression, and this freedom both necessitates and enables her independence from the community. According to Jacques Lacan's theories of human development, "because language is what identifies us as gendered subjects, identity truly occurs only when we enter into speech." But because the use of language initiates us into the law of the father, the phallocentric universe, and because the feminine is linked to the silence of the unconscious that precedes discourse, apparently only the male gender can reap the full benefits of language. By talking and fucking, Sally and Justine claim their own identity and reject the symbolic order that separates their sex from language itself and that makes both language and sexuality masculine tools. Their strategy is similar to that advocated by Hélène Cixous in resisting the hierarchical arrangement of sexual difference on which language and discursive practices are based: "In telling it, in developing it, even in plotting it, I seek to undo it, to overturn it, to reveal it, to expose it."[34]

Sally's voice is that of the authentic woman artist, speaking freely with her mind and body, and as such, she finally destroys the curse of Red

34. Corinne Dale, "The Power of Language in Lee Smith's *Oral History*," *Southern Quarterly* 28 (1990): 32; Wilfred L. Guerin et al., *A Handbook of Critical Approaches to Literature,* 3d ed. (New York: Oxford University Press, 1992), 200; Sellers, *Hélène Cixous Reader,* 6.

Emmy. Sally narrates the last section of the novel, and she has the final word on the Cantrell mystery. Smith comments here and in other works on alternate definitions of art as well as on women's roles. Artists in Smith's works often use "low" or "popular" forms such as oral storytelling, cake baking, letter writing, or country singing. Sally's ability to speak her own story in her own way, distinct from the legend handed down to her, makes her an artist. She ends the curse by renaming it, retelling it, and demythologizing it. Preparing to tell her family's story to her husband and to us, Sally says of the clan, "People say they're haunted and they are—every one of them all eat up with wanting something they haven't got. . . . Roy says that watching my family carry on is better than TV" (*OH* 239). No longer the victims of a scorned witch's curse, they are victims of a society that stifles their inner passions.

After she has told her tale, Roy begins to think of it while they make love, romanticizing the legend and retelling it for himself. But Sally, the artist, maintains her control, firmly placing the story where it belongs and pointing Roy in what she sees as the right direction, both in their lovemaking and in their talk: "'That's the *past*,' I said. 'It's nothing to talk about now. Now it's you and me. It's what happens after this, and if Roger gets into college or not, and if Rosy ever gets married again, and if Al gets to be a double ruby or whatever the hell else it is he takes it into his mind to do next'" (*OH* 284). By claiming her linguistic and sexual freedom, Sally refuses to allow the curse to haunt her. As narrator, she presides over Ora Mae's disposal of the gold earrings that had been passed on to Pricey Jane's daughter and granddaughters. To Sally, however, these gold loops are not the carrier of Red Emmy's curse, as they are for the older Ora Mae; they are the emblem of the constrained passions of her female predecessors.

By destroying the vilified image of the sexually assertive woman, Sally takes control of the narrative and frees herself on many creative levels. But Sally's action does not signify the same liberation for all younger women artists. In the novel's final section, Jennifer, the last female descendant of Almarine Cantrell and Pricey Jane, prepares to return to college. Jennifer's attempts to impress her anthropology professor control her language, causing her to ignore the truths about her past, hinted at by her Uncle Al, and to view all she hears as rustic folklore. Her ability to mimic her professor's language and to tell him what he wants to hear earn her high marks in school and something more: "*Jennifer will make an A for the course. Jennifer will marry Dr. Bernie Ripman the summer after she graduates from college*" (*OH* 291). Smith's description links Jennifer's success in school, brought about by her ability to see the world as her professor sees it, to her later marriage to this same professor, in which it is assumed he exercises a similar control. Like her foremothers, Jennifer takes her place in the traditional social order, submitting to the sexual and verbal domination of male authority. But how long will she be satisfied with imitation? With Ora Mae's musings that Jennifer is so much like her mother, Pearl, the reader is left to wonder if Jennifer has also inherited Red Emmy's curse.

KAYE GIBBONS

Kaye Gibbons (1960–), the youngest of the contemporary writers in this study, still struggles to free herself from her society's concept of creative and powerful women. Born in a poor, rural family and reared by relatives and foster parents after her mother's suicide (when Gibbons was a preadolescent) and her father's death a few years later, Gibbons lacked the traditional advantages afforded by the comfortable backgrounds of Welty, Spencer, and even Smith, who at least *felt* like a princess in Grundy. One would imagine that Gibbons's background would also free her from some of the traditional limitations of the woman's role in the South. But in her essay "My Mother, Literature, and Life Split Neatly into Two Halves," Gibbons states she found a new grounding and identity in literature that enabled her to "'read' [her]self out" of rural North Carolina and that provided another world, at times unhealthily divorced from reality, during her college years. The writers she mentions frequently, Poe and Faulkner, as well as other literary greats, seem to have shaped her identity as much as anyone in Polk County and became almost surrogate parents. The fact that Gibbons mentions only male writers, when one would assume such a voracious reader would have also encountered Glasgow, Mitchell, and Welty, shows she still struggles with the prejudice against creative women. Though Gibbons probably did not encounter the bad belle in Polk County, as Spencer said she did in her daily life, she no doubt encountered her through Poe and Faulkner.[35] These male writers repeatedly use versions of this figure in a traditional way, allowing her to destroy men and to be destroyed in

35. Kaye Gibbons, "My Mother, Literature, and Life Split Neatly into Two Halves," in *The Writer on Her Work,* Janet Sternburg, ed. (New York: Norton, 1991), 2: 56; Elizabeth Spencer, letter to the author, 25 November 1997.

turn when the proper patriarchal order is reestablished. Gibbons's attack on the bad belle, therefore, challenges her literary forebears as much as it reacts against traditional southern society.

Like many other southern women writers, Gibbons manifests the tensions of her dual role as an artist and a woman in the South as destructive sexuality, a connection that appears in her autobiography and in her fiction. And like her predecessors, she uses this figure as a means to critique the society that imposes silencing limitations. For Gibbons, both the creativity and the sexuality are rooted in madness, recalling the nineteenth-century British women writers who often used the character of the madwoman to manifest their dis-ease within their society. Gibbons manifests what Gilbert and Gubar have termed an anxiety of authorship, though she is fully conscious of this anxiety, and it stems as much from her class background and her illness as from her gender. The purpose of dramatizing her anxiety in her work is not, as Gilbert and Gubar claim to be the case for the nineteenth-century writers they study, to punish herself for the sin of writing, but is a means, as it is for the other southern women studied here, to exorcize the negative images she inherited from her culture that might keep her from writing. A manic-depressive, Gibbons writes that her greatest periods of creativity come during her manic upswing, at a stage called "hypomania," when her energy is high and thoughts come with greater ease and intensity than normal. She wrote her first novel, *Ellen Foster* (1987), over a period of six to eight weeks during such a manic phase (*FF* 7). This stage is a precursor to the full-blown mania, when her thoughts are moving so quickly she cannot write them down. The most noticeable symptom of this final manic stage is a dramatically increased libido, during which Gibbons says she makes sexual "assaults" on her husband, draining his energies to such an extent that he must spend her depressed cycle, when she neither writes nor pursues him sexually, recovering (*FF* 11).

In her description of her illness, destructive sexuality follows on the heels of creative energy, stifling that creativity and leading to a period of dormancy on all creative fronts. Though Gibbons clearly recognizes and acknowledges the connection between her illness and her art, she has ambiguous feelings about them both. She worries about the effect of her mood cycles on her children, fearing that her disorder makes her an ineffective parent and role model, but she refuses some types of medication that "have made [her] too normal to do art" (*FF* 19). Gibbons also romanticizes her illness, believing that it is responsible for her art: "All I can do, and all I ever will do, is write, and if it takes an illness to trigger creativity, that is what my family and I will have to bear" (*FF* 20). If earlier women struggled against the assertion that their writing made them abnormal women, Gibbons depends on her abnormality to make her write. Both cases imply that uninhibited artistic expression is, at least for women, not normal. But in a recent novel, *Sights Unseen* (1995), Gibbons appears to recognize the danger of this implication and to try to reverse some of the damage it has caused.

In *Sights Unseen,* Gibbons expresses her ambiguous feelings toward her illness, paradoxically creating art directly out of it while figuratively destroying the madness that both inspires and silences her creative drives. The novel details the experiences of Maggie, a manic-depressive woman who torments her family while being sheltered by them from the rest of the world. As with the other contemporary southern women's novels explored, the central intelligence of *Sights Unseen* is a daughter-artist figure, Hattie, whose life, after the mother's madness is treated, achieves some measure of normality, from the perspective of which the daughter speaks her story. Though in her nonfiction works Gibbons focuses on the connection between writing and madness while only briefly mentioning the link between her illness and the manic surges in her libido, in the novel the link between madness and destructive sexuality takes center stage. Both of these outlets are sources of creative power traditional society has controlled for women— in both of these realms, women have been traditionally silenced.

Although she is ill and therefore cannot be held accountable for the evil intentions of the sane femme fatale, Maggie in her manic state plays the role of the belle gone bad. Outwardly proper and demure, as a southern lady should be, Maggie wears "white gloves to church and cross[es] her feet at the ankles" (*SU* 41), but behind this decorous exterior, her illness unleashes the bad belle's destructive desire to manipulate men. Confident in her good looks, she concocts plans to control men with her wiles, and the attractive male actors on television are the primary victims of her allure. Obsessing over a tentative love affair from *As the World Turns,* Maggie devises a plan to win the male protagonist for herself: "She thought she could take Bob away from Kim, who was a weakling. Nice Kim. Well, nice Kim could watch her man being snatched. Bob would be drawn to Mother. . . . My mother . . . told my father that he would just have to understand that she had been put on the planet to be worshiped by all men" (*SU* 21–22). Though delusional, Maggie possesses Scarlett O'Hara's ruthlessness, delighting in her own power over men and viewing other women as unworthy rivals for their affections.

We see here a progression from Welty to Gibbons in the authors' treatment of the bad belle. Welty uses this figure so much as a type or symbol that her bad belles become grotesques. In Spencer's *Night Travellers,* the reader can see that Kate has been seduced by the same stereotypes she represents but cannot feel much sympathy for her in light of her actions. And although a narrator never offers sympathy to Red Emmy, Smith allows the reader to see the fate of other strong women in her society, so the reader eventually may realize that the mountain woman is a victim of her time and place. Finally, through Maggie's illness, Gibbons allows the reader to feel sympathy for the bad belle from the start, in spite of her destructive actions. At the same time, however, Gibbons's destruction of the bad belle (through her cure) is more assertive and final than in any of the other writers' works. Perhaps the more conscious the writer becomes of the threat negative images of powerful women pose for her and for other women writers, the more sensitive she becomes to the fact that real women in the past have been seduced by this image and are in need of enlightenment and sympathy.

Maggie's manipulations are not all delusional fantasies; she also has control over actual men. Always a caretaker and protector of Maggie, her father-in-law Mr. Barnes, the family patriarch, especially delights in escorting her around town during her manic shopping sprees. And Hattie, the narrator from whose memory the novel springs, sexualizes this relationship. After hearing a story about an old senator who married his young secretary and then died on his honeymoon six hours later, Hattie mentally projects this destructive power onto her mother: "Mr. Barnes no doubt had a fine time squiring her about town, dressed as she would have been in a stylish suit, high heels, and seamed stockings. . . . Mr. Barnes pleased her most by taking her to Hertzberg Furs and to A Stone's Throw jewelry store. Townspeople who did not know them might have thought he was her sugar daddy. They might have wondered if she would board a train with him and cause his corpse to be hauled off somewhere down the line" (*SU* 84). Maggie's energetic charm fascinates her husband and Mr. Barnes, but it is also dangerous, both financially and sexually, as her extreme demands threaten to sap their resources. Once again, we see the link between destructive sexuality and financial greed. Maggie's illness resembles Gibbons's own, but the author sets the main action of the novel about 1967, so Maggie is a contemporary of Gibbons's mother and Maggie's daughter, Hattie, is a contemporary of the author. Interestingly, in this autobiographical novel, the economically well-to-do Maggie does not resemble Gibbons's mother, who, according to the author, lived a life "surrounded by heat and poverty and the sad certainty that life will not be any other way" (*FF* 20). Rather than make the mother figure a poor white, Gibbons places her in the class from which belles and ladies arise, so that she more closely fits the stereotype of southern womanhood Gibbons would have encountered primarily in books. But in this book, the family's money comes mainly from the father's side, so Maggie is a social climber, embodying stereotypes that link free expression of sexuality with lower classes. The character seems to represent not only Gibbons's feelings toward her mother; she also represents Gibbons's anxieties about her illness and conceptions of southern ladyhood, two seemingly antithetical abstractions that are, Gibbons reveals, paradoxically empowering and debilitating.

Gibbons links Maggie's madness to destructive sexuality more strongly through Maggie's husband, Frederick, giving her the power of a female vampire to drain all strength from him. More than once, Hattie describes her mother's manic sexual drives as deadly. During one particularly bad manic episode, "when she was substituting him for actors, writers, and politicians, she nearly killed him. Sometimes I would come off the bus in the afternoons to find him adrift in the house in khaki pants and a rumpled undershirt, looking like a hallwalker in a veterans' hospital, spent and forlorn" (*SU* 35). Frederick resembles the Knight at Arms, "Alone and palely loitering," in Keats's "La Belle Dame sans Merci."[36] Every time he tries to leave the bedroom for a rest break, Maggie growls for him to come back and "finish what [he's] started" (*SU* 36), until he finally escapes to a family friend's house for a nap. Hattie later reflects, "If my mother had not been married during those six weeks of 1967, if she had been just another untreated manic depressive, God knows how many men she could have wasted" (*SU* 73). Maggie is a woman out of control.

As in Gibbons's life, however, this madness in Maggie inspires artistic creativity, which men of traditional patriarchal society also find threatening—at least in women. Also as in Gibbons's life, the madness at its peak deprives Maggie of mental focus. During one manic episode, she believes what she wants most is to be a poet, but, she thinks, "It would be very hard

36. Keats, "La Belle Dame sans Merci."

to write poems down on a piece of paper when words fly away like scared robins from their nest" (*SU* 89). By using the simile of the birds and the nest, Gibbons invokes an image of a traditionally acceptable woman's role, motherhood. The madness that is necessary for any kind of creative freedom makes Maggie a bad mother—a bad woman in the traditional sense—but it ultimately limits her ability as an artist as well.

Gibbons links her own and her character's physical and mental creative drives to madness, showing that the madness frees one from the constraints of normal life and allows one to step beyond expected roles. But the madness is ultimately harmful to its victims as well as to future generations of women, who would suffer from lack of strong, healthy female role models and who would learn that only through this destructive form of escape could they achieve creative freedom. Hattie is repulsed and fascinated by her mother's manic sexuality. She stands mesmerized outside her parents' bedroom door, wondering at the noises she hears beyond, fearing for her father's health, but she is also in awe of her mother's power over him and of her unflagging energy. Pearl, the black housekeeper, expresses her own fear that the younger female members of the house, especially Pearl's niece Olive, will be influenced by Maggie's behavior (*SU* 76). Maggie is a sometimes brilliant woman, but her physical and mental creativity veers out of control. As a role model, she seems to signal that any step beyond the normal boundaries of feminine behavior will lead to chaos. To break free of this threatening idea, that different means sick, Gibbons must destroy the negative role model and learn to write while still maintaining her life as a sane woman.

As did Smith in *The Last Day the Dogbushes Bloomed,* Gibbons uses the black housekeeper as the moral and physical counterpart of the corrupt white lady. Dark, sturdy, and asexual, Pearl is the visual opposite of the thin, glamorous Maggie. Pearl is also practical, firm, and virtuous, like a traditional mammy. Just as Mammy monitored Scarlett, Pearl looks after Maggie, deciding when she is well enough to leave the house, entertaining and protecting her when she is ill. It is Pearl who shelters Hattie from her mother's manic displays and Pearl who explains the facts of life, from her own conservative perspective, to the young girl. Like the other contemporary southern women in this study, Gibbons's story is about writing and influence, at least on the allegorical level. It is the artistic mother, not the real mother, whose influence is most important and at times most dangerous to the woman writer. The traditionally negative image of powerful women is incapable of nurturing other women, so the daughter-artist must look elsewhere for emotional and physical comfort. In a society that categorizes women into types, the daughter-artist is forced to seek nurturance in another stereotype rather than in a real, balanced female role model who offers both power and support. By having her character seek guidance from the asexual Pearl rather than from the maniacally sexual mother, Gibbons also seems to reject sexuality. But when Maggie becomes a more balanced woman, Pearl disappears from the picture, and through her mother's influence, Hattie eventually achieves controlled but uninhibited artistic and sexual expression.

In the end, like the other contemporary southern women writers explored, Gibbons destroys the negative image of powerful women to free the next generation of women artists. But Gibbons removes this negative type by curing Maggie, not by destroying her. Following a minor car accident in which she bumps a woman wearing a coat identical to her own, Maggie is hospitalized and successfully treated with medication and electroconvulsive therapy. When she returns home, Maggie amazes her family with her propriety, firmness, and practicality as she takes control of the household management. And as Hattie tells her mother's story, we see that Maggie's newfound authority aids her daughter's growth into womanhood:

> A girl cannot go along motherless without life's noticing, taking a compensatory tuck here and there in the heart and in the mind . . . . I could have lurched on ahead to adulthood, straining to be a good girl, not ever learning what to do when my own children were placed in my arms. . . . But we caught each other just in time, right on the edge of my puberty. She pulled me back from the rim of an abyss. . . . Boys, when they finally took notice of me, had to wait for my mother and me to learn each other, to learn our habits and our ways. (*SU* 6–7)

A strong, healthy mother, Gibbons says, is not only necessary to this one young girl, but to all young girls, including those yet to be born. After Maggie's cure, the mother and daughter direct their attentions toward themselves and each other rather than toward boys or men. Hattie does not say she rejects sexuality altogether, only that it must wait until she has learned from her mother how to be a woman. Upon Maggie's return from the hospital, one of her first acts of intimacy with her daughter is to call her to her bedroom to read and nap after lunch. At first Hattie distrusts her mother, as the once sex-crazed woman removes her stockings, conjuring images of her former manic appetites. Despite the girl's fears, the pair lie together calmly reading, sharing a controlled artistic connection.

Though Maggie does not go on to create great works of art, her healthy influence frees her daughter's creativity. *Sights Unseen,* told from the perspective of the grown daughter, is inspired by the mother's illness but made possible by her cure. Hattie narrates the story in homage to her mother who, fifteen years after her recovery, has died, right after Hattie discovers she is pregnant with her first daughter. Hattie explores her mother's past to create her story, but in maintaining control, she refuses to be influenced by it. Her mother's cure allows Hattie's growth into a strong, healthy woman with the freedom to create and allows her to become a strong influence for her daughter. Though the loss of Maggie's illness is healthy for Hattie, it does silence Maggie. Hattie as the ostensible author takes readers through Maggie's manic swings up to and immediately after her recovery, and then she shields her mother's life as a healthy woman from us until the day of Maggie's death, fifteen years later. Fittingly, this former madwoman dies from an accidental fall as she climbs too quickly down her attic steps. Like Gibbons's expressed fear of losing her creativity along with her madness, Maggie's cure ends her creative freedom—making her "too normal" for art.

Maggie is cured when Hattie is twelve, approximately the same age as Gibbons was when her mother committed suicide. In both Gibbons's and her character's lives, the daughter must free herself from the unhealthy mother to write in her own voice. As the author writes about herself, "My mother's death both freed me and marked me. When she died I was able to physically leave the place I'd been making little mind excursions from ever since I learned to read. If she was still living, I would still be bound to my old home, and I would not have turned to literature and used it as I have."[37] Gibbons's rejection of Maggie as a sexually destructive madwoman reflects her liberation from her mother's influence. At the same time, it dramatizes the contemporary woman artist's rejection of the bad belles, who dominate the literature that became Gibbons's surrogate parent and that perpetuate the negative stereotype of powerful women while stifling the woman artist's independent voice.

Like Welty, Spencer, and Smith, Gibbons rejects the influence of her literary forebears to focus on positive feminine power that strengthens the budding

---

37. Gibbons, "My Mother, Literature, and Life," 60.

woman writer. In reacting against the destructive sexuality used as a weapon by Southern Renascence women writers, these contemporary authors claim new territory for women writing in the South. From Welty to Gibbons, each writer becomes more sensitive to this figure's threat to actual women, causing the writer to reveal that the bad belle has herself been seduced by the images of sexually manipulative women. Although in slightly different ways, all of these contemporary writers destroy the influence of the belle gone bad to construct a world in which women can create from their own minds, hearts, bodies, and experiences and still be, not vilified freaks of nature who threaten the social order, but normal women.

CONCLUSION
For Whom the Belle Told

This study began with Baym's assertion that the most popular literature of the nineteenth century was written by and about women. Baym goes on to say, "Today, we hear of this literature, if at all, chiefly through detractors who deplore the feminizing—and hence degradation—of the noble art of letters." Baym's 1978 study helped to reclaim many of these nineteenth-century women writers, but they and their literary heirs are still overshadowed by their male counterparts' reputations. The women authors often are rejected by literary critics because they are thought to focus too narrowly on domestic settings and concerns and ignore more universal issues. But Faulkner's greatest works also focus on the home and family, and like him, these southern women writers use the relationships and routines of their characters as lenses through which to view more sharply the entire society and its beliefs. Some scholars also believe these women writers are too conservative in their supposed failure to challenge, as do such greats as Faulkner and Tennessee Williams, those southern institutions and conventions that society now condemns. Richard King, for example, in *A Southern Renaissance,* excludes southern women authors because, he says, they do not "take the South and its tradition as problematic," as do their male contemporaries. And Patricia Yaeger points out Louis Rubin's intended defense of Welty in *The Faraway Country* includes "odd diminutions of Welty's abilities. While Faulkner's Mississippi contains combatants 'larger than life,' Welty's Mississippi is a 'tidy, protected little world.'" The implicit message in Rubin's defense is that Welty is very good—for a woman.[1]

But, as suggested in the introduction, these women writers had a far greater impact on the works of their male counterparts than normally is acknowledged, and this topic deserves further investigation. The popular women writers' portrayals of women characters influenced male writers and, in the long run, influenced cultural conceptions of women. Faulkner and Wolfe get credit for directing a newly critical glance at the South, but Glasgow preceded them by a generation. This study also suggests a literary tradition and intertextuality among southern women writers, evidence they took their craft and its power in their society seriously. The belle gone bad is a recurring and consistent figure, which is revised by each new generation of southern women writers.

Though Baym's examination of domestic writers inspired many other critical surveys devoted to the works of nineteenth- and twentieth-century women writers, many surveys continue to perpetuate the notion that these writers as a group accepted the sexist and racist social structure they inhabited. For example, Elizabeth Moss asserts that "popular literature helped to formalize and codify the elite southern female's conservative world view, familiarizing readers with the issues separating North and South by translating political rhetoric into easily accessible language and images." This statement insults the intelligence of southern females, many of whom were capable of grasping political rhetoric without having it dumbed down into "easily accessible language and images," and it ignores the language and images—such as the bad belle—that compete against the conservative southern world view in many of the most popular works by southern women writers. Some recent collections, however, have explored the less-than-conservative political messages contained in the works of nineteenth- and twentieth-century women writers, giving them credit for a "historical consciousness" that King and others have overlooked.[2] And this study examines

1. Baym, *Woman's Fiction*, 11; Richard King, *A Southern Renaissance: The Cultural Awakening of the American South, 1930–1955* (New York: Oxford University Press, 1980), 8; Patricia Yaeger, "Beyond the Hummingbird: Southern Women Writers and the Southern Gargantua," in *Haunted Bodies*, 288.

2. Moss, *Domestic Novelists*, 18; King, *Southern Renaissance*, 8. Two excellent new collections are Manning's *Female Tradition in Southern Literature* and Jones and Donaldson's *Haunted Bodies*.

in detail one subtle strategy these women writers consistently employed to critique their culture and challenge its conceptions of race, class, and gender relations.

The bad belles that appear in the works of southern women writers from the antebellum period to the present reflect at once a parody of the negative stereotypes of powerful women and the writers' critique of the society that created such confining images. Their parodies are theatrical performances that expose through exaggeration and violation the "ritualized repetition of conventions" that produce gender. By using exaggerated feminine qualities to mask conventional masculine qualities, the bad belle, like Butler's drag queen, "imitates the imitative structure of gender, revealing gender itself to be an imitation," challenging her culture's notion of "true womanhood" or "true manhood."[3] What unites these bad belles used by generations of women writers in the South, then, is not their power to destroy men so much as their role in liberating women.

The perfect figure with which to attack the Old South was one that combined its ideal, as the southern belle, with the sexual knowledge and power of the dark seductress. In this society, the culture's primary obsession, linked to its views on family honor, slavery, and white supremacy, was the physical and moral purity of the white lady. The ancient moral dichotomy between lady and whore was reinforced in the Old South by the visual differences between white and black women. The South's white lady became the visual epitome of the European ideal of light, pure virgin, and the black woman was the ultimate dark, evil seductress. In this society, there was no moral or physical gray area. One was either white or black, good or bad, and each moral pole was firmly tied to its physical counterpart. But the bad belle blurs that distinction, and her muddling of traditional boundaries has possibly serious repercussions. When read by the masses of women readers, the bad belle's actions have the potential to destroy all the society's valued institutions; for if white women began to act as black women were reputed to, where was the justification for slavery and white supremacy? As Helena Michie points out, "'Dark' and 'Fair' are positions that must be occupied and inhabited; if one sister switches roles, the other must do the same."[4]

Many of the intellectual and social restrictions placed on women (and

3. Butler, *The Psychic Life of Power: Theories in Subjection* (Stanford, Calif.: Stanford University Press, 1997), 144, 145.

4. Helena Michie, *Sororophobia: Differences among Women in Literature and Culture* (New York: Oxford University Press, 1992), 29.

blacks) in the Old South were erected in the name of protecting the lady's legendary and holy virtue, a symbolic state through which the society's institutions of slavery and white supremacy were rationalized. When women strayed from their culturally imposed mental and spiritual roles, they threatened all other conventions linked to their position. As a result, nineteenth-century women writers were often accused of immorality (if they crossed one boundary, they had surely crossed others), and their intellectually powerful women characters also appear as morally and racially tainted. Through their belles gone bad, E.D.E.N. Southworth, Caroline Lee Hentz, and Augusta Jane Evans exaggerate the connection between the crossing of intellectual boundaries and the moral and physical taints their culture's mythos said must surely follow. Southworth's Juliette, Sinai, and Faustina, Hentz's Florence and Claudia, and Evans's Creola have the dark features that, though they are not overtly described as African in origin, resemble the traditional descriptions of the mulatta in antebellum literature. To varying degrees, each of these dark ladies also violates her culture's code of moral purity by openly expressing and relying upon her sexuality.

This blurring of color lines conveys a social critique in the novels. By quietly pointing out the similarities between their light heroines and their dark villainesses, these writers expose, as did abolitionist writers, the arbitrariness of race distinction, which assigns black and white women to equally confining, though antithetical, sexual roles based on a drop of blood. Also, by revealing the troubled pasts that led to the wayward lives of the belles gone bad, showing the ways in which they are victims of the social structure, the writers encourage their readers to feel sympathy for these bad women—perhaps even, through their common victimization, to identify with them. Reading the silences in these novels, we begin to see the subtle messages insinuating that, instead of black and white, the South is colored gray and the bad belle's manipulation is the only avenue to power for women in a corrupt system.

Most important for understanding this character's link to the author's critique of gender conventions is the fact that each of the bad belles (or in the case of Evans, the main character Beulah, who must alter her path so she does not turn into the dark fallen lady) is criticized by her community for using her intellect in ways unbecoming to a lady. Significantly, each author links at least one of her bad belles to artistic expression: Faustina is a singer, Claudia is a dancer, and Beulah—who is reformed by the negative example of Creola—is a writer. Though the bad belle's main attribute is her destructive sexuality, the writers' use of this figure seems to indicate that the culturally imposed asexuality of the white lady is only one of many means of denying her power. The bad belles violate the culture's sexual expectations for women, just as they and their creators violate its expectations of female voicelessness and passivity.

But because most antebellum southern writers were dependent on this culture's patronage for their livelihood, they destroy their bad belles to restore proper patriarchal authority at their novels' ends. Before their villainesses' deaths, however, these writers allow the bad belles to usurp the patriarch's control and quietly expose the power structure's flaws. Their belles gone bad reveal the abuses and hypocrisies inherent in the patriarchal system and show that to one who is willing to manipulate the system, through using her status and allure as belle for self-serving ends, both the good lady and southern gentleman are made vulnerable by the very traits southern society viewed as their greatest strengths.

The belle gone bad not only blurs the color lines established by traditional southern society, but she also blurs gender and class lines. Laura Kipnis's discussion of the political implications of the body and control over it in "White Trash Girl" echoes Judith Butler's theories of theatrical gender performance as a form of protest. But Kipnis considers the value of theatrical performance as a protest against classist hegemonies in a way that is relevant to understanding the Southern Renascence women writers' social protest:

> [I]f, as anthropologist Mary Douglas has pointed out, the body invariably symbolizes the social and is universally employed as a symbol for human society, then control over the body is always a symbolic expression of social control. And if the body and the social are both split into higher and lower strata, with images or symbols of the upper half of the body making symbolic reference to the society's upper echelons—the socially powerful—while the lower half of the body and its symbols makes reference to the lower tiers, to those without social power . . . then symbolic and aesthetic inversions of these hierarchies have a certain political resonance.
>
> Symbolically deploying the improper body as a mode of social sedition also follows logically from the fact that the body is the very thing that these various modes of power—whether state, religious, or class privilege—devote themselves to keeping "in its place."[5]

5. Laura Kipnis, "White Trash Girl: An Interview," in *White Trash: Race and Class in America,* Matt Wray and Annalee Newitz, eds. (New York: Routledge, 1997), 114.

In traditional southern culture, each group within the social hierarchy is associated with a different part of the stratified body. The culture identified blacks and some poor whites with the genitals because of these groups' supposed promiscuity and animal nature, white ladies with the heart and womb because of their supposed sensitivity and maternal instincts, and white gentlemen with the head because of their supposed capacity for rational thought and leadership. It is the bad belle's subversion of the normal hierarchy that makes her so dangerous. By using her sexuality, her genitals—the symbolic territory of the African American or poor white—and her mind, the symbolic territory of the white man, to gain control of the patriarch, the bad belle blurs race, class, and gender lines and threatens the traditional power structure.

The fact that the power structure was already shaken by the Civil War and Reconstruction—though, as suggested earlier, many of the ideals still lingered—meant that Southern Renascence women writers could more openly express their discontent with traditional society. These modern authors' attitudes toward their bad belles are, like those of their antebellum predecessors, complex—a mixture of admiration and contempt. But the destruction and manipulation wrought by these belles gone bad, who survive while the so-called good ladies and gentleman around them perish, seem to serve at least in part as an outlet for authors' rage against their limiting society. The dangerous lady's mind, created by the mind of the woman author, executes this release, but that the release makes use of the body as an instrument of power, though inconsistent with the culture's conception of southern ladyhood, is not surprising. As John Shelton Reed points out in his discussion of southern types, "[W]omen who are denied or who have foregone conventional sorts of power cannot be persuasive villains except in the spheres where they *do* have power." In the South of the twenties, thirties, and forties, where most women did not have access to money and political power, all they had was their bodies and others' emotional attachment to them.[6] The bad belles unleash their rage through their bodies, using them as a means to manipulate the emotions of others, shaking the foundations of the culture that worshiped or feared those bodies so much that it wanted to hide them behind hoop skirts and pretend they did not exist.

6. John Shelton Reed, *Southern Folk, Plan and Fancy: Native White Social Types* (Athens: University of Georgia Press, 1986), 58.

Ellen Glasgow's Annabel and Stanley, Evelyn Scott's Julia, Margaret Mitchell's Scarlett, and Caroline Gordon's Isabel and Cynthia are all so dangerous and so successful because, though they continue to look like traditional women on the outside, soft and inviting, on the inside they think like men—about money, family, and most threateningly, about sex. They expose the patriarchy's frailties by using its supposed strengths—pride and the obligation to protect and control—against it, claiming power from those who expect them to follow traditional social codes. That the Southern Renascence belles gone bad look more like their authors and readers than an Africanist double suggests the southern woman's more open discontent with traditional power structures and increased comfort with her own quest for power. But the issue of race has not disappeared from the works of Southern Renascence women writers. The African American woman appears as a shadow figure who distantly presides over the white lady's sins, marking and judging her sexuality, recalling the sexual abuse sanctioned in the Old South.

Contemporary southern women writers have the mixed blessing of more than a century of female antecedents. On the one hand, their female literary predecessors cleared the path for them as women authors, but on the other hand the predecessors unintentionally perpetuated images that equate female power (including the creative power as artist) with exploitation and immorality. For example, though Mitchell's Scarlett O'Hara survives and prospers independently, she immortalizes the image of the strong southern woman as a cold, calculating, selfish, and manipulative femme fatale. This image seems to say that while one can defy tradition, to do so one must become like Scarlett.

By destroying the belle gone bad, contemporary southern women writers Eudora Welty, Elizabeth Spencer, Lee Smith, and Kaye Gibbons finally destroy this image, which their society created to silence women like them, the same image their literary foremothers invoked as a way of talking back against their society's prohibitions. The bad belle's destruction exorcizes this figure's lingering influence from the women writers' conceptions of themselves as artists. No longer must the powerful woman fear that she is, or will be perceived as, dangerous and evil. The mother-daughter conflict these writers employ in their works reflects the debilitating influence negative images of powerful women can have on future generations of women. The artists project themselves into the daughter-artist characters in their works to illustrate their own struggle against the influence of their literary foremothers. By destroying the femme fatale mother, then, the writers free the daughter's body and mind at the same time they free themselves from their troubling heritage as women writing in the South.

But the belle gone bad is just one strategy employed by southern women writers to challenge their culture and heritage. Schmidt identifies numerous mad or outcast women in Welty's short stories; he believes these characters embody the author's commentary on the powerful woman's fate in the South. And Yaeger sees a different hyperbolic character, the female "gargantua" or grotesque, functioning as a vehicle for critique in the work of twentieth-century southern women writers including Welty and Flannery O'Connor. The grotesque in Welty's and O'Connor's works has been studied before, but Yaeger sees in them a serious political message that has not been previously discussed. These gargantua—outsized women who serve as the butt of community ridicule, such as Welty's Miss Eckhart in "June Recital" and the unnamed obese woman on the beach in "A Memory"—are "symbol[s] for female artistry and self-empowerment threatening beyond words." Yaeger believes that "[i]n reworking the image of the southern lady—in creating her grotesque or giant antitype—southern women writers do more than protest the burdens of ladyhood. Their grotesque heroines help bring the hard facts of southern racism and sexism into focus."[7]

The bad belles explored herein are usually more subtle and more rounded than the grotesque; both these figures, however, are often dismissed as having no serious import because they are unrealistic and sometimes comic. But these characters parody society's concept of powerful women, and parodies, which are unrealistic and often comic by definition, have been used since ancient times as vehicles for political messages. Is it only because these parodies are crafted by and about women that most readers cannot see the message behind them? Or are their serious meanings disregarded because so many of these works concentrate on the home and family, the normal sphere of women that has been historically slighted by society?

Southern women writers' methods of social criticism are often subtle, so subtle as to have been overlooked, and they are not new to the twentieth century. The bad belles that appear in southern women writers' works from the antebellum period to the present reveal the women's discomfort with their status as icons and with the injustices committed reputedly in defense

7. Schmidt, *Heart of the Story;* Yaeger, "Beyond the Hummingbird," 295, 301–2.

of their honor. These works also contradict the notion of the southern lady's passivity, for the works served as active, though indirect and gradual, means of changing society and woman's role in it. Hopefully, the bad belle's destruction in the works of contemporary writers announces a more open society where women writers no longer need to disguise their cultural critiques and strong women no longer need to disguise themselves.

BIBLIOGRAPHY

Allsup, Judith. "Feminism in the Novels of Ellen Glasgow." Ph.D. diss., Southern Illinois University, 1973.

Andersen, Hans Christian. *Favorite Tales of Hans Andersen*. Translated by M. R. James. Boston: Faber and Faber, 1978.

Auerbach, Nina. *Woman and the Demon: The Life of a Victorian Myth*. Cambridge, Mass.: Harvard University Press, 1982.

Bartley, Numan V. *The New South, 1945–1980*. Baton Rouge: Louisiana State University Press, 1995.

Bauer, Margaret D. "'Put Your Heart in the Land': An Intertextual Reading of *Barren Ground* and *Gone with the Wind*." In *Ellen Glasgow: New Perspectives*, edited by Dorothy M. Scura, 162–82. Knoxville: University of Tennessee Press, 1995.

Baym, Nina. "The Myth of the Myth of Southern Womanhood." In *Feminism and American Literary History: Essays*, 183–96. New Brunswick, N.J.: Rutgers University Press, 1992.

———. *Woman's Fiction: A Guide to Novels by and about Women in American, 1820–1870*. 2d ed. Urbana: University of Illinois Press, 1993.

———. "Women's Novels and Women's Minds: An Unsentimental View of Nineteenth-Century American Women's Fiction." *Novel* 31 (1998): 335–50

Beauvoir, Simone de. *The Second Sex*. Translated and edited by H. M. Parshley, with an introduction by Margaret Crosland. New York: Knopf, 1993.

Belsey, Catherine. "Constructing the Subject: Deconstructing the Text." In *Feminisms: An Anthology of Literary Theory and Criticism,* 2d ed., edited by Robyn R. Warhol and Diane Price Herndl, 657–73. New Brunswick, N. J.: Rutgers University Press, 1997.

Benjamin, Jessica. "The Bonds of Love: Rational Violence and Erotic Domination." In *The Future of Difference,* edited by Hester Eisenstein and Alice Jardine, 41–70. Boston: G. K. Hall, 1980.

Boyd, Belle. *Belle Boyd in Camp and Prison, Written by Herself.* New edition, prepared from new materials by Curtis Carrol Davis. South Brunswick, N.J.: T. Yoseloff, 1968.

Boyle, Regis Louise. *Mrs. E.D.E.N. Southworth, Novelist.* Washington, D.C.: Catholic University of America Press, 1939.

Breur, Josef, and Sigmund Freud. *Studies in Hysteria.* Translated by A. A. Brill. New York: Nervous and Mental Disease Publishing, 1936.

Broadwell, Elizabeth Pell, and Ronald Wesley Hoag. "A Conversation with Elizabeth Spencer." In *Conversations with Elizabeth Spencer,* edited by Peggy Whitman Prenshaw, 56–76. Jackson: University Press of Mississippi, 1991.

Brooks, Cleanth. "A Conversation between Eudora Welty and Cleanth Brooks." In *More Conversations with Eudora Welty,* edited by Peggy Whitman Prenshaw, 154–57. Jackson: University Press of Mississippi, 1996.

Broughton, Irv. "Interview with Lee Smith." In *The Writer's Mind: Interviews with American Authors,* edited by Irv Broughton, 279–97. Fayetteville: University of Arkansas Press, 1989.

Burchell, Sonya Smith. "Female Characterization in Lee Smith's *Oral History:* Superstition, Sexuality, and Traditional Roles." *North Carolina Folklore Journal* 42 (1995): 105–12.

Butler, Judith. *Bodies that Matter: On the Discursive Limits of "Sex".* New York: Routledge, 1993.

———. *Gender Trouble: Feminism and the Subversion of Identity.* New York: Routledge, 1990.

———. *The Psychic Life of Power: Theories in Subjection.* Stanford, Calif.: Stanford University Press, 1997.

Callard, D. A. *"Pretty Good for a Woman": The Enigmas of Evelyn Scott.* London: J. Cape, 1985.

Capote, Truman. *Breakfast at Tiffany's: A Short Novel and Three Stories.* New York: Random House, 1958.

Carby, Hazel V. *Reconstructing Womanhood: The Emergence of the Afro-American Woman Novelist.* New York: Oxford University Press, 1987.

Cash, W. J. *The Mind of the South.* New York: Knopf, 1941.

Cheney, Brainard. "Caroline Gordon's *The Malefactors.*" *Sewanee Review* 79 (1971): 360–72.

Cixous, Hélène. "The Laugh of the Medusa." In *Feminisms*, 334–49.

Clark, William Bedford. "The Serpent of Lust in the Southern Garden." *Southern Review* 10 (1974): 805–22.

Clinton, Catherine. *The Plantation Mistress: Woman's World in the Old South*. New York: Pantheon Books, 1982.

Conrad, Susan Phinney. *Perish the Thought: Intellectual Women in Romantic America, 1830–1860*. New York: Oxford University Press, 1976.

Dale, Corinne. "The Power of Language in Lee Smith's *Oral History*." *Southern Quarterly* 28 (1990): 21–34.

Dew, Thomas Roderick. "Dissertation on the Characteristic Differences of the Sexes, and Woman's Position and Influence in Society." *Southern Literary Messenger* 1 (1835): 493–512.

Dinnerstein, Dorothy. *The Mermaid and the Minotaur: Sexual Arrangements and Human Malaise*. New York: Harper and Row, 1976.

Dixon, Thomas. *The Sins of the Father: A Romance of the South*. New York: Grosset and Dunlap, 1912.

Dobson, Joanne. "The Hidden Hand: Subversion of Cultural Ideology in Three Mid-Nineteenth-Century American Women's Novels." *American Quarterly* 38 (1986): 223–42.

Donaldson, Susan V., and Anne Goodwyn Jones. "Haunted Bodies: Rethinking the South through Gender." In *Haunted Bodies: Gender and Southern Texts*, edited by Jones and Donaldson, 1–19. Charlottesville: University Press of Virginia, 1997.

Douglass, Frederick. *Narrative of the Life of Frederick Douglass, an American Slave*. 1845. Reprint, New York: Penguin, 1982.

Eaton, Clement. *A History of the Old South*. New York: MacMillan, 1949.

Edwards, Laura F. *Gendered Strife and Confusion: The Political Culture of Reconstruction*. Urbana: University of Illinois Press, 1997.

Egenreither, Ann E. "Scarlett O'Hara: A Paradox in Pantalettes." In *Heroines of Popular Culture*, edited by Pat Browne, 120–27. Bowling Green, Ohio: Bowling Green State University Popular Press, 1987.

Ellison, Ralph. "Twentieth-Century Fiction and the Black Mask of Humanity." In *Shadow and Act*. New York: Random House, 1953.

Ellison, Rhoda Coleman. "Caroline Lee Hentz's Alabama Diary, 1836." *Alabama Review* October (1951): 254–69.

———. "Mrs. Hentz and the Green-Eyed Monster." *American Literature* 22 (1950): 345–50.

Entzminger, Betina. "Interview with Elizabeth Spencer." *Mississippi Quarterly* 47 (1994): 599–618.

Evans, Augusta Jane. *Beulah*. New York: Carleton, 1859.

———. *Vashti; or, Until Death Us Do Part*. New York: Carleton, 1869.

Evans, Sara M. "Women." In *The Encyclopedia of Southern History,* edited by David C. Roller and Robert W. Twyman. Baton Rouge: Louisiana State University Press, 1979.

Faulkner, William. *Requiem for a Nun.* New York: Random House, 1951. Reprint, New York, Vintage, 1975.

———. *Sanctuary: Corrected Text.* New York: Random House, 1987.

———. *Sartoris.* New York: Harcourt, Brace, 1929. Reprint, New York: Signet, 1964.

———. *Soldier's Pay.* New York: Boni and Liveright, 1926. Reprint, New York: Liveright, 1954.

Faust, Drew Gilpin. *Mothers of Invention: Women of the Slaveholding South in the American Civil War.* Chapel Hill: University of North Carolina Press, 1996.

Felman, Shoshana. "Women and Madness: The Critical Phallacy." In *Feminisms,* 7–20.

Fidler, William Perry. *Augusta Evans Wilson, 1835–1909: A Biography.* University: University of Alabama Press, 1951.

Fiedler, Leslie. *Love and Death in the American Novel.* New York: Criterion Books, 1960.

Flax, Jane. "Postmodernism and Gender Relations in Feminist Theory." *Signs* 12 (1987): 621–43.

Fox-Genovese, Elizabeth. *Within the Plantation Household: Black and White Women of the Old South.* Chapel Hill: University of North Carolina Press, 1988.

Frazer, Sir James. *The Golden Bough: A Study in Magic and Religion.* New abridgment from the 2d and 3d editions. Edited with an introduction by Robert Fraser. New York: Oxford University Press, 1994.

Fredrickson, George M. *The Black Image in the White Mind: The Debate on Afro-American Character and Destiny, 1817–1914.* New York: Harper and Row, 1971.

Freud, Sigmund. "Female Sexuality." In *Collected Papers,* vol. 5, translated by James Strachey. London: Hogarth Press, 1953.

———. "On Narcissism: An Introduction." In *Collected Papers,* vol. 4, authorized translation under the supervision of Joan Riviere. London: Hogarth Press, 1934.

———. *The Origin and Development of Psychoanalysis.* Washington, D.C.: Gateway, 1910.

Fuller, Margaret. "Woman in the Nineteenth Century." In *The Heath Anthology of American Literature,* 3d ed., edited by Paul Lauter et al., 1: 1714–35. Boston: Houghton Mifflin, 1998.

Gebhard, Caroline. "Reconstructing Southern Manhood: Race, Sentimentality, and Camp in the Plantation Myth." In *Haunted Bodies,* 132–55.

Gibbons, Kaye. *Frost and Flower: My Life with Manic Depression So Far.* Decatur, Ga.: Wisteria Press, 1995.

———. "My Mother, Literature, and Life Split Neatly into Two Halves." In *The Writer on Her Work*, vol. 2, edited and with an introduction by Janet Sternburg. New York: Norton, 1991.

———. *Sights Unseen*. New York: Avon Books, 1996.

Gilbert, Sandra M., and Susan Gubar. *The Madwoman in the Attic: The Woman Writer and the Nineteenth-Century Literary Imagination*. New Haven: Yale University Press, 1979. Reprint, 1984.

———. *The War of Words*. Vol 1. of *No Man's Land: The Place of the Woman Writer in the Twentieth Century*. New Haven: Yale University Press, 1988.

Gilman, Sander. "Black Bodies, White Bodies: Toward an Iconography of Female Sexuality in Late Nineteenth-Century Art, Medicine, and Literature." In *"Race," Writing, and Difference*, edited by Henry Louis Gates Jr. Chicago: University of Chicago Press, 1986.

Glasgow, Ellen. *A Certain Measure: An Interpretation of Prose Fiction*. New York: Harcourt, Brace, 1943.

———. *In This Our Life*. New York: Harcourt, Brace, 1941.

———. *The Romantic Comedians*. Garden City, N.Y.: Doubleday, Page, 1926.

———. *The Wheel of Life*. New York: Doubleday, 1906.

———. *The Woman Within: An Autobiography*. Edited and with an introduction by Pamela R. Matthews. Charlottesville: University Press of Virginia, 1994.

Gordon, Caroline. *The Malefactors*. New York: Harcourt, Brace, 1956.

———. *The Strange Children*. New York: Scribner, 1951.

Graulich, Melody. "Pioneering the Imagination: Eudora Welty's *The Robber Bridegroom*." In *Women and Western American Literature*, edited by Helen Winter Stauffer and Susan Rosowski, 283–96. Troy, N.Y.: Whitston Publishing, 1982.

Greene, Sally. "Re-Placing the Hero: *The Night Travellers* as Novel of Female Self-Discovery." *Southern Quarterly* 33 (1994): 33–39.

Gretland, Jan Nordby. "An Interview with Eudora Welty." In *Conversations with Eudora Welty*, edited by Peggy Whitman Prenshaw, 211–29. Jackson: University Press of Mississippi, 1984.

———. "Component Parts: The Novelist as Autobiographer." In *The Late Novels of Eudora Welty*, edited by Jan Nordby Gretland and Karl-Heniz Westarp, 163–75. Columbia: University of South Carolina Press, 1998.

Guerin, Wilfred L., et al. *A Handbook of Critical Approaches to Literature*. 3d ed. New York: Oxford University Press, 1992.

Gwin, Minrose. *Black and White Women of the Old South: The Peculiar Sisterhood in American Literature*. Knoxville: University of Tennessee Press, 1985.

Gygax, Franziska. *Serious Daring from Within: Female Narrative Strategies in Eudora Welty's Novels*. New York: Greenwood Press, 1990.

Haggard, H. Rider. *She*. Edited with an introduction by Daniel Karlin. New York: Oxford University Press, 1991.

Hall, Caroline King Barnard. "'Telling the Truth about Themselves': Women, Form, and Ideas in *The Romantic Comedians.*" In *Ellen Glasgow: New Perspectives,* 183–95.

Hanson, Elizabeth I. *Margaret Mitchell.* Boston: Twayne Publishers, 1991.

Hardy, John Edward. "Marrying Down in Eudora Welty's Novels." In *Eudora Welty: Critical Essays,* edited by Peggy Whitman Prenshaw, 93–119. Jackson: University Press of Mississippi, 1979.

Hays, H. R. *Dangerous Sex: The Myth of Feminine Evil.* New York: Putnam, 1964.

Henderson, Mae. "Toni Morrison's *Beloved:* Re-Membering the Body as Historical Text." In *Comparative American Identities: Race, Sex, and Nationality in the Modern Text,* edited with an introduction by Hortense J. Spillers, 62–86. New York: Routledge, 1991.

Hentz, Caroline Lee. *De Lara; or, The Moorish Bride.* Tuscaloosa, Ala.: Woodruff and Olcott, 1843.

———. *Marcus Warland.* 1852. Reprint, Philadelphia: T. B. Peterson, 1869.

———. *The Planter's Northern Bride.* With an introduction by Rhoda Coleman Ellison. Chapel Hill: University of North Carolina Press, 1970.

Hersh, Blanche Glassman. *The Slavery of Sex: Feminist-Abolitionists in America.* Urbana: University of Illinois Press, 1978.

Hill, Dorothy Combs. "An Interview with Lee Smith." *Southern Quarterly* 28 (1990): 5–34.

Hundley, Daniel R. *Social Relations in Our Southern States.* Edited and with an introduction by William J. Cooper Jr. Baton Rouge: Louisiana State University Press, 1979.

Inge, Tonette Bond, ed. *Southern Women Writers: The New Generation.* Tuscaloosa: University of Alabama Press, 1990.

Irigaray, Luce. "Another 'Cause'—Castration." In *Feminisms,* 404–12.

Irvin, Helen Deis. "Gea in Georgia: A Mythic Dimension in *Gone with the Wind.*" In *Recasting: "Gone with the Wind" in American Culture,* edited by Darden Asbury Pyron, 57–68. Miami: University Presses of Florida, 1983.

Jacobs, Harriet. *Incidents in the Life of a Slave Girl Linda Brent.* Edited by Maria L. Child. New introduction and notes by Walter Teller. New York: Harcourt Brace Jovanovich, 1973.

Johnston, Mary. *Hagar.* New York: Houghton Mifflin, 1913.

Jones, Anne Goodwyn. *Tomorrow Is Another Day: The Woman Writer in the South, 1859–1936.* Baton Rouge: Louisiana State University Press, 1981.

Jonza, Nancylee Novell. *The Underground Stream: The Life and Art of Caroline Gordon.* Athens: University of Georgia Press, 1995.

Jordan, Winthrop D. *White over Black: American Attitudes toward the Negro, 1550–1812.* Chapel Hill: University of North Carolina Press, 1968.

Jung, Carl. *The Essential Jung.* Selected and introduced by Anthony Storr. Princeton, N.J.: Princeton University Press, 1983.

———. *Psyche and Symbol: A Selection from the Writings of C. G. Jung.* Edited by Violet S. de Laslo. Garden City, N.Y.: Doubleday, 1958.

Keats, John. "La Belle Dame sans Merci." In *The Norton Anthology of Poetry,* 3d ed, edited by Alexander W. Allison et al., 658. New York: Norton, 1983.

Kieft, Ruth M. Vande. "The Love Ethos of Porter, Welty, and McCullers." In *The Female Tradition in Southern Literature,* edited by Carol S. Manning, 235–58. Urbana: University of Illinois Press, 1993.

King, Richard H. *A Southern Renaissance: The Cultural Awakening of the American South, 1930–1955.* New York: Oxford University Press, 1980.

Kipnis, Laura. "White Trash Girl: An Interview." In *White Trash: Race and Class in America,* edited by Matt Wray and Annalee Newitz, 113–30. New York: Routledge, 1997.

Larsen, Nella. *Quicksand; and, Passing.* Edited and with an introduction by Deborah E. McDowell. New Brunswick, N.J.: Rutgers University Press, 1986.

Leach, Maria, ed. *Funk and Wagnalls Standard Dictionary of Folklore, Mythology, and Legend,* vol. 2. New York: Funk and Wagnalls, 1950.

Levy, Helen Fiddyment. "Coming Home: Glasgow's Last Two Novels." In *Ellen Glasgow: New Perspectives,* 220–34.

Longstreet, Augustus Baldwin. "The Charming Creature as a Wife." In *Georgia Scenes.* 1835. Reprint, Upper Saddle River, N.J.: Literature House, 1969.

MacKethan, Lucinda H. *Daughters of Time: Creating Woman's Voice in Southern Story.* Athens: University of Georgia Press, 1990.

Makowsky, Veronica A. *Caroline Gordon: A Biography.* New York: Oxford University Press, 1989.

Manning, Carol S. "The Real Beginning of the Southern Renaissance." In *The Female Tradition in Southern Literature,* 37–56.

Mark, Rebecca. *The Dragon's Blood: Feminist Intertextuality in Eudora Welty's "The Golden Apples."* Jackson: University Press of Mississippi, 1994.

Matthews, Pamela R. Introduction to *The Woman Within,* by Ellen Glasgow. Charlottesville, University of Virginia Press, 1954.

McCandless, Amy Thompson. "Concepts of Patriarchy in the Popular Novels of Antebellum Southern Women." *Studies in Popular Culture* 10 (1987): 1–16.

McDowell, Deborah E. Introduction to *Quicksand and Passing,* by Nella Larsen, ix–xxxv. New Brunswick, N.J.: Rutgers University Press, 1986.

Michie, Helena. *Sororophobia: Differences among Women in Literature and Culture.* New York: Oxford University Press, 1992.

Miner, Madonne. *Insatiable Appetites: Twentieth-Century American Women's Bestsellers.* Westport, Conn.: Greenwood Press, 1984.

Mitchell, Juliet, ed. *The Selected Melanie Klein*. New York: Penguin Books, 1986.

Mitchell, Margaret. *Gone with the Wind*. New York: MacMillan, 1936.

Moi, Toril. *Sexual/Textual Politics: Feminist Literary Theory*. New York: Methuen, 1985. Reprint, New York: Routledge, 1995.

Moore, John Hammond, ed. *A Plantation Mistress on the Eve of the Civil War: The Diary of Keziah Goodwyn Hopkins Brevard, 1803–1886*. Columbia: University of South Carolina Press, 1993.

Morris, Willie. *The Last of the Southern Girls*. New York: Knopf, 1973.

Morrison, Toni. *Playing in the Dark: Whiteness and the Literary Imagination*. Cambridge, Mass.: Harvard University Press, 1992.

Mortimer, Gail L. *Daughter of the Swan: Love and Knowledge in Eudora Welty's Fiction*. Athens: University of Georgia Press, 1994.

Moss, Elizabeth. *Domestic Novelists in the Old South: Defenders of Southern Culture*. Baton Rouge: Louisiana State University Press, 1992.

Muhlenfeld, Elisabeth. "The Civil War and Authorship." In *The History of Southern Literature,* edited by Louis D. Rubin Jr. et al., 178–87. Baton Rouge: Louisiana State University Press, 1985.

Mulvey, Laura. "Visual Pleasure and Narrative Cinema." In *Visual and Other Pleasures: Language, Discourse, Society,* 14–26. Basingstoke, England: MacMillan, 1989.

The New English Bible, with the Aphocrypha. Samuel Sandmel, general editor. New York: Oxford University Press, 1976.

Noppen, Martha van. "A Conversation with Eudora Welty." In *Conversations with Eudora Welty,* 236–51.

O'Brien, Kenneth. "Race, Romance, and the Southern Literary Tradition." In *Recasting,* 153–66.

Painter, Nell Irvin. "'Social Equality,' Miscegenation, Labor, and Power." In *The Evolution of Southern Culture,* edited by Numan V. Bartley, 47–67. Athens: University of Georgia Press, 1988.

Pennington, Estill Curtis. "Anglo-American Antebellum Culture." In *The Encyclopedia of Southern Culture,* edited by Charles Reagan Wilson and William Ferris. Chapel Hill: University of North Carolina Press, 1989. 595–96.

Poe, Edgar Allan. *Great Tales and Poems of Edgar Allan Poe*. New York: Simon and Schuster, 1951.

Prenshaw, Peggy Whitman. *Elizabeth Spencer*. Boston: Twayne Publishers, 1985.

———. "Southern Ladies and the Southern Literary Renaissance." In *The Female Tradition in Southern Literature,* 73–88.

———. "The True Happenings of My Life: Reading Southern Women Autobiographers." In *Haunted Bodies,* 443–63.

Raper, Julius Rowan. *From the Sunken Garden: The Fiction of Ellen Glasgow, 1916–1945*. Baton Rouge: Louisiana State University Press, 1980.

Reed, John Shelton. *Southern Folk, Plain and Fancy: Native White Social Types.* Athens: University of Georgia Press, 1986.

Rieves, Amélie. *The Quick or the Dead? A Study.* Philadelphia: J. B. Lippincott, 1888.

Roberts, Diane. *The Myth of Aunt Jemima: Representations of Race and Region.* New York: Routledge, 1994.

Roberts, Terry. *Self and Community in the Fiction of Elizabeth Spencer.* Baton Rouge: Louisiana State University Press, 1994.

Rocks, James E. "The Christian Myth as Salvation: Caroline Gordon's *The Strange Children.*" *Tulane Studies in English* 16 (1968): 149–60.

Rouse, Blair. *Ellen Glasgow.* New York: Twayne, 1962.

Rubin, Louis D., Jr. *A Gallery of Southerners.* Baton Rouge: Louisiana State University Press, 1982.

Russ, Joanna. "Aesthetics." In *Feminisms,* 194–211.

———. "Why Women Can't Write." In *Images of Women in Fiction: Feminist Perspectives,* compiled by Susan Koppelman Cornillon. Bowling Green, Ohio: Bowling Green State University Popular Press, 1972.

Samuels, Shirley. "The Identity of Slavery." In *The Culture of Sentiment: Race, Gender, and Sentimentality in Nineteenth-Century America,* edited by Shirley Samuels, 157–71. New York: Oxford University Press, 1992.

Sanchez-Eppler, Karen. "Bodily Bonds: The Intersecting Rhetorics of Feminism and Abolition." In *The Culture of Sentiment,* 92–114.

Schmidt, Peter. *The Heart of the Story: Eudora Welty's Short Fiction.* Jackson: University Press of Mississippi, 1991.

Scott, Anne Firor. *The Southern Lady: From Pedestal to Politics, 1830–1930.* Expanded paperback ed. Charlottesville: University Press of Virginia, 1995.

Scott, Evelyn. *Background in Tennessee.* New York: R. M. McBride, 1937.

———. *A Calendar of Sin: American Melodramas.* New York: J. Cape and H. Smith, 1931.

———. *Narcissus.* New York: Harcourt, Brace, 1922.

Seidel, Kathryn Lee. *The Southern Belle in the American Novel.* Tampa: University of South Florida Press, 1985.

Sellers, Susan, ed. *The Hélène Cixous Reader.* Preface by Hélène Cixous and foreword by Jacques Derrida. New York: Routledge, 1994.

Showalter, Elaine. "The Female Tradition." In *Feminisms,* 269–88.

———. *Sexual Anarchy: Gender and Culture at the Fin de Siècle.* New York: Viking, 1990.

Silber, Nina. *The Romance of Reunion.* Chapel Hill: University of North Carolina Press, 1993.

Simpson, Lewis P. *The Brazen Face of History: Studies in the Literary Consciousness in America.* Baton Rouge: Louisiana State University Press, 1980.

Sims, Anastasia. *The Power of Femininity in the New South: Women's Organizations and Politics in North Carolina, 1880–1930.* Columbia: University of South Carolina Press, 1997.

Smith, Lee. Telephone interview with the author. 6 January 1998.

———. *The Last Day the Dogbushes Bloomed.* New York: Harper and Row, 1968. Reprint, Baton Rouge: Louisiana State University Press, 1994.

———. *Oral History.* New York: Putnam, 1983. Reprint, New York: Ballantine, 1984.

Smith, Lillian. *Killers of the Dream.* 1949. Reprint, New York: Norton, 1978.

Smith, Rebecca. "A Conversation with Lee Smith." *Southern Quarterly* 32 (1994): 19–29.

Southworth, E.D.E.N. *Retribution, A Tale of Passion; or, The Vale of Shadows.* New York: G. W. Dillingham, 1849.

———. *Self-Raised; or, From the Depths.* New York: A. L. Burt, 1900.

———. *The Three Beauties.* Philadelphia: T. B. Peterson, 1858.

Spencer, Elizabeth. "Judith Kane." In *The Stories of Elizabeth Spencer,* 243–59. Garden City, N.Y.: Doubleday, 1981. Reprint, New York: Penguin, 1983.

———. *Landscapes of the Heart: A Memoir.* New York: Random House, 1998.

———. *The Night Travellers.* New York: Viking, 1991.

———. Letter to the author. 25 November 1997.

Spenser, Edmund. *The Faerie Queene.* In *The Norton Anthology of English Literature,* 3d ed., edited by M. H. Abrams et al., 305–456. New York: Norton, 1975.

Sponza, Lucio. "Italians in London." In *The Peopling of London: Fifteen Thousand Years of Settlement Overseas,* edited by Nick Merriman, 129–37. London: Museum of London, 1993.

Stanesa, Jamie. "Caroline Lee Whiting Hentz." *Legacy* 13 (1996): 130–41.

———. "Slavery and the Politics of Domestic Identities: Ideology, Theology, and Region in American Women Writers, 1850–1860." Ph.D. diss. Emory University, 1993.

Stowe, Stephen M. "The Not-So-Cloistered Academy: Elite Women's Education and Family Feeling in the Old South." In *The Web of Southern Social Relations: Women, Family, and Education,* edited by Walter J. Fraser Jr., R. Frank Saunders Jr., and Jon Wakely, 90–102. Athens: University of Georgia Press, 1985.

Tate, Allen. *Collected Essays.* Denver: A. Swallow, 1959.

Taylor, Helen. *Scarlett's Women: "Gone with the Wind" and Its Female Fans.* New Brunswick, N.J.: Rutgers University Press, 1989.

Taylor, William R. *Cavalier and Yankee: The Old South and American National Character.* 1957. Reprint, Cambridge, Mass.: Harvard University Press, 1979.

Thompkins, Jane. "Sentimental Power: *Uncle Tom's Cabin* and the Politics of Literary History." In *Feminisms,* 20–39.

Thompson, Stith. *Motif Index of Folk Literature.* Bloomington: Indiana University Press, 1955.

Tridon, André. *Psychoanalysis: Its History, Theory, and Practice.* New York: B. W. Huebsch, 1919.

Wagner, Linda W. *Ellen Glasgow: Beyond Convention.* Austin: University of Texas Press, 1982.

Wagner-Martin, Linda. "Glasgow's Time in *The Sheltered Life.*" In *Ellen Glasgow: New Perspectives,* 196–203.

Walker, Alice. *Meridian.* New York: Harcourt Brace Jovanovich, 1976.

Welty, Eudora. *One Writer's Beginnings.* Boston: Harvard University Press, 1984.

———. *The Optimist's Daughter.* New York: Random House, 1972. Reprint, New York: Vintage, 1978.

———. *The Robber Bridegroom.* Reprint, New York: Harcourt, Brace, 1970.

———. "The Wanderers." In *The Golden Apples,* 230–77. New York: Harcourt, Brace, 1949. Reprint, New York: Harcourt Brace Jovanovich, 1977.

Westling, Louise. "Fathers and Daughters in Welty and O'Connor." In *The Female Tradition in Southern Literature,* 110–24.

———. *Sacred Groves and Ravaged Gardens: The Fiction of Eudora Welty, Carson McCullers, and Flannery O'Connor.* Athens: University of Georgia Press, 1985.

Wheeler, Marjorie Spruill. *New Women of the New South: The Leaders of the Woman Suffrage Movement in the Southern States.* New York: Oxford University Press, 1993.

White, Mary Wheeling. *Fighting the Current: The Life and Work of Evelyn Scott.* Baton Rouge: Louisiana State University Press, 1998.

Whites, LeeAnn. *The Civil War as a Crisis in Gender: Augusta, Georgia, 1860–1890.* Athens: University of Georgia Press, 1995.

Willis, Ellen. "Bring in the Noise." In *Reading Culture: Contexts for Critical Reading and Writing,* edited by Diana George and John Trimbur, 34–37. New York: Longman, 1999.

Winsbro, Bonnie. *Supernatural Forces: Belief, Difference, and Power in Contemporary Works by Ethnic Women.* Amherst: University of Massachusetts Press, 1993.

Williams, Tennessee. *A Streetcar Named Desire.* Edited by E. Martin Browne. New York: New Directions: 1947. Reprint, New York: Penguin, 1984.

Williamson, Joel. "How Black Was Rhett Butler?" In *The Evolution of Southern Culture,* 87–107.

Winter, Kari J. *Subjects of Slavery, Agents of Change: Women and Power in Gothic Novels and Slave Narratives, 1790–1865.* Athens: University of Georgia Press, 1992.

Woodward, C. Vann, ed. *Mary Chesnut's Civil War.* New Haven, Conn.: Yale University Press, 1981.

Wyatt-Brown, Bertram. *Southern Honor: Ethics and Behavior in the Old South.* New York: Oxford University Press, 1982.

Yaeger, Patricia. *Honey-Mad Women: Emancipatory Strategies in Women's Writing.* New York: Columbia University Press, 1988.

———. "Beyond the Hummingbird: Southern Women Writers and the Southern Gargantua." In *Haunted Bodies*, 287–318.

Yates, Gail Graham. "My Visit with Eudora Welty." In *More Conversations with Eudora Welty*, 87–99.

INDEX

Abolition, 32, 36, 44, 53, 57, 76, 181
Agrarians. *See* Southern Agrarians
Artist figure, 34–35, 40, 52, 63–64, 67–69,
    81, 83, 89–90, 96, 98, 106–07, 115–21,
    126, 128–29, 132–35, 137–41, 143–51,
    153–54, 156–61, 167–68, 171, 173–76,
    181, 184

Baym, Nina, 1, 2, 33, 58–59, 178, 179
Beauvoir, Simone de, 4, 99
Boyd, Belle, 74–75
Brontë, Charlotte, 43, 70
Butler, Judith, 7, 8, 16, 42, 111, 112, 123,
    180, 182

Cash, W. J., 9, 28
Castration, 4, 5, 90, 101, 111
Chesnut, Mary, 18–19, 23, 39, 53, 55, 63
Chopin, Kate, 73, 79
Civil War, 25–26, 33–34, 50, 54, 66–67, 72,
    74–75, 77–78, 104–105, 108, 112, 115,
    117–18, 183
Cixous, Hélène, 15, 124, 167
Clark, William Bedford, 36, 55

Class, 125, 130, 136–37, 145, 154–55, 162,
    164–65, 167, 169, 170, 173, 180–83
Clinton, Catherine, 33, 60

Dark double, 16, 17, 19, 21, 24, 30, 56, 68,
    70, 184
Daughter figure, 121, 126–31, 134,
    138–39, 141, 143, 145–47, 153–54,
    156–57
Dew, Thomas Roderick, 11, 92
Dixon, Thomas, 25–26

Edwards, Laura, 13, 17, 76
Ellison, Rhoda, 54, 63
Evans, Augusta Jane, 1, 23, 66–72, 79, 80,
    119, 181

Fairy tale, 129–31, 133–34, 143–44, 146,
    149, 150, 156–57
Father figure, 127–28, 132, 144, 146, 148,
    161
Faulkner, William, 20, 26–28, 35–36,
    78–80, 93, 105, 136, 169, 178, 179
Faust, Drew, 7–8, 67, 74–75

Fiedler, Leslie, 5, 81, 85, 151
Fitzgerald, F. Scott, 5, 81, 82, 151, 152
Fox-Genovese, Elizabeth, 18, 159
Fredrickson, George, 52–53
Freud, Sigmund, 4, 84, 96–100, 126–27

Gebhard, Caroline, 76–77
Gibbons, Kaye, 30, 123, 125, 127, 130,
    138, 141, 160, 169–77, 184
Gilbert, Sandra, and Susan Gubar, 4, 6–7,
    14, 70, 124, 131, 157, 170
Gilman, Charlotte Perkins, 7–8, 9, 86,
    102–103
Gilman, Sander, 56, 102–103
Glasgow, Ellen, 26, 28, 73, 74, 79, 80,
    82–95, 96, 98, 102, 106, 108, 112, 114,
    117, 118, 121, 127, 137, 169, 179, 184;
    A Certain Measure, 82, 95; *In This Our
    Life*, 85, 89–95; *The Romantic
    Comedians*, 85–89; *The Woman Within*,
    82–83, 84
Gordon, Caroline, 28, 80, 90, 98, 114–21,
    127, 184; *The Malefactors*, 114–15,
    120–21; *The Strange Children*, 115–20,
    121
Gubar, Susan. *See* Gilbert, Sandra
Gwin, Minrose, 12, 18–19

Haggard, H. Rider, 5, 124
Harem, 44–45, 47, 56–57
Hentz, Caroline Lee, 1, 23, 54–67, 69, 71,
    72, 79, 81, 89, 90, 162, 181; *Marcus
    Warland*, 54–57, 60; *The Planter's
    Northern Bride*, 54, 55, 57–66, 107

Italians, 19, 36–38, 43, 59–60, 81

Jacobs, Harriet, 18–19, 22
Jezebel, 17, 22, 45, 72, 155, 159
Johnston, Mary, 73–74, 79
Jones, Anne Goodwyn, 9, 68, 79, 109

Keats, John, 3, 4, 19, 116, 117, 118–19,
    120, 173
Ku Klux Klan, 25, 53, 103, 111

Lacan, Jacques, 42, 59, 90, 162, 167
Lilith, 2, 30, 58, 163

Madness, 6–8, 28, 42–43, 49, 69–71, 104,
    115–16, 119, 131, 134, 139, 166,
    170–76, 185
Matron, 36, 38, 44, 55, 61, 69, 72, 87, 100
Mermaid, 4, 143, 144, 148–49, 150, 153
Milton, John, 50, 106
Miscegenation, 19, 25, 33, 35–36, 38, 39,
    46, 55, 59–60, 63, 105, 108, 159
Mitchell, Margaret, 28, 29, 79, 80, 98,
    104–15, 116, 117, 118, 121, 124, 127,
    130, 156, 169, 171, 174, 184
Morrison, Toni, 20, 56–57, 93
Moss, Elizabeth, 2, 179
Mother figure, 30, 61–62, 82, 87–88, 97,
    99–101, 112, 125, 126–27, 129–31,
    139, 144, 146–48, 153–54, 156, 157,
    159–61, 164, 172, 174–76, 184–85
Mulvey, Laura, 24, 59

Narcissism, 99–101, 142, 149

Patriarch, 36, 38, 40, 44, 46, 48, 61, 63, 71,
    92–93, 100, 161, 163, 172
Phallus/phallic 4, 14, 19, 21, 42–43, 49,
    59, 90, 98, 101, 111, 160, 162, 167
Poe, Edgar Allan, 20, 23, 64–65, 169
Prenshaw, Peggy Whitman, 14, 78, 80, 143
Prostitute, 33, 36, 52, 74, 103

Roberts, Diane, 16, 33, 44–45

Sanchez-Eppler, Karen, 20, 46
Schmidt, Peter, 130, 139, 141, 185
Scott, Anne Firor, 9, 12, 14–15, 75
Scott, Evelyn, 28, 80, 90, 95–104, 106,
    108, 112, 114, 117, 118, 119, 121, 127,
    142, 184
Seidel, Kathryn Lee, 9–11, 79n, 100, 149
Shadow figure, 82, 93–94, 102–103, 108,
    118–19, 137, 160, 184
Showalter, Elaine, 4–5, 41, 124
Silber, Nina, 74, 77

Slavery, 1, 2, 17, 20–21, 23, 24, 33–36, 40,
  43, 49, 52–54, 57, 62, 65, 67, 70, 76,
  180, 181
Smith, Lee, 30, 123, 125, 127, 130, 138,
  141, 154–69, 176, 184; *The Last Day the
  Dogbushes Bloomed*, 156–61, 174; *Oral
  History*, 160, 161–69, 172
Smith, Lillian, 9, 10, 17, 19
Southern Agrarians, 78, 114–16, 121, 142
Southern Renascence, 28–29, 78–82, 106,
  107, 110, 112, 114–15, 121–24,
  126–27, 129, 134, 137, 140, 142, 159,
  182–84
Southworth, E.D.E.N., 1, 23, 34–54,
  58–60, 64–67, 69–72, 79–81, 89, 90,
  97, 106, 109, 119, 161, 162, 181;
  Retribution, 35–44, 49, 50, 52, 54, 66,
  69; *Self-Raised*, 50–54, 63; *The Three
  Beauties*, 44–51, 54, 66, 69, 87
Spencer, Elizabeth, 29–30, 123, 125, 127,
  130, 141–57, 169, 176, 184
Spenser, Edmund, 4, 16
Stowe, Harriet Beecher, 16, 54, 61
Suffrage, 13, 28, 74–76

Tate, Allen, 78, 114, 115, 118, 121
Twain, Mark, 5, 53

Vampire, 4, 96, 104, 125, 130, 145, 157,
  162, 165, 173
Vietnam War, 142, 150, 153

Wagner, Linda W., 83, 95
Welty, Eudora, 14, 30, 123–25, 127–42,
  145, 146, 149–51, 155–57, 163–65,
  169, 172, 176–79, 184, 185; *One
  Writer's Beginnings*, 14, 128, 129, 134,
  135, 139–40; *The Optimist's Daughter*,
  129, 134–41, 154, 163; *The Robber
  Bridegroom*, 129–35, 138, 146, 150,
  155, 165
Whiteness, 17, 108
White supremacy, 12, 180, 181
Williams, Tennessee, 27–30, 178
Witch, 4, 109, 131, 143, 161, 163–65, 168
Women's clubs, 75–76
Wolfe, Thomas, 26, 179
World War I, 26, 76, 78, 104–105
Wyatt-Brown, Bertram, 9, 10, 12, 60, 62–63

Yaeger, Patricia, 178–79, 185